SOCIOLOGY OF EDUCATION SERIES
Aaron M. Pallas, Series Editor

Advisory Board: Sanford Dornbusch, Adam Gamoran, Annette Lareau,
Mary Metz, Gary Natriello

D1226174

FROM THE SERIES EDITOR

Spurred by the threat of international competition, the students and teachers who inhabit American schools are being held to higher standards for academic performance than ever before. Memorization of facts and formulas is no longer enough; instead, our educators are striving to teach for understanding, an approach that emphasizes giving *all* children access to powerful ideas. It is not hyperbole to claim that teaching for understanding represents a revolution in teaching. But revolutions do not come easily; teaching for understanding is a new and challenging practice that obliges teachers to engage with student thinking, and to develop a new repertoire of instructional practices that allow for nimble responses to the uncertainties of the classroom.

Adam Gamoran and his colleagues recognize a truism about educational reform: It is much easier to *identify* good practice than to figure out how to move from poor practice to good practice. It is also difficult to *sustain* good practice. This book argues that teaching for understanding requires professional expertise, and professional expertise requires professional development. At the heart of the argument is the organizational context for teaching for understanding, a unique blend of sociological thinking about schools as organizations and state-of-the-art ideas about the teaching of mathematics and science. The authors suggest that the capacity for schools and school districts to change is not fixed; rather, through the strategic use of resources, change can be developed and sustained.

One of the most innovative features of this analysis is its conception of resources in schools. We are accustomed to thinking about the material and human resources at the heart of the educational enterprise: textbooks, buildings, and people, all of which are tangible, and have costs that show up on an accounting ledger. Moreover, we usually view schools as *consuming* resources. Gamoran and his collaborators suggest that the most important resources for cultivating teaching for understanding may be social rather than material. Teachers can, for example, form groups that enable them to share their expertise, and can import new knowledge about teaching from outside of these groups. In this way, professional communities of teachers can *create* resources to support teaching for understanding.

Think of this volume as a narration of the road to the reform of teaching at the school and district levels. I hope that you find the journey as rewarding as I did.

Aaron M. Pallas

Transforming Teaching
in Math and Science

HOW SCHOOLS AND DISTRICTS
CAN SUPPORT CHANGE

Adam Gamoran
Charles W. Anderson
Pamela Anne Quiroz
Walter G. Secada
Tona Williams
Scott Ashmann

TEACHERS COLLEGE PRESS

Teachers College, Columbia University
New York and London

Published by Teachers College Press, 1234 Amsterdam Avenue, New York, NY 10027

This study was conducted at the National Center for Improving Student Learning and Achievement in Mathematics and Science, supported by funds from the U.S. Department of Education, Office of Educational Research and Improvement (Grant No. R305A60007). Findings and conclusions are those of the authors and do not necessarily reflect the views of the supporting agencies.

Library of Congress Cataloging-in-Publication Data

Transforming teaching in math and science : how schools and districts can support change / Adam Gamoran . . . [et al.].
    p. cm. — (Sociology of education series)
    Includes bibliographical references and index.
    ISBN 0-8077-4310-0 (acid-free paper) — ISBN 0-8077-4309-7 (pbk. : acid-free paper)
    1. Mathematics—Study and teaching—United States.   2. Science—Study and teaching—United States.   I. Gamoran, Adam, 1957–   II. Sociology of education series (New York, N.Y.)

    QA13 .T73 2003
    510'.71'073—dc21   2002040922

ISBN 0-8077-4309-7 (paper)
ISBN 0-8077-4310-0 (cloth)

Printed on acid-free paper
Manufactured in the United States of America

10 09 08 07 06 05 04 03   8 7 6 5 4 3 2 1

Contents

Acknowledgments

I had the privilege of leading this project, but it was truly a collaborative effort, and this book is a fully collaborative work. Although each chapter has its own author or authors, the entire team of authors read and discussed all the chapters as they developed. The book as a whole reflects our joint contributions. Working with this diverse, interdisciplinary team has been a rewarding intellectual experience from which I have benefited tremendously.

As authors, we have many others to thank. First and foremost are the teachers and administrators who willingly shared their time and experiences with us. Confidentiality requirements mean we cannot list them by name, but we thank them deeply for their professional commitment and for their participation in this professional service. We also owe an extraordinary debt to our colleagues at the National Center for Improving Student Learning and Achievement in Mathematics and Science, who led the professional development groups upon which this research is based. Their deep commitment to reform and their tireless efforts to work hand in hand with teachers instead of remaining in the ivory tower of the university are reflected in these pages.

We also thank other members of our research team who participated in earlier phases of the study, particularly Cora B. Marrett, Vice President of the University of Wisconsin System; Marcy Singer Gabella, Assistant Provost for Initiatives in Education at Vanderbilt University; Eric Grodsky, Assistant Professor of Sociology at the University of California–Davis; Patricia Berman, a researcher at the Wisconsin Center for Education Research; and Abel Mercado, a Ph.D. candidate in education at the University of Illinois–Chicago. We appreciate the support staff of our research center, especially the talented Cathlin Foy, who provided remarkable assistance in keeping our project moving forward during the past 4 years. We are grateful for helpful comments on portions of this work from Okhee Lee, Francisco Ramirez, James Rosenbaum, Miriam Gamoran Sherin, James Spillane, and our anonymous reviewers. We further appreciate the encouragement and advice of our editors at Teachers College Press.

All of us owe debts of gratitude to those in our personal lives who support our professional careers with patience, love, and understanding. For me, the person who fills this role is my wife, Marla N. Gamoran, who shows me every day what understanding is and what it means to support understanding in our lives together.

—*Adam Gamoran*

Introduction

School teachers and administrators across the nation are striving to improve teaching and learning, often with the help of outside experts, such as leaders of change movements, designers of comprehensive reforms, and university researchers. How can schools and districts best support these efforts to improve? For teachers attempting to "teach for understanding"—focusing on student thinking, examining powerful scientific and mathematical ideas, and providing equitable opportunities for learning—what supports and barriers are presented by their schools and districts? How can the supports be enhanced and the barriers overcome? Schools and districts with the *capacity for change* develop material, human, and social resources and allocate them strategically to enhance teaching and learning.

This book reports the results of a 5-year study of the context of changes in teaching, carried out at the National Center for Improving Student Learning and Achievement in Mathematics and Science (NCISLA/MS). Teachers and researchers in six "design collaboratives" (four in Wisconsin, one in Massachusetts, and one in Tennessee) strove together to enhance teaching for understanding. Our research team examined the school and district contexts of these reform efforts. In our investigation, we followed the perspective of Gamoran, Secada, and Marrett (2000) by taking a broad view of resources, identifying teacher professional development as the primary engine of change, and viewing school organization as a dynamic system in which cause and effect flow in multiple directions.

THE PROBLEM

The organizational context in which most teachers work is designed to support teaching that follows predictable routines (Rowan, 1990). When teaching does not change much from day to day, a predictable flow of material resources—mainly time and curricular materials to use with students in classrooms—is the primary element of support for teaching (Barr & Dreeben, 1983; Gamoran & Dreeben, 1986). In this conception of teaching, teachers obtain knowledge largely through preservice training, and the purpose of inservice education is to keep teachers abreast of new techniques and accountability demands (Fullan, 2001).

However, the usual configuration of resources in schools is not designed to support teachers who use student thinking as a basis for guiding instruction. When teachers focus on student understanding, they encourage students to construct relationships, extend their knowledge, articulate their ideas, and make knowledge their own (Carpenter & Lehrer, 1999). A predictable flow of material resources, while still important, is not sufficient to support teaching for understanding, which may take off in unexpected directions and requires new knowledge and collegial ties that are often unavailable (Cohen, McLaughlin, & Talbert, 1993; Fennema & Romberg, 1999; Wiske, 1998). To support teaching for understanding, schools must increase their *capacity for change*, by developing new resources—not only material, but also human and social resources—and by allocating resources in ways that support teachers' efforts.

Many leading science and mathematics educators advocate teaching for understanding. The current national goals and standards for science and mathematics curricula and teaching contain ideas about what it means and how it might be achieved (American Association for the Advancement of Science, 1989, 1993; National Council of Teachers of Mathematics, 1989, 1991, 2000; National Research Council, 1996). Yet teaching for understanding embodies substantial new demands on teachers, and on the contexts in which teachers work. Teaching for understanding draws attention to the need for providing all students with access to powerful scientific and mathematical ideas and practices, which until now have been reserved for students in "high-level" classes. These reforms call for new ways of organizing and supporting teachers' work. They recognize the centrality of professional development for mathematics and science teachers, yet little has been said about how schools and districts can acquire the capacity to nurture and support these reforms. Addressing this dimension of educational reform is crucial for the success of many current initiatives.

In an effort to improve teaching and learning, districts and schools around the country are bringing in outside expertise and adopting new models of teaching. Although the troubles of urban districts receive most attention from the news media, suburban districts also are heavily involved in educational reform. In both urban and suburban districts, one often finds a disjuncture between the ideals of good practice and the means to achieve such practice. Sustained, reflective professional development, while an important element in the reform, is not sufficient in itself but needs to occur in the context of a larger supportive environment. Access to six sites of reform in teaching activities in mathematics and/or science has provided us a unique opportunity to identify the challenges of supporting teaching for understanding, and to observe successful and unsuccessful responses to these challenges. This book tells the story of those challenges and responses.

ORGANIZATION OF THE BOOK

The book is divided into three parts. In Part I, we explain what we mean by teaching for understanding in mathematics and science, and we identify the key challenges that districts and schools face if they wish to support this practice. Then we present the ideas and concepts we will use throughout the other parts of the book to answer the question of how districts and schools can support teaching for understanding. Also in Part I, we describe the six reform sites—partnerships between teachers and researchers—that we examined in our research.

In Part II, we use the six cases to draw evidence about possible responses to the challenges of supporting teaching for understanding. We show how important organizational resources are to the change process, and how investments in professional development can generate new resources that help sustain the change process. We highlight issues of equity, leadership, and community in this part of the book.

In Part III, we place our findings in a broader context. We examine the district policy environment as a context for change and consider the prospects for sustaining change over the long term. Following our conclusions at the end of Part III, we provide an Appendix that offers details about the methodology of our study.

Transforming Teaching
in Math and Science

PART I

Challenges of Supporting Teaching for Understanding

What does it mean to support teaching for understanding? We can hardly begin to answer that question until we have a clear notion of what teaching for understanding means. Chapter 1 explains that teaching for understanding in mathematics and science refers to instruction that focuses on student thinking, emphasizes powerful scientific and mathematical ideas, and offers equitable learning opportunities to students. Based on this conception, Chapter 1 identifies the key challenges to supporting teaching for understanding: providing resources to classroom teachers; aligning purposes, perceptions, and commitments; and sustaining change. In Chapter 2, we present the conceptual model that we use to examine six cases of collaborative efforts among teachers and researchers to develop teaching for understanding. Where other models have adopted narrow conceptions of resources focusing only on money and other material conditions, our model considers human and social resources alongside material resources as essential aspects of a school or district's capacity for change. Moreover, our model recognizes that resources may flow in many different directions—not just from school to teacher, for example, but from teacher to school, as schools may increase their capacities by responding to new teacher commitments. In our model, teacher professional development is at the fulcrum of the change process, because although it is costly in material resources, it has the potential to generate new human and social resources. Once equipped with these conceptual tools, we will be ready to introduce the cases of change that we examined empirically. In Chapter 3, we present the six cases. For each case, we describe the district and school contexts and the character of the teacher–researcher collaboration.

CHAPTER 1

How Can Schools Support Teaching for Understanding in Mathematics and Science?

Charles W. Anderson

This is a book about how schools respond to new demands and use new resources. The demands include expectations that schools will adopt improved methods of science and mathematics teaching, and that they will produce evidence (generally in the form of achievement test scores) that these methods are improving student understanding. The resources include research-based knowledge of how students learn mathematics and science, and teaching tools and materials based on that knowledge.

We are in the midst of a revision of science and mathematics curricula that states "understanding for all" as its goal. This revision is represented by the current national goals and standards for science and mathematics curricula and teaching (American Association for the Advancement of Science, 1989, 1993; National Council of Teachers of Mathematics, 1989, 1991; National Research Council, 1996). These documents are the products of general trends that are changing American education. One such trend is toward greater accountability for student learning. Elmore (1997) describes this trend as follows:

> Schools will be subjected to more or less unrelenting pressure over the foreseeable future to focus on demonstrable student learning and to seek external guidance from states, professional communities and commercial enterprises for how to solve the difficult problems of what to teach and how to teach it. (p. 17)

As Elmore points out, sustained pressure to produce demonstrable student learning differs from traditional expectations for most schools. Schools traditionally have operated through dispersed control and political pluralism where teachers and administrators responded primarily to local constituents. Large-scale attempts to assess students' understanding were relatively rare, and the results of those assessments had few consequences for teachers and administrators.

These circumstances are changing irrevocably. The standards movement is here to stay. The impact of standards is enhanced by large-scale assessment programs such as the Third International Mathematics and Science Study (TIMSS; Beaton, Mullis, Martin, Gonzalez, Smith, & Kelly, 1996), the National Assessment of Educational Progress (NAEP; National Center for Education Statistics, 1999), and assessment programs in almost every state (Elmore, 1997). Accountability for student learning is becoming a fact of life for teachers and administrators.

In principle, schools also have access to new resources that can help them meet these new expectations. During the past 2 decades, educational researchers, often working in school environments, have developed new insights into the nature of student understanding. They have designed improved strategies for classroom teaching, better teaching materials, and improved teaching tools that incorporate modern information technology. These developments could support teachers in their efforts to help their students learn with understanding.

In combination, these new demands and new resources have the potential to promote professionalism in teaching. As Elmore points out, teachers and administrators traditionally have been more craftspeople than professionals, seeking to satisfy their local constituents and paying relatively little attention to national or international developments in their fields. As state- and national-level standards increase their influence on local educational practices, teachers and administrators could become more like professionals in other fields, using the results of large-scale research and development programs to meet high and uniform standards throughout the nation.

It is by no means certain, however, that the current changes will benefit schools. In particular, accountability pressures can have positive effects only if teachers have the personal and professional resources to respond. New standards and testing programs could demoralize teachers and school systems that lack adequate resources. Pressure to "teach to the test" could obliterate the pockets of excellent teaching that currently exist, and educational practitioners could perceive the best new tools and resources as irrelevant to their quest to improve standardized test scores.

So which of these views of the future will become a reality? Will schools respond to pressure by using new tools and resources to improve the professionalism of their teachers and the quality of their teaching, or will they develop bureaucratic control systems that encourage mediocrity? This question ultimately will be answered locally, in schools and classrooms throughout the nation. In this introductory chapter we consider the nature of teaching for understanding, the demands that it places on teachers, and the challenges that it poses for schools as organizations.

THE NATURE AND DEMANDS OF TEACHING FOR UNDERSTANDING

The more hopeful image for the future envisioned above assumes that school professionals will use tools from educational research to enact new and more effective teaching practices. In this section we look at the nature of those practices and the demands they make on teachers.

Learning with Understanding

"Teaching for understanding for all" encompasses two goals for students in our schools: (1) understanding of science and mathematics content, and (2) equity among students of different races, cultures, social classes, and levels of ability. We have abundant evidence (from TIMSS and NAEP) that neither of these goals is being achieved now. American students generally are poorly prepared for work and citizenship in a complex technological society. American students score lower on international achievement tests than do students from other industrialized nations. Furthermore, middle-class European American and Asian American students do far better than students of other races and cultures or students from poor families.

In this book we study the practices of researchers, teachers, and administrators who are working in schools to do better. Their work begins with a critique of current curricula, which treat mathematics as a hierarchically organized sequence of skills in symbol manipulation and formal reasoning, and science as a large set of facts and concepts to be learned. In their view, these curricula misrepresent the nature of the disciplines and lead to poor performance in student learning.

Classroom research studies indicate that curricula emphasizing facts and skills really make sense to only a few students (e.g., Erlwanger, 1973). Most students who appear to be successful actually rely on memorization and symbol manipulation. These students generally make reasonably good grades through "procedural display"—producing acceptable answers without understanding the symbols and facts in any depth. Other students show active or passive resistance and alienation. Thus, meaningful learning of science and mathematics is limited to a small group of elite students.

The projects that we studied in this book shared an alternative view of science and mathematics curricula. This vision begins with a deeper look at scientific and mathematical reasoning as it is practiced in disciplinary communities. Symbols and facts play a role, but are used for collective sense making. At the core of these projects is a search for *patterns* in number and space (math) or in the phenomena of the material world (science). Scientifically and mathematically literate people work collectively to explore and explain these patterns and to use them for real-world problem solving. The specialized symbols and vocabulary of science and mathematics are used in the service of this collective pattern-finding and sense-making activity.

This view of the nature of science and mathematics encourages an alternative view of the curriculum, in which the goal of instruction is to engage students in *collective pattern finding and sense making*. Learning with understanding takes place in classroom communities wherein teachers have established norms and practices with careful attention to students' understanding. Lehrer, Carpenter, Schauble, and Putz (2000) point out that successful learning is a social activity.

> Thinking is brought into being and develops within contexts that are fashioned by people. Whether or not we are aware of it, these contexts include norms for the kinds of questions worth pursuing, the activities that are valued, the forms of argumentation deemed convincing, and the criteria for a satisfactory explanation. (p. 81)

This view of the curriculum reveals what Warren, Ballenger, Ogonowski, Rosebery, and Hudicourt-Barnes (2001) describe as "generative continuities" between the language and reasoning of children, including children who are poorly prepared for procedural display, and the language and reasoning of scientists and mathematicians. For example, children are like scientists in their tendencies to generate preliminary explanations that use informal or metaphorical language, or to imagine themselves in the circumstances of plants or animals that they are studying. By building on these generative continuities, it is possible to engage a wider range of children in rigorous reasoning about scientific and mathematical problems and in meaningful learning of science and mathematics.

Teaching for Understanding

Teaching that emphasizes pattern finding and sense making is empowering for students, but it is also demanding on teachers, who must lead classroom communities that differ from traditional classrooms in their priorities and orientations, patterns of classroom practice, and organizational resources. Although they are diverse, classrooms that exhibit teaching for understanding share some common characteristics, including *attention to student thinking*, a focus on *powerful scientific and mathematical ideas and practices*, and the development of *equitable classroom learning communities*. We briefly illustrate and discuss each of these below.

Attention to Student Thinking. Teaching for understanding begins with careful consideration of students' thinking, interests, language, and practices. Students bring ideas, ways of understanding the world, and patterns of practice that are the starting points for building understanding. Successful teachers are able to discover and understand their students' personal perspectives and build the language and activities of their classrooms upon those resources. For example, Lehrer, Carpenter, Schauble, and Putz (2000) have described how teachers in Verona, Wisconsin, built their teaching around questions that children generated about Wisconsin Fast Plants (a plant that completes its entire growth cycle within 40 days):

EXAMPLE 1.1. TEACHING FOR UNDERSTANDING IN A THIRD-GRADE CLASSROOM

☐ Most questions that one class of third-graders generated before planting seeds to grow Wisconsin Fast Plants looked to endpoints of growth: "How tall will they grow?" A few concerned timing of events in the life cycle. During its second round of growing Fast Plants, however, the class generated more subtle questions. Some were oriented toward function, such as the role of petals and pollen, others toward development: for instance, the typical shape of the growth curve. Interval—"On what day?"—raised issues. Still others involved comparison: for example, the effects of different amounts of fertilizer. Over cycles of inquiry, questions became increasingly elaborated: "how long does it take" gave way to "how many more days" and then to "what day." From "flower buds" to "role of petals" and "what makes pollen," questions grew more specific. They also reflected increasing cognizances of variation: the words "usually," "normally," and "mainly" begin to be used to qualify statements. Students also turned from queries about endpoints to questions about change over time and rates of growth.

One way to begin examining and evaluating questions is to record them on index cards and ask small groups to arrange and rearrange them into categories. Then each group of students describes its category system, a process that encourages children to read and become familiar with the range and variety of questions, as well as to consider additional ways of categorizing. We have observed similarities in the ways that students in the third grade through the fifth (and groups of teachers!) categorize questions. Some categorize by words that appear in the question; for example, all questions containing the word "flower" are grouped together. Others group by concepts. Questions about living organisms may be sorted into groups labeled "growing," "size," or "environment." Some groups classify questions into the familiar format who–what–when–where–why–how. Occasionally, a student suggests that the questions be sorted by the type of answer expected. This insight often helps students understand that many questions that can be answered by a simple "yes" or "no" are less interesting than queries that call for more complex answers. Students may separate from problems that they think unsolvable others that can be addressed by authorities such as books and experts or by investigation. It can also be useful to ask the class which questions are interesting or simple, and what makes them so. The class may consider which questions they could investigate within a given amount of time and which would take longer. Class discussions about how a question can be investigated are as important as later discussions about what has been learned from the investigation.

As students evaluate their questions, the teacher will also be considering which questions are most likely to be productive for extended class work. This will require attention to children's prior knowledge, the tasks and tools the question calls for, and the potential for developing reasoning and argument at both the planning stage and the resolution. . . . Time spent in helping students work at posing and revising questions also pays off in a deeper understanding of the results. (pp. 92–93)   ■

The children in the Verona classrooms were learning science in the traditional sense of mastering facts and skills, but they also were learning science in the deeper sense of being engaged in collective pattern finding and sense making about the material world. These activities were rewarding for students, but they also were demanding for teachers. Rather than just being aware of students' general levels of ability, the teachers had to understand and make use of students' thinking. These teachers used their students' ideas and practices as resources for building understanding.

Thus, teaching for understanding requires teachers to attend closely to patterns in students' language and activities, incorporate these patterns into classroom practice, and help students to change them when they are inadequate. Well-designed teaching materials that engage students' interests, reveal their ways of thinking, and utilize their ideas and language can help teachers in these tasks.

Powerful Scientific and Mathematical Ideas and Practices. Although students' ideas and practices are important in teaching for understanding, they must be challenged and changed. Teachers must work to change students' initial curiosity into more mature scientific and mathematical interests: exploring pattern in number and space, describing and understanding nature and technology. These teachers engage their students in powerful scientific and mathematical ideas and practices and develop commonly held standards that support those practices. For example, Cobb and Bauersfeld (1995) describe the mathematical practices of students in inquiry mathematics classrooms:

> The standards of argumentation established in an inquiry classroom are such that the teacher and students typically challenge explanations that merely describe the manipulation of symbols. Further, acceptable explanations appear to carry the significance of acting on taken-as-shared mathematical objects. Consequently, from the observer's perspective, the teacher and students seem to be acting in a taken-as-shared mathematical reality, and to be elaborating that reality in the course of their ongoing negotiations of mathematical meanings. (pp. 2–3)

An example of a powerful mathematical idea is *distribution*. This concept plays a critical role in statistical reasoning and scientific experimentation. Distributions of data points enable us to compare ranges of experiences in situations where there is a lot of variation. As citizens we regularly encounter situations that call for understanding and comparing distributions. For example, we must choose schools for our children, vote on propositions and bond issues, or decide what to make of statistically based advice about diet and health. Distributions are equally important in the natural and social sciences. For example, an evolutionary biologist studying speciation, an ecologist studying the effects of environmental toxins, a sociologist studying immigrant populations, and an educator studying the effects of collaborative groupwork must all compare distributions. McClain (2000) has described how she helped her seventh-grade students take an important step toward understanding distributions:

EXAMPLE 1.2. TEACHING FOR UNDERSTANDING IN MIDDLE SCHOOL MATHEMATICS

☐ The particular task asked the students to analyze the T-cell counts of two groups of AIDS patients who had enrolled in different treatment protocols. A lengthy discussion revealed that the students were quite knowledgeable about AIDS and understood the importance of finding an effective treatment. Further, they clarified the relation between T-cell counts and a patient's overall health (increased T-cell counts are desirable). In the task, students were given data on the T-cell counts of 46 patients in a new, experimental treatment and the T-cell counts of 186 patients in a standard protocol [see accompanying figure]. The students were asked not only to make a recommendation about which protocol was more effective, but were also asked to develop inscriptions that could be used to support their arguments.

The teacher began the whole-class discussion by posting the reports and the inscriptions that the students had created on the white board. In discussing the reports, students were asked to decide if the reports were "adequate" for another person who had not seen the data to use to make a good decision. In

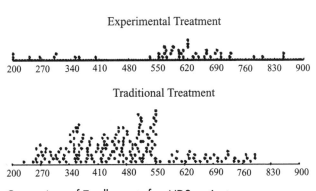

Comparison of T-cell counts for AIDS patients.

one of the first reports that was discussed, the students had partitioned the data at a T-cell count of 550 and found that "the majority" of the data in the standard protocol was below a 550 T-cell count and "the majority" of the data in the experimental protocol was above a 550 T-cell count. Towards the end of the discussion, Val asked the following:

> *Val:* Uhm, why did they pick 550? Why is 550 so important? 'Cause the median is really 500, but it's not 550.

Here, Val was asking for a backing for the warrant. She wanted to understand why the group had decided to partition the data at 550 since it did not represent any particular value of the data set such as the median. At this point, the teacher clarified that these students had chosen the T-cell count of 550 because the "hill" of one data set was mostly below this value and the "hill" of the other was mostly above. The teacher then pointed to the next report in which the students had noted the number of patients in each protocol that fell within the range of 200 to 525 and then 525 to 850.

> *Teacher:* This group did a similar thing. Because they said they looked at how many of the T-cell counts were between 200 and 525 and they looked at how many were between 525 and above. So they used 525 and these people use 550 so they were doing like you were talking about, Meg, looking at where the hills started to change on the graphs. Questions or comments about these two ways? Mari?
> *Mari:* I would think the second one would be more confusing since the old program has more numbers than the new program.
> *Teacher:* Ah, so it looks like it's more . . . they had 56 that were above 525 and they only had 37?
> *Mari:* So it's like so I guess what I'm trying to say is that it's harder to compare.
> *Teacher:* What about what Mari said? She just said there were more people in the old program so if you actually look at the actual numbers of people you find out they had 56 that are in this upper range where we want to be and these only had 37 so somebody might say the old program was better because it had more.

In sequencing the choice of solutions to be shared, the goal had been to move from more qualitative descriptions, such as looking at the "hills" and "the majority" of the data, to quantitative comparisons that might then become problematic due to the unequal N's of the two data sets. Mari's comment provided the perfect opportunity to highlight this dilemma. In this way, the teacher was able to advance her mathematical agenda by building from the students' reports. In particular, the ensuing discussion involved students actually discussing ways to "make them equal" so that they could compare the two data sets. The notion of using percentages was suggested and students then calculated the percentage of patients in both treatments in each interval. From these values, the students were able to make judgments about which program was more effective. (pp. 21–23)   ■

This kind of teaching demands of teachers a deep appreciation of the core scientific and mathematical ideas that they are teaching and of how students can engage those ideas. The teachers must understand the language and practices of scientists and mathematicians and help students to use that language and engage in those practices. They must be able help their students develop standards for explanation and argumentation that approach the rigor of scientific and mathematical standards. Teaching materials that incorporate powerful scientific and mathematical ideas and practices in ways that are accessible to students can help teachers meet these difficult demands. Teaching for understanding engages students with the core ideas and principles of a discipline (see also Newmann & Associates, 1996), and encourages students to make connections among ideas, in contrast to the fragmentation that characterizes much of contemporary schooling. Understanding is meaningless without rigorous content, and content is trivialized if understanding is superficial.

Equitable Classroom Learning Communities. If the goal of understanding for *all* is to be achieved, then classroom learning communities must give all students access to resources and to meaningful and productive opportunities to participate. This means that teachers must help students to develop rigorous and democratic social norms and to find appropriate roles and responsibilities in the classroom community. Equitable classroom learning communities recognize the individual and cultural differences among students and overcome the effects of stigma and stereotype threat (Steele, 1992, 1999). For example, Rosebery, Warren, Conant, and Hudicourt-Barnes (1992) have described how a group of seventh- and eighth-grade Haitian immigrant students at the Graham and Parks Alternative Public School (K–8) in Cambridge, Massachusetts, were able to engage in scientific sense making and to make connections with European American students in their school:

EXAMPLE 1.3. TEACHING FOR UNDERSTANDING IN A JUNIOR HIGH SCIENCE CLASS

☐ The Water Taste Test was an investigation the students designed to investigate the "truth" of a belief held by most of the junior high students (mainstream and bilingual) that the water from the fountain on the third floor (where their classrooms are located) was superior to the water from the other fountains in their school. Challenged by their teacher, the students set out to determine whether they actually preferred water from the third-floor fountain or only thought they did. As a first step, they designed and then took a blind taste test of water from the first-, second-, and third-floor fountains. To their surprise, they found that two-thirds of them chose the water from the first-floor fountain, although they all said they preferred drinking from the third-floor fountain.

But the students did not believe the data. They held firmly to their belief that the first-floor fountain was the worst because "all the little kids slobber in it." (The first-floor fountain is located near the kindergarten and first-grade classrooms.) Their teacher was also suspicious of the results because she had expected no differences among the three water fountains. These suspicions motivated the class to conduct a second taste test with a larger sample drawn from the other junior high classes.

The students decided where, when, and how to run their experiment. They discussed methodological issues: how to collect the water, how to hide the identity of the sources, and, crucially, how many fountains to include. They decided to include the same three as before so they could compare results. They worried about bias in the voting process: what if some students voted more than once? Each student in the class volunteered to organize a piece of the experiment. About 40 mainstream students participated in the blind taste test. When the class analyzed their data, they found support for their earlier results: 88% of the junior high students thought they preferred water from the third-floor fountain, but 55% actually chose the water from the first floor.

Faced with this evidence, the students' suspicion turned to curiosity. Why was the water from the first-floor fountain preferred? How could they determine the source of the preference? They decided to analyze the school's water along several dimensions, among them acidity, salinity, and bacteria. They found that all the fountains had unacceptably high levels of bacteria. In fact, the first-floor fountain (the one most preferred) had the highest bacterial count! They also found that the water from the first-floor fountain was 20 degrees colder than the water from fountains on the other floors. Based on their findings, they concluded that temperature was probably a deciding factor in taste preference. They theorized that the water was naturally cooled as it sat in the city's underground pipes during the winter months (the study was conducted in February), and warmed as it flowed from the basement to the third floor. (p. 16) ∎

Although they were "educationally disadvantaged," these Haitian students conducted a scientifically rigorous investigation leading them to unexpected results. The teacher found generative continuities between students' and scientists' strategies and helped students to use these strategies in their collective and individual sense-making efforts. She accomplished this because she had a deep understanding of the nature and sources of differences among students and could fashion a community where students respected those differences as assets. Teachers in diverse classrooms must understand how culturally based norms affect students, and they must find ways of managing cooperation and competition so that all students are working hard in an atmosphere where they feel personally secure.

Successful Classrooms as Resource-Rich Communities

The ideals described above are widely shared but rarely achieved in practice. It is difficult for teachers to marshal the full array of personal resources that it takes to develop a classroom learning community: commitment, knowledge of students, subject matter, and strategies for building equitable learning communities. Few schools have successfully supported teachers' efforts to teach for understanding. Why should we believe that these high ideals can become models for real practice?

There is hope, in the form of a growing knowledge base that includes new theories, tools, and practices that enable teachers to be responsive to students around powerful disciplinary ideas. These new forms of understanding and practice include the following:

- New intellectual frameworks that connect students' thinking with scientific or mathematical reasoning, enabling teachers to understand both students' thinking and disciplinary reasoning in greater depth, and to see how the two can be connected (e.g., ways of understanding students' questions about plants and arguments about AIDS treatments)
- New tools for classroom teaching and learning, including tools that make use of new information technologies as well as textbooks and materials for hands-on activities (e.g., the computer tool that students used to create the figure presented earlier)
- New pedagogical techniques that engage students, individually and collectively, with significant scientific and mathematical problems and help them to develop the skills and knowledge to solve those problems (e.g., ways of encouraging student discourse that lead to student-led investigations)

Taken together, these new frameworks, tools, and techniques constitute a powerful and demanding technology for teaching. This technology has the potential to make "understanding for all" an achievable goal. But, like many other complex and powerful technologies, it is resource-intensive, placing substantial demands on teachers and schools. Teaching for understanding for all requires teachers to shift their attention from presenting information and managing students' activities to "bridging the gap" between their students' reasoning and powerful scientific and mathematical ideas. This requires both a commitment by teachers to putting extra time and effort into their teaching, and the extensive professional and craft knowledge necessary to make that extra effort pay off.

Beyond that, teachers must be willing to invest their time and energy without being certain that their investments will pay off. Teaching, even in its more conventional forms, is an uncertain practice (Cohen, 1988). By uncertain we mean that teaching is contingent, involving instructional decisions that are based on how well students are learning; it is complex, requiring attention to many students; it is risky, in that it will not always be successful; and it is ambiguous, that is, the goals of teaching are often multiple, and ways of judging success are often contradictory.

Uncertainty is not a problem to be solved, since it is an inherent part of teaching. Rather, it is a dilemma to be managed. Teachers manage this dilemma in several ways. Most have a wide repertoire of routines that they can apply in many different settings with a high probability of success. They have elaborated knowledge of what works and why it works, and when things go wrong, they can implement backup plans. Expert teachers have an extensive repertoire of knowledge about teaching, practices, and other human resources that allow them to manage much of the uncertainty in teaching.

Teachers also depend on one another to manage this uncertainty collectively. Colleagues working together within a professional group, for example, establish norms governing how new members join the group, how they share information among each other, and what practices are acceptable and unacceptable, and they support one another's adoption of those norms and the associated practices. Within a school setting, individual teachers receive support and encouragement to adopt practices that have been tacitly sanctioned, if not actively pursued, by their departmental colleagues, teachers within the larger school, or others within their profession.

A *shift* from conventional teaching to teaching for understanding makes uncertainty more salient because it takes away the routines and practices that teachers have developed over years and that were successful according to old criteria. For example, teachers must forgo the kinds of bargains that Doyle (1983, 1986) describes, in which teachers and students reduce risk and ambiguity by making academic work predictable and routine. Teachers must decide which practices remain viable and which will no longer work. Many potential strategies to manage this uncertainty are themselves under question.

Teachers who try to enact new ideas about teaching for understanding face the uncertainty that comes with being pioneers; there is no set of readily available routinized "teaching for understanding" practices that are comparable to the routines of conventional teaching. That is, while conventional teaching has a well-developed body of technical knowledge, teaching for understanding does not. Furthermore, it is not clear which of the practices that some very gifted teachers have developed under unique conditions and/or with strong support (e.g., Ball & Rundquist, 1993; Fennema & Romberg, 1999; Hiebert et al., 1997; Lampert, 1986, 1990) can be used by conventional teachers who are shifting over to teaching for understanding.

The lack of ready-made routines saddles teachers with the added burden of having to create and validate a new set of practices that support teaching for understanding. Moreover, teaching for understanding can disrupt professional communities because it requires teachers to question norms and beliefs that they share with colleagues. Hence, a shift to teaching for understanding makes explicit the uncertainty that is inherent in teaching in general, and it may well create increased uncertainty through the loss of routines that help teachers with curricular decisions, instruction, and assessment (Fennema & Romberg, 1999).

These fundamental changes in teaching practice and resources form the context for the study described in this book. These changes make new demands, not only on teachers, but on the organizations within which they work. Schools, school districts, and other organizations that provide resources or expertise to educators also will have to alter their accustomed practices and provide new resources to teachers. The focus in this book is on school organizations and the professionals within them. We seek to understand the organizational conditions and resources that enable schools to support teaching for understanding for all in science and mathematics classrooms.

CHALLENGES FOR SCHOOLS AND SCHOOL DISTRICTS

To summarize the argument to this point, we are currently in the midst of large-scale changes in our expectations for science and mathematics curricula. In particular, schools are increasingly expected to produce demonstrable improvements in measures of student learning. It is conceivable that schools will be able to respond to the new demands with more professional approaches to science and mathematics teaching that will bring "understanding for all" closer to reality. Current research has produced many "existence proofs"—examples of resource-rich classrooms that have these qualities and help all students to learn with understanding.

Yet most teachers today cannot teach for understanding within their present organizational contexts. They lack the human resources (their own knowledge and abilities) and the material resources (teaching tools and facilities) to create and sustain classroom communities that will support understanding by all students.

Thus, the existence proofs developed in research contexts can become widespread practice only if schools can deliver new kinds of support to teachers. Our purpose in this study is to investigate how a number of schools and school districts are responding to this challenge. We want to know more about the challenges they face and the strategies they use to meet these challenges. We hope to understand how our current existence proofs in the form of individual classrooms can become existence proofs in the form of entire schools or school districts, and ultimately how teaching for understanding might become accepted professional practice on a large scale.

Previous research and experience suggest something of the nature of the challenges that school professionals—teachers, administrators, and professional developers—must face in order to make teaching for understanding for all a widespread practice. In this section we review the most important of those challenges:

1. Providing resources for classroom teaching
2. Aligning purposes, perceptions, and commitments
3. Sustaining teaching for understanding

Challenge 1: Providing Resources for Classroom Teaching

The first challenge that schools face as organizations is that they must "deliver the goods" to classroom teachers. They must help teachers to develop or acquire the knowledge (human resources) and tools (material resources) to teach for understanding for all in their classrooms. The same researchers who have demonstrated the possibility of teaching for understanding in some classrooms also have documented how difficult this challenge will be for our schools (e.g., Lehrer, Schauble, Carpenter, & Penner, 2000; McClain, 2000). The available research evidence indicates that this requires (1) long-term professional development, and (2) human resources (experts) and material from outside the school community.

A large body of empirical research has investigated the knowledge and tools that teachers need to teach science and mathematics for understanding. The evidence from this research indicates that teaching for understanding requires all the knowledge and material resources needed to support competent traditional teaching, and more besides. Several good reviews of this research are available (e.g., Cohen, McLaughlin, & Talbert, 1993; Kennedy, 1991), and we will not attempt to summarize them in this chapter. Instead, we will focus on a few essential resources discussed in the section on the nature and demands of teaching for understanding above, including the following:

- Tools and teaching materials that support student engagement
- Understanding and ability to respond to students' reasoning
- Understanding of powerful ideas in science and mathematics and the ability to relate them to students' ideas
- Understanding of differences among students that focuses on qualitative resources that students bring to the classroom rather than on quantitative differences in ability and motivation
- The ability to develop social norms in classroom learning communities that promote engagement and learning for all students

The difficulties of providing such an impressive array of resources in every classroom are obvious, yet this is precisely the first challenge that schools face. How can they do it? Much of the remainder of this book is devoted to answering this question. Some characteristics of the answer, though, are dictated by the organizational conditions of schools.

Schools as organizations are set up to support routinized, predictable forms of practice that (1) are responsive to a variety of different demands, and (2) can be supported with limited organizational resources. In contrast, the examples that we have of successful teaching for understanding involve teaching practices that are complex, demanding, not reducible to predictable routines, and based on new tools and knowledge that most teachers currently lack. Thus, providing teachers with the new resources listed above will require fundamental changes in school budgets, staffing patterns, time allocations, and many other aspects of life for professionals working in schools. Two of these changes are especially notable.

First, this challenge requires *long-term professional development* that engages teachers in professional learning communities with many of the characteristics of successful classroom learning communities described above. The teachers and other professionals in these communities will have to develop common purposes, they will have to engage in meaningful reasoning about essential professional knowledge, and they will need the support of a rich array of material, human, and social resources.

Second, this challenge requires *partnerships between school professionals and outside agents*, such as university-based researchers, professional developers, or members of teachers' professional networks. That is, teachers' and administrators' support for their professional communities and professional development activities is necessary, but not sufficient. They will need the long-term involvement of other professionals who can provide knowledge and materials that they lack.

Challenge 2: Aligning Purposes, Perceptions, and Commitments

As Labaree (1997) and others (e.g., Cohen, McLaughlin, & Talbert, 1993; Tyack & Cuban, 1995) have pointed out, American schools today provide the general public with a variety of services. Schools provide custodial care for children; they provide credentials and rankings to students aspiring to different kinds of jobs; they prepare workers and citizens. Our society's expectations for its schools are complex and sometimes contradictory. Schools must use their limited resources to accommodate multiple demands and balance conflicting priorities. How can school professionals deal with the multiple expectations placed on them (of which teaching for understanding is only one) and the sometimes conflicting practices associated with those expectations?

Most schools have an infrastructure devoted to maintaining traditional teaching in its diverse forms. Many teachers, students, and parents value the benefits that this infrastructure provides in a traditional school that is working well:

- Parents may value a school that provides a safe and predictable environment for children, credentials for advancing in the educational system, and preparation for work and citizenship (cf., Labaree, 1997). Many parents also like schools in which the curriculum resembles the curriculum that they remember from their own schooling.
- Administrators may value a school that works in smooth and predictable ways, satisfies parents and other influential members of the local community, and does not make excessive demands for material or human resources.
- Teachers may value a work environment that is secure, stable, socially friendly, egalitarian, and not excessively demanding of their time or intellectual energies, and that allows them to work autonomously in their classrooms.

- Well-run traditional schools also can succeed in accommodating a variety of ideals and practices within their classrooms and within their professional groups. Teachers with very different pedagogical theories and classroom communities can work side by side without interfering with one another.

Given these virtues of traditional schooling, it is predictable that not everyone will be enamored of attempts to shift the emphasis of schooling to teaching for understanding. In schools that have these traditional virtues, there will be questions about whether the costs of a shift to teaching for understanding exceed the benefits—why devote time and energy to disruptive attempts to "fix what ain't broke"? In schools that are struggling to achieve these virtues, there will be questions of priorities—why worry about teaching for understanding when kids are fighting in the halls and the school's annual budget for paper runs out by January? (Tyack & Cuban, 1995).

As Gamoran, Secada, and Marrett (2000) noted, there is little evidence that schools know how to manage the complex array of internal and external relationships necessary to engender, in all teachers, the kind of commitment and sustained effort necessary for teaching for understanding. Schools are not well equipped to deal with professional cultures in which teachers play differentiated roles and feel social and administrative pressure to enable their students' understanding. Yet it seems unlikely that teaching for understanding can become a widespread practice without these changes in professional cultures. In Gamoran and colleagues' (2000) terms, most schools function as "loosely coupled systems" (see Chapter 2), but it is doubtful that such systems can support as complex and difficult an endeavor as teaching for understanding.

Thus, the most likely outcomes of reform efforts are not the complete transformations of schools' professional groups, as described above, but a variety of partial alternatives in which professional groups devoted to reform and to traditional teaching compete for and divide organizational resources. Gamoran and colleagues (2000) describe some of the alternatives that the current literature documents:

- *Constant conflict.* The professional development group and other members of the school professional group engage in sustained conflict over resources, standards, and practices.
- *Compromise—accommodation instead of transformation.* Members of the professional development group choose not to challenge essential parts of the existing professional culture. This kind of compromise often becomes "innovation without change."
- *Coexistence—change as an alternative structure alongside traditional structures.* The professional development group becomes a "school within a school" that coexists with a more traditional school professional group.

Thus, we can expect conflict and confusion about purposes, perceptions, and commitments to be a major issue in schools that are undergoing organizational change. Teachers and administrators must balance multiple demands on their time and energy and address multiple purposes that society has for schools. Even teachers and administrators who believe that they support teaching for understanding and the reform movement in general often perceive the entailments of teaching for understanding differently from university researchers and leaders of the reform movement.

Challenge 3: Sustaining Teaching for Understanding

Our society benefits from teaching for understanding only if it becomes a practice that is sustained over time. We see little reason to believe that teaching for understanding will turn out to be like riding a bicycle—an activity that can be learned once and then sustained with little additional effort or attention. Teaching for understanding will continue to be more like top-quality professional practice in other fields—a complex and demanding activity that requires continuing commitment and new resources as the state of the art changes over time. Thus, teachers as individuals and schools as communities will have to sustain their commitment and efforts indefinitely.

Our reading of the research literature and our thinking about the cases presented in this book suggest three important points about sustaining teaching for understanding: (1) it will require *collective as well as individual efforts*, (2) it will depend on *interdependence rather than independence*, and (3) it will depend on *leadership of professional communities*. Each of these points is discussed below.

Collective as Well as Individual Efforts. It seems unlikely that even the most dedicated teachers will be able to sustain the resources and commitment necessary for teaching for understanding by themselves. They will need the support of colleagues and continuing access to new developments in their fields. Thus, sustaining teaching for understanding is a challenge for professional communities, not just for individual professionals.

Interdependence Rather than Independence. Successful professional communities will generate many of the resources that they need to sustain their activities and high-quality teaching by their members. However, it is unlikely that they will ever become self-sustaining in the sense that they will no longer need external resources. Rather, we might hope that successful professional communities will become integrated into networks of people and institutions that exchange resources and work together for mutual benefit. Thus, the key question is whether the exchange of resources can be sustained, *not* whether the community can continue without outside resources.

Leadership of Professional Communities. The responsibility for sustaining professional communities will depend ultimately on their leaders, but leadership in schools that support teaching for understanding is likely to take a different form from leadership in traditional schools. Leadership will become more a set of functions that are filled by different individuals than roles that are assigned to particular people. Spillane, Halverson, and Diamond (2001) suggest that school leaders have the following functions:

- Constructing and selling an instructional vision
- Building norms of trust, collaboration, and academic press
- Supporting teacher development
- Monitoring instruction and innovation

Professional communities that are able to sustain teaching for understanding will find ways to allocate these functions among administrators, teachers, and professional developers and to sustain them over time.

Summary

Even as resources in the school and district context can foster and sustain professional development, ongoing change requires a process that allows professional development to alter the nature of resources available in the school and district. Leadership for teachers, administrative roles recast as facilitators rather than managers, changes in the allocation of time during the school day, and materials to implement new teaching practices may all result from professional development. Schools and districts that promote such "contagion"—modifying resources to fit new teaching endeavors—enhance their capacity for change. Schools and districts that force new initiatives to conform to existing arrays of resources risk stifling or marginalizing potential change.

CONCLUSIONS

We began this chapter with a discussion of demands and resources—demands on schools for improved student achievement in mathematics and science, and resources in the form of powerful but demanding new technologies for developing student understanding. We have argued that schools will need substantial resources themselves to use these technologies. Teachers will need knowledge, commitment, and material resources to create classroom learning communities that support teaching for understanding. School organizations will need to create and sustain forms of professional development that support teachers' classroom work.

Few school organizations will have the capacity to meet these challenges without outside help. They will need to form partnerships with outside agents, researchers, or professional developers who have expertise in the technologies of teaching for understanding. These will have to be sustained partnerships, both because building capacity in schools and classrooms is a long process and because the technologies are changing. The remainder of this book describes and discusses six such partnerships. Each of these partnerships faced the challenges described above. We will share what we have learned from studying their successes and their failures.

CHAPTER 2

A Dynamic Model of Organizational Support

Adam Gamoran and Charles W. Anderson

What conceptual tools do we need to understand how schools and districts engage in the complex process of moving toward teaching for understanding? As we prepared for our research on six cases of teacher–researcher partnerships, we found that existing models did not provide all the concepts we needed in order to study how school organizations respond to the challenges. We therefore have developed our own model, which we explain in this chapter and use to frame the remaining chapters.

We begin with another vignette of the professional work of teachers who teach science for understanding. Unlike the vignettes in Chapter 1, this focuses on teachers' work outside of the classroom as they met to improve their teaching. We discuss how our key ideas from Chapter 1—characteristics of teaching for understanding and challenges for schools—can help us appreciate the significance of these teachers' activities. We also discuss the limitations of these concepts for understanding organizational change. We then present the key elements of our model and compare our model to related models and theories.

AN EXAMPLE FROM A WORKING PARTNERSHIP

In all of the partnerships we studied, teachers and researchers collaborated to build knowledge necessary for teaching for understanding and to enact their ideas in classrooms. Indeed, the lines between teachers and researchers were often blurry, with researchers frequently teaching in classrooms and teachers participating as members of research teams. The teachers and researchers often met to learn from one another and to develop classroom teaching strategies. Example 2.1, from a different study by Rosebery and Puttick (1998), exemplifies one kind of discussion that took place in the meetings we observed. This excerpt describes a discussion focusing on a videotape of a small group of sixth-grade science students in the class of Elizabeth Cook Dennis. Liz and her colleagues had been participating for 16 months in a project that involved both intensive science learning and discussions of videotapes and classroom transcripts. During the second year of their collaboration, Liz showed her colleagues a videotape of a small-group discussion in her classroom. The group, which included Brian and Dylan, was exploring the nascent theory that the "gravitational pull of the sun and the moon caused the tides."

EXAMPLE 2.1. SHARING AN INSTRUCTIONAL EXPERIENCE IN PROFESSIONAL DEVELOPMENT

☐ Liz told her colleagues that she had chosen this episode because she valued the effort her students were making to understand the data and to use them to try to support their "theory." She pointed out how they struggled to figure out if there is a relationship among moonrise and -set times, high and low tides, and sunrise and -set times, and what this might have to say about their theory.

Liz also spoke about the value she saw for individual students. This, for example, is what she said about Brian:

> Brian, I mean his whole expression was, "wait a minute, I need to figure this out, I need to think about this." And—and later on in the tape they—they start to talk about, when Brian was talking about "around midnight the moon rises," what he says shortly after that is, "and then it's low tide right around that same time" and Dylan will say, "What do you mean? What are you trying to say?" And so he tries to explain by using that and then they try to look at the other tides, the A.M. tides and see if that coincides with anything that they found. But I—I guess what I see is kids who know they have the right answer starting to question themselves. Or you know, where, in the group's needing to, to make that more—to make sense to the other kids in the groups. . . . So I think it made them think a little more about how exactly it would work. (December 13, 1993)

Liz described how she saw Brian engage with the tides data and how he "need[ed] to figure this out." She pointed out how he used the data to probe his thinking and that of the group. She was pleased that Brian, a student who usually thinks he has the right answer, was forced to think hard about his own ideas and . . . she highlighted the role she believed the group played in challenging him to explain himself.

During their discussion of the video segment, Liz's colleagues asked her whether she thought her students had difficulty understanding the textbook theory. She said that, while they had talked about it for a long time and their work in the library had prepared many of them to understand it, she worried that, while some students like Brian and Dylan had understood it pretty well, others had not. She went on to tell her colleagues how she was still struggling with "how to set up" her science classes to enable all her students to learn. (pp. 669–670) ■

How might we understand what Liz and her colleagues were doing and its role in the development of schools that support teaching for understanding? Our answer to this question has several parts. First, consider the *content of the discussion* between Liz and her colleagues and its relation to the characteristics of teaching for understanding discussed in Chapter 1: attention to student thinking, powerful scientific and mathematical ideas and practices, and equitable classroom learning communities. Even in the short excerpt above, it is clear that each of these characteristics played a key role in Liz's discussion with her colleagues. They studied a classroom videotape in order to understand her students' thinking about powerful ideas, including the nature of gravity and how life on earth is affected by the gravity of other bodies in addition to the earth. Liz and her colleagues also discussed their concerns about how the unit worked for all the students in the class, including those not usually successful in science.

The ideas about teaching for understanding from Chapter 1 also can help us to understand the *nature of professional development activities* in which Liz and her colleagues participated. Just as Liz and her colleagues based their teaching on attention to student thinking, the workshop organizers paid careful attention to the teachers' thinking. The workshops also were built around a set of powerful ideas about teaching and learning science, including ideas about science content, about students and how they learn, and about teaching strategies. Finally, the organizers were committed to creating the equitable professional community in which Liz and her colleagues participated. Thus, the professional development activities were themselves a form of teaching for understanding focused on science content, students and their thinking, and teaching strategies.

We also can understand Liz and her colleagues' activities in terms of how they address the *challenges for schools and school districts* discussed in Chapter 1. We can see that these professional development activities are addressing the three challenges: providing resources for classroom teaching; aligning purposes, perceptions, and commitments; and sustaining teaching for understanding. Although Liz and her colleagues did not receive resources in the narrow sense of teaching materials that they could carry into the classroom, they were developing themselves as human resources in the broader sense discussed in Chapter 1. They were developing knowledge and skills essential to their successful classroom teaching. This new technical knowledge would help them respond to the uncertainties evident in Liz's struggle "to enable all her students to learn." At the same time, they were developing shared histories and experiences that helped them to align their purposes, perceptions, and commitments. We also can see how the workshops might help to achieve some of the aspects of sustained change discussed in Chapter 1. For example, the workshops promote both collective and individual efforts, and they promote interdependence among teachers and researchers.

Although the ideas from Chapter 1 are useful for understanding the excerpt above, they clearly are not sufficient for understanding the work of the partnerships that we investigated. Here are just a few of the essential questions that are not considered by an analysis based solely on ideas from Chapter 1:

- What is the role of principals and other administrators? How do they support or hinder the efforts of these teachers and researchers?
- What happens to teachers who are not participating in these workshops? How will their relationships with Liz and her colleagues affect the change process?
- Do teaching materials make a difference?
- How do teachers find the time to participate in these activities? Who pays for it?

To investigate these questions and many others, we need a more inclusive conceptual framework, which we present next.

A DYNAMIC, MULTIDIRECTIONAL MODEL FOR UNDERSTANDING ORGANIZATIONAL CHANGE

To understand fully how districts and schools can support teacher change, we need to describe and analyze the complex relations among school organization, teaching, and learning. Because we wish to make comparisons across different cases of teacher–researcher collaborative partnerships, we have articulated the cases around a framework that includes three key elements: *groups*, *practices*, and *organizational resources*. In this section we define these key terms and consider how they apply to the partnerships we studied.

Key Concepts

We could summarize our view of teaching for understanding by saying that learning with understanding occurs when teachers and students develop classroom groups that (1) engage all students in meaningful scientific and mathematical practices, and (2) are rich in resources for teaching and learning. When we say this, we are using the terms *groups*, *practices*, and *resources* with special meanings that require explanation.

Groups. A group is any collection of individuals who share activities that involve direct personal interaction. Groups can be distinguished from professional *communities*, which are generally bound together by shared jargons or technical language, values, and social norms (Newmann & Associates, 1996; Swales, 1990). Similarly, a classroom *group* becomes a *community* only after its members have developed shared interests, concerns, norms, and values.

Members of a professional community have a history of joint work leading to a sense that they are engaged together in a common enterprise. In addition to this shared sense of purpose, they develop shared norms and values, ways of deprivatizing their teaching practices, habits of collaboration, and traditions of reflective dialogue focusing on student learning. Thus, in the excerpt above, we know that Liz and her colleagues are members of a professional group simply because they worked together on some common activities. There is also some evidence that they have formed a professional community, although we would need more evidence than the vignette provides to reach this conclusion with confidence.

In the collaborations that we studied, some teachers worked directly with the researchers, while others did not. Thus, these sites included at least two overlapping professional groups. The *school professional group* included all the teachers and administrators in the school. The *professional development group* included the teachers and researchers who were developing new approaches to teaching for understanding.

Practices. Distinctions among groups are important inasmuch as the groups engage in distinct practices. The shared activities of school professional groups, for example, often focused on schedules, budgets, and policies, while the shared activities of professional development groups focused on understanding student thinking and teaching for understanding in mathematics and science. Although our data focus mostly on verbal activities—speaking, writing, listening, and reading—other activities, such as scientific experimentation or shared social events, are also important.

Organizational Resources. Organizational resources both enable and constrain the activities of a group. We distinguish among three kinds of resources: material, human, and social:

- *Material resources* can be exchanged among groups as materials or information. They include money and anything that money can buy, electronic information, and physical objects and structures. Classroom learning communities may use a variety of material resources, including teaching tools and materials, computers, databases, and so forth. They also generate new material resources of their own: records of data, written explanations, drawings, tools, and models that provide records of joint activities and enable more sophisticated scientific and mathematical practices to be built.
- *Human resources* are qualities of individuals that can be exchanged among groups through overlapping membership. When the members of one group participate

in the activities of another, they make their knowledge, skills, and commitments available to the members of the other group. Teachers provide essential human resources for classroom learning communities: commitments, understanding of students, scientific and mathematical ideas and practices, and knowledge of the cultural and social aspects of classroom groups—all constitute human resources for the classroom. When a teacher who has learned new content and practices through professional development brings those innovations to her classroom, the human resources inherent in the teacher move from the professional development community to the classroom community. Classroom learning communities also are built on the human resources that students bring to them—students' ideas, interests, practices, and language abilities. "Student achievement" is another term for the human resources that students develop in classrooms and can use outside of school.

- *Social resources* are attributes of roles, relationships, or methods of communication that each new group develops separately (although they are built from the human and material resources available). When the teacher and students in a class come together, or when the members of a professional group meet, they must negotiate common purposes; develop shared norms, expectations, and ways of communicating; and establish roles and relationships. With time, they share a history that supports or disrupts their sense of community and trust.

Thus, classroom or professional groups can become learning communities if their practices are well supported by material, human, and social resources. Note that *resources are also constraints*. Teaching materials, for example, enable some activities and modes of reasoning, while making others more difficult. Similarly, teachers' and students' ideas and abilities, or classroom social norms and expectations, make some activities possible and others difficult or impossible.

Groups, Practices, and Organizational Resources in the School Context

For the purposes of this study, we treat schools as consisting of professional groups (the school professional group and the professional development group) and a number of classroom groups whose members engage in relatively stable patterns of practice. Material, human, and social organizational resources enable and constrain the activities of each group. Material and human resources can be exchanged or shared among groups, and groups sometimes develop new resources through their activities. We attempt to understand how the organizational resources of each group enable some practices and constrain others. We are also interested in how groups acquire human and material resources from other groups or develop new resources through their own activities. By considering how resources enable activities and are created by activities, we seek to understand the progress, productivity, and sustainability of the practices of professional groups.

Table 2.1 displays some of the relationships we saw among groups, practices, and organizational resources in the partnerships that we studied. We will discuss the detailed contents of the cells of Table 2.1 in later chapters. For now, we use the table to illustrate some key elements of the ways that we have organized and analyzed our data.

The columns of Table 2.1 represent three major roles of professionals in schools: leadership, professional communication and development, and classroom teaching. As the table indicates, each role is distinguished by certain practices, but not necessarily by the positions or titles of the people in those roles. In some schools different professionals played distinct, clearly defined roles. Other schools, however, carried out these roles in more fluid ways, so that leadership, professional development, and classroom teaching practices were distributed across professionals in different positions.

The last three rows of Table 2.1 suggest the organizational resources that are necessary for people to carry out the activities associated with each role. We suggest that each of these activities requires material, human, and social resources. Many of our analyses focus on how these organizational resources are created and exchanged within and among the professional groups in each partnership.

The Dynamics of Organizational Support

District- and school-based resources such as time and materials constrain teachers, but teachers are not passive recipients. On the contrary, teachers' commitments to particular practices may influence their organizational environments—their schools and districts—to change policies and modify available resources. Consequently, we propose that districts and schools that are responsive to teacher practices can support teachers' efforts to change, while those that refuse to adapt by maintaining an unresponsive process of resource allocation and decision making tend to stifle change and innovation. While we recognize that school systems are hierarchical organizations, composed of classrooms nested within schools, and within districts, we maintain that the flow of resources is not necessarily limited to adjacent levels of the hierarchy, nor is it restricted to a one-way path.

Our emphasis on material, human, and social resources places teacher professional development in a theoretically central position. As Example 2.1 illustrates, professional development expends material resources (time, money, supplies), but it has the potential to create new human and social resources. Groups, practices, and activities thus are placed in a dynamic relation with one another through the medium of teacher professional development (Gamoran, Secada, & Marrett, 2000).

We propose that material, human, and social resources each contribute to schools' and districts' capacity to support teacher change. This is particularly important in the case of teaching for understanding, which demands especially high levels of human and social resources. Because it does not rely on predefined in-

Table 2.1. Activities and Resources of Schools That Support Teaching for Understanding

	Leadership	Professional Communication and Development	Classroom Teaching
People	Teachers Researchers Administrators	Teachers Researchers Administrators	Teachers
Activities or practices	Developing vision Allocating resources Building norms of trust, collaboration, and academic focus Supporting teacher development Monitoring instruction and innovation	Learning about students, content, pedagogy, and equity Planning curriculum, teaching, and assessment of student learning Reflection and revision Maintaining school schedules, climate, and policies	Building on students' ideas and personal resources Engaging students with powerful scientific and mathematical ideas Developing equitable classroom learning communities
Material resources	Money	Time Professional literature Curricular materials	Time Teaching materials and tools
Human resources	Commitment to teaching for understanding for all Organizational skills and knowledge Understanding of classroom teaching Commitment to professional autonomy	Commitment to teaching for understanding for all Understanding of classroom teaching	Commitment to teaching for understanding for all Insight into students' thinking Understanding of powerful scientific and mathematical ideas Qualitative understanding of differences among students Ability to create and sustain equitable classroom communities
Social resources	External linkages Administrative consistency and support Trust	Professional community (shared norms and values, focus on student learning, reflective dialogue, deprivatized practice, and collaboration) Shared technical language Professional autonomy (teacher classroom control and influence on school policies)	Classroom learning community (shared purpose of learning with understanding)

structional scripts, teaching for understanding calls for teachers to have a rich knowledge of content and of students' potential responses to instruction. With these resources, teachers can adapt instruction to furthering students' understanding. Also, teaching for understanding requires teachers to confront the uncertainties inherent in teaching. Since there is no single best way to teach, teachers may be unsure about how to respond to students, and a strong social network of colleagues may help them manage these uncertainties (Gamoran et al., 2000).

Our theoretical model both builds on and departs from earlier research on school organization and school effects. We also have taken some of our key ideas from other research traditions, including economic sociology and sociocultural research on teaching and learning. In the next sections we review these other models and discuss the connections with our model.

EARLIER MODELS OF SCHOOL ORGANIZATION AND SCHOOL EFFECTS

Early studies of the effects of schools ignored what occurred inside schools to focus solely on "inputs" (material resources such as expenditures, books, and facilities) and "outputs" (student achievement). These studies had little success in identifying aspects of schools that enhanced achievement, because they treated schools as "black boxes" without looking at what was happening inside them (e.g., Coleman et al., 1966). By the 1980s, sociologists had moved beyond this "input–output" model to take into account what occurs within schools and classrooms. To this day, however, there is no agreement on the best theoretical model for understanding the relation between schools and their effects on students. The reason for the lack of consensus is that neither of the two most prominent models, "nested layers" and "loose coupling," consistently accounts for the associations they are attempting to understand.

The Nested-Layers Model

One view holds that school systems are arranged in layers, and the way districts and schools affect student achievement is by regulating the flow of resources to classroom teachers. Each layer is embedded in a higher level of organization (i.e., students are nested in classrooms, classrooms in schools, and so on), and resources flow from higher to lower layers in the system. For example, textbooks are chosen at the district level, allocated to schools, and distributed to teachers, who use them with students. Textbooks affect what and how much students learn, so districts can affect learning by choosing better textbooks. The nested-layers model recognizes that teachers have a lot of autonomy in their classrooms, but views resources as constraints that limit what teachers can do. In this conception, an "output" from one level of the school system becomes an "input" at the next. For example, the school day is divided into class periods; that is a school-level output that constitutes an input for classroom teachers. The nested-layers model constitutes a major advance over the older "input–output" model because it attends to what happens inside schools and focuses on teaching and learning, through which achievement is produced.

The best example of a successful application of the nested-layers model is Barr and Dreeben's (1983) classic analysis of first-grade reading. These authors showed that allocations of time, curricular materials, and students have strong influences on what teachers teach and how much students learn. Attempts to apply the perspective in other subject areas and other grade levels have met with more limited success (e.g., Gamoran, 1987). The problem is that as instruction becomes more complex, with older students and more sophisticated curricular areas, it is difficult to trace the flow of resources along the layers of the school system. Moreover, in more complex subject areas teachers may not narrowly conform to a textbook approach, but select at their discretion and incorporate material outside of what they have been allocated. Consequently, the impact of district and school resource allocations is often attenuated. This is not to deny the importance of resources as constraints, but to suggest that the way resources are allocated and used may be more complicated than a simple one-way flow.

Despite these limitations, the nested-layers approach is the dominant perspective in research on schools and student achievement. Most studies that examine school types or school characteristics (private schools, magnet schools, school community, and so on) implicitly adopt the view that school conditions affect achievement through their influence on classroom instruction (e.g., Gamoran, 1996b; Lee & Smith, 1997). At the same time, another view challenges the nested-layers model and tries to account for the weak associations between school characteristics and student outcomes in many studies.

The Loose-Coupling Model

Why are school conditions such as expenditures and facilities often unrelated to achievement? According to the loose-coupling view, structure and activities are weakly connected to one another in school systems, and professional activities tend to be disconnected from student outcomes (Meyer & Rowan, 1977, 1978; Weick, 1976). Events occurring in one part of the school system—for example, the district office—typically have minimal impact on other parts—such as a given classroom. Schools generally orient themselves to fit society's expectations of what a school should look like, instead of focusing on technical activities such as teaching and learning. Because of conflicting opinions about the goals of schooling, the absence of agreement on the best way to teach, and continual changes in the student and teacher populations, we tend not to judge schools on their technical performance. Instead, schools are considered legitimate if their outward appearance fits our expectations, that is, if they are divided into grade levels, have certified teachers, offer the usual subjects, and so on. In this conception, both school structure and student learning respond to societal expectations, without a necessary connection between the two.

If schools are loosely coupled, how is it that any coordination occurs? How can they possibly manage to move students from grade to grade, and teach a curriculum with a semblance of order? According to Weick (1982), schools maintain some degree of coherence and coordination because teachers have engaged in a common socialization and training. Even though schools do not operate through giving commands and directives, teachers' work is coordinated because they have been conditioned to carry it out in a common framework.

The loose-coupling model captures important aspects of school systems. It helps us understand why researchers sometimes fail to find a link between school conditions and student outcomes. It correctly identifies the aspects of bureaucracy that tend to be missing in school systems: commands, directives, and close supervision. It also draws our attention to how teacher socialization and training influence what teachers do. At the same time, the loose-coupling perspective has two salient weaknesses. First, it is inconsistent with studies that have found associations between aspects of school organization and student learning. Research on Catholic schools, public magnet schools, school academic demands, and other policies show that loose coupling is not entirely pervasive (e.g., Bryk, Lee, & Holland, 1993; Gamoran, 1996b; Lee & Smith, 1997). For example, part of the advantage of Catholic schools over public schools for student achievement is that Catholic schools place more academic demands on students. In this case, academic policies, students' experiences, and achievement outcomes are closely linked rather than loosely connected. A second weakness of the loose-coupling paradigm, which is even more important for our purposes, is that it offers little help in understanding how districts and schools can help teachers who are attempting to improve their teaching. If structure, activities, and outcomes are disconnected, how can schools intervene, or even support teachers' own efforts? Loose coupling offers no guidance on this question.

Limitations of Both Models for Understanding Responses to the Reforms of Today

Neither nested layers nor loose coupling is adequate for understanding contemporary reform efforts, particularly in light of new demands for accountability that are sweeping the country. Almost every state now requires public schools to test students, and many use test results as a basis for making judgments about the quality of individual schools. This might be understood using a nested-layers approach, in that states and districts are providing curricula—either explicitly or implicitly in the form of tested content—that become inputs at the school and classroom levels. A nested-layers approach would identify these curricula as resources that constrain teachers' activities, but it offers little guidance on how teachers can become better decision makers through considering both the opportunities and con-straints that resources offer. Moreover, there is often little connection between classroom activities and what appears on tests (Boser, 2000)—a clear signal of loose coupling between the state's design and the classroom implementation. A loose-coupling analysis might recognize this disconnect, but would have little to say about how schools can be better organized to respond to the state's demands. Finally, neither approach is well suited to suggesting how schools and districts can respond to demands for high standards that come not from the state, but from teachers and professional organizations. Yet reforms that emphasize teaching for understand-ing in mathematics and science, our chief concern in this book, tend to come from professionals rather than from politicians or bureaucrats (American Association for the Advancement of Science, 1989, 1993; National Council of Teachers of Mathematics, 1989, 1991, 2000).

THE DYNAMIC MODEL IN RELATION TO OTHER MODELS AND APPROACHES

The new conceptual model we propose draws on elements of the nested-layers and loose-coupling models as well as other theoretical approaches, but moves beyond them in the effort to understand contemporary reform. In particular, our approach allows us to capture and analyze how districts and schools both support and im-pede teachers who are attempting to teach for understanding in mathematics and science.

Addressing the Limitations of Earlier Models

Our approach has more in common with the nested-layers model than with loose coupling. Recognizing the norm of teacher autonomy in the classroom, however, we draw one key insight from loose coupling about supporting change: Teacher practice is responsive to socialization and training, so *teacher professional develop-ment is an essential engine of change in school systems that aim for higher standards.* This insight is consistent with recent studies of restructured schools, which con-clude that changes in school structure often fail to result in changes in teacher practice. Rather, explained Peterson, McCarthey, and Elmore (1996):

> Changing practice is primarily a problem of [teacher] learning, not a problem of organization. . . . School structures can provide opportunities for the learning of new teaching practices and new strategies for student learning, but structures, by them-selves, do not cause learning to occur. . . . School structure follows from good practice not vice versa. (p. 149)

Opportunities for teacher learning help provide new knowledge and skills by enhancing teachers' human resources, but in the case of teaching for understanding, that is not enough, because social resources are also essential. As we have argued, teaching for understanding usually does not emerge in isolation because teachers rely on their colleagues to help them address the classroom uncertainties that arise when they attempt to teach for understanding. Some forms of professional development may enhance these social resources as well as contributing to teachers' human resources. When professional development emphasizes reflection and inquiry in a community of teachers, particularly when it is based in a school, it tends to enhance not only teachers' knowledge and skills, but their sense of community—that is, the social resources of the school as a whole (Grodsky & Gamoran, in press). Professional development, therefore, not only responds to resources, but also helps *generate* resources, particularly human and social resources that teachers can draw on as they attempt to teach for understanding.

In the loose-coupling model, classroom activities and student outcomes are disconnected. Research following the nested-layers paradigm, however, has shown that student learning is responsive to instruction, particularly when instruction is measured as content coverage, and learning as content mastery (e.g., Barr & Dreeben, 1983; Gamoran, 1987). We accept the point that student learning reflects classroom activities more than events that occur elsewhere in the system, such as district and school offices. That is, classroom experiences mediate the impact of district and school influences on outcomes for students. In the case of teaching for understanding, however, the pattern of influence is not one-way: Students respond to instruction, but instruction is also responsive to students. That, in fact, is the essence of teaching for understanding. Thus, to understand how schools can support teaching for understanding, we need a conception that recognizes that instruction may respond to students and cannot be entirely scripted in advance. Districts that rely entirely on accountability systems for raising standards—that is, by prescribing a curriculum and testing for mastery—are following an approach that is incompatible with teaching for understanding. Districts that blend professional growth with accountability mechanisms are more likely to allow room for teaching for understanding and, depending on the nature of professional development, may even encourage teaching for understanding in the context of creating and meeting standards.

Other Theoretical Connections

The construct of organizational resources is important in part because it enables theoretical links among research traditions that have developed along separate paths. Macroeconomic theorists have been concerned with how nations and institutions expand their capacity for productive economic activity and accumulate wealth. Learning theorists have been concerned with how individuals and groups develop new ideas and abilities. Researchers studying organizational change in schools have been concerned with how policies and forms of organization affect teaching practices and student achievement. The construct of organizational resources provides us with an exciting opportunity to develop links among these traditions and create more coherent accounts of how schools change in response to new demands and opportunities. Developments in two other fields—economic sociology and sociocultural research on teaching and learning—also lend depth and resonance to this conception of organizational resources.

Connections to Economic Sociology. Macroeconomic theories traditionally have concerned themselves with forms of wealth (capital) and productivity (goods and services) that are measured in monetary terms. Some economists have become concerned in recent years, however, that monetary measures of wealth and productivity do not capture the true value of a nation's or a corporation's capital, goods, and service. These concerns have led economists to consider ways of considering "human capital" and "social capital" as forms of wealth and productivity. Woolcock (1997) describes the development of more inclusive economic theories as follows:

> The classical economists identified land, labor, and *physical* capital (i.e., assets that generate income) as the three basic factors shaping economic growth. In the 1960's neo-classical economists such as T. W. Schultz and Gary Becker introduced the idea of *human* capital, arguing that a society's endowment of educated, trained, and healthy workers determined how productively the orthodox factors could be utilized. The latest equipment and most innovative ideas in the hands or mind of the brightest, fittest person, however, will amount to little unless that person also has access to others to inform, correct, assist with, and disseminate their work. . . . To physical and human capital, sociologists and political scientists (and some economists) working within the field of the so-called "new economic sociology" have thus begun to speak of *social* capital, a broad term encompassing the norms and networks facilitating collective action for mutual benefit. (pp. 154–155, emphasis in original)

By developing more inclusive measures, economists and sociologists hope to make better judgments about the promise and sustainability of different forms of economic activity, and about which changes in our economies can be accepted as "true progress"—real increases in our wealth and productivity. Similarly, our concerns about sustainability and progress lead us to use the concept of organizational resources in schools (Gamoran et al., 2000; Spillane, Diamond, Walker, Halverson, & Jita, 2001). In addition to entities or activities to which society has assigned monetary value (such as professional time, school buildings, or teaching materials), other worthwhile "things" (such as knowledge, commitments, and shared values) are important resources affecting teachers' commitments and abilities to sustain teaching for understanding. As Gamoran and colleagues (2000) explain:

> Collaboration, collegial relations, and opportunities for reflective discussion about teaching help build social capital . . . in the case of schools, social capital among teachers helps them improve their knowledge and skills (i.e. their human capital) by pro-

viding a normative environment that encourages experimentation, offers a place to discuss uncertainties, and rewards improvement. This portrait differs substantially from the standard picture of schools in which teachers' activities are largely unseen by other adults and their unique contributions are unrecognized and unacknowledged. (pp. 51–52)

Connections to Sociocultural Research on Teaching and Learning.

The classroom work of the teacher–researcher collaboratives we observed was influenced by sociocultural analyses of the nature of teaching and learning. This perspective views classrooms as communities where students learn through participation in culturally significant practices (not just as places where individual students develop conceptual, procedural, and dispositional knowledge). It builds on the work of sociolinguists such as Gee (1991), Heath (1983), and Wertsch (1991), and of scholars interested in relationships among cognition, culture, and written language such as Vygotsky (1978), Olson (1986), and Latour (1990).

Our research applies a similar perspective to issues of design and policy in professional development. Rather than focusing on professional development as a way of changing the knowledge, skills, and dispositions of individual teachers, we seek to understand professional development as the development of communities of educational practice. Thus, many important sociocultural concepts are applicable to professional communities in schools as well as classroom communities.

One key aspect of sociocultural theory involves a focus on activities or practices as units of analysis. Rather than focusing on individuals using knowledge and skills, sociocultural theorists focus on activities that may be distributed across individuals or between people and their material environment. When a person is working on a computer, for example, we can describe the activity, but it may not make sense to try to decide whether the person or the computer is doing the work. Similarly, members of a small group may devise a teaching strategy by working together, and it may not be possible to decide "whose idea" the strategy is. Thus, sociocultural theory helps us to understand how groups use resources to accomplish tasks, rather than tying our analyses to individuals.

Two consequences of the connection between activity theory and our model for understanding schools as organizations, are noteworthy. First, *resources and activities are reflexively related.* That is, resources enable activities that, in turn, can generate resources. Second, *human and social resources must be inferred from patterns in activities.* In contrast to material resources, which we can observe directly, our assertions about human and social resources are based on observations of the language and activities of individuals or groups. (Many important scientific concepts are similarly inferred from patterns in phenomena. Energy, for example, is not something that we observe directly, but an inferred quantity that explains consistent patterns in diverse phenomena such as light, sound, heat, and chemical reactions.)

CONCLUSIONS

The model presented in this chapter is a resource that we have used to understand the issues discussed in the remainder of the book. As we consider how the six partnerships that we studied addressed the challenges of teaching science and mathematics for understanding, we will use our dynamic model to examine the professional groups in each partnership, the activities of the members of those professional groups, and the ways in which they created, exchanged, and used material, human, and social resources.

CHAPTER 3

Six Cases of Change by Design

Tona Williams

> I think all of us teachers also have to have this one common goal, or some focus or vision that we can work together . . . . Teaching for understanding, [for] the kids, it is hard because a lot of them don't come from the same background. But I don't think it is an impediment because . . . they are bringing . . . their own, wherever they are, bringing their understanding, and we can share that. (Bilingual elementary school teacher in Callisto, a Massachusetts urban district)

As the statement above suggests, while teaching for understanding requires a tremendous amount of effort, it also provides powerful opportunities for building professional communities and connecting with students. In this chapter we introduce six sites wherein teachers and researchers collaborated with the goal of developing teaching for understanding practices. To gain insight into the school and district contexts of this work, we followed these groups for periods of 1–3 years. Here, we describe the context and character of each group and identify how it approached the three challenges outlined in Chapter 1.

We refer to the groups of teachers and researchers that we observed as *design collaboratives*. This term emerged from what Cobb (2001) calls "design experiments," where teachers and researchers together analyze classroom activities and design instruction in cycles that allow research and teaching practice to influence one another. A design experiment's goal is to develop and systematically analyze new instructional materials and techniques that contribute to both a body of research and individual teachers' practices. The aim is not merely to test existing ideas or demonstrate that a particular instructional design works. In utilizing the methodology of design experiments, the design collaboratives in this study relied on extensive interactions among teachers and researchers in classrooms and group meetings.

CHARACTERISTICS OF THE DESIGN COLLABORATIVES

The six cases varied in relation to one another along several dimensions. Tables 3.1A and 3.1B summarize the school and district context and the composition of each design collaborative. Specifically, they outline six areas: community demographics; reform context; school organization; subject, grade level, and size; relationships with researchers; and primary activities of the group. They also pair the sites according to how each site met the three challenges: some met all three while we observed them; others met the initial two, but the sustainability of their practices remained less certain; and still others collaborated for a shorter time and faced more difficulties in meeting the first two challenges. The many dimensions of variation meant that we could not draw conclusions based on carefully controlled comparisons, but that would not have been possible with this type of research anyway. Meanwhile, the distinctiveness of each case offers the advantage of allowing us to explore a broad range of scenarios.

One important basis of difference was the urban districts' greater diversity in terms of students' race, ethnicity, language background, and family income. The suburban districts had much higher percentages of students who were White, spoke only English, and did not qualify for free or reduced-price lunch programs.

Second, the existing reform contexts both facilitated and complicated the efforts of the design collaboratives. In Janus, the pressures of conforming to new standards and curriculum mandates dissuaded the teachers from continuing the collaboration. At the other extreme, standards requirements energized and supported Europa teachers, who had more flexibility to experiment. The large urban districts focused more than the smaller districts on adopting large-scale and ambitious programs, although such initiatives did not necessarily coincide with the design collaboratives' goals.

Third, organizational factors influenced cohesion among teachers and the ease with which the design collaboratives developed. Planning time differed, with some teachers interacting daily and others meeting only once or twice per month. Mimas High and Europa Middle revolved around cross-disciplinary teams of teachers and their students, while others, such as Oberon High, reinforced strong departmental affiliations. Also, some schools had bilingual programs, while others were monolingual.

A fourth dimension of difference was that some collaboratives encompassed several schools, while others were based in only one, and the grade levels that they covered varied. Both Europa groups initially addressed mathematics and science teaching, while the other collaboratives focused on one subject or the other. The size of the groups and the schools differed, in that the two high school and one of

Table 3.1A. Summary Characteristics of the Design Collaboratives: Contexts for Collaboration

Site	Community Demographics	Reform Context	School Organization
GROUPS THAT MET THE CHALLENGES AND CONTINUED TO GROW			
Europa Elementary	Small, suburban Wisconsin district Predominantly White and middle class District recently has doubled in size and is diversifying	Test scores above state and national averages District philosophy that teachers should continually develop their strengths Many reforms, committees, and use of site councils	Four elementary schools Single-grade and multiage classrooms
Oberon High	Small rural-suburban Wisconsin district Predominantly White and middle class	Above-average science test scores Recent state and district push toward standards and assessment School- and district-sponsored professional development grants K–12 science curriculum rewrite in progress	One high school Strong departmental structure Daily science department meetings Department does not assign textbooks Integrated science curriculum rather than separate subjects
GROUPS THAT MET THE INITIAL CHALLENGES			
Europa Middle	Same community context as Europa elementary	Includes the district context of Europa elementary District-sponsored coaching teams that paid teachers to observe one another's practice	One middle school School organized into both departments and thematic houses Daily meeting time for teachers in each house
Callisto Elementary and Middle	Mid-sized, urban district in Massachusetts Students from a wide variety of racial/ethnic, sociolinguistic, and socioeconomic backgrounds	Many separate school programs and missions District equity and diversity goals District supports teaching for understanding District supports professional development District-wide school choice program	Four participating schools that contain elementary and middle grades Bilingual programs in each school, with five language groups represented Both single-grade and multiage classrooms Weekly school team meetings
COLLABORATION ENDED WITHOUT MEETING THE CHALLENGES			
Mimas High	Large, urban Wisconsin district Wide range of student backgrounds; over half Hispanic and one-fifth African American	Administration open to new ideas District-wide effort to help more students pass the graduation test National project to increase ninth-grade algebra course taking	One high school Many bilingual, Spanish–English classrooms Organized into thematic families Weak departmental structure; no common planning periods for math
Janus Middle	Urban district in Tennessee Relatively balanced student population; nearly half African American and a similar number non-Hispanic White	District focus on improving below-average test scores Core curriculum that conflicts with teaching for understanding Mandatory use of benchmarks Limited, structured professional development time	Four participating middle schools Relatively weak school departments with no common planning periods for math

Table 3.1B. Summary Characteristics of the Design Collaboratives: Composition of the Collaboratives

Site	Subject, Grade Level, and Size	Relationships with Researchers	Primary Activities
GROUPS THAT MET THE CHALLENGE AND CONTINUED TO GROW			
Europa Elementary	Math and science Grades 1–5 Grew from 25 to 34 teachers during the collaboration	Pilot project that involved teachers and university researchers 3 years of larger-scale research collaboration The teacher group was continuing to meet 2 years later	Focus on scientific and mathematical modeling within a group called SAMM Summer workshops of 1–2 weeks and large- and small-group workshops throughout the year
Oberon High	Science Grades 9–11 Seven of the eight science department teachers participated	Decade-long collaboration between the lead university researcher and one teacher who also had a research center appointment 2-plus years of department-wide collaboration One researcher taught half time for 1 year	Created original curricular units that emphasized modeling approaches to teaching science Intense summer collaboration of a few weeks and semiregular meetings after school during the rest of the year
GROUPS THAT MET THE INITIAL CHALLENGES			
Europa Middle	Math and science, with primary focus on math Grades 6–8 Grew from 4 to 12 teachers in 3 years of collaboration	A 3-year grant that the researchers brought initiated the project Teachers were aware of the Europa elementary group Researchers began to provide formal curricular support through the district	Developed a multigrade algebra curriculum that focused on student understanding using Math in Context materials Monthly meetings after school, 4 half-day meetings per year, and a few days each summer
Callisto Elementary and Middle	Science Grades K–8 Both bilingual and monolingual teachers Included 22 teachers during the first year of collaboration, with 13 participating by the third year	Organized primarily by two researchers from an educational development firm A smaller-scale collaboration with bilingual teachers lasted for 8 years For 3 additional years, an expanded program included monolingual teachers	The group, called Uhuru, focused on teaching science for understanding to students whose first language was not English 1 week of summer meetings, semiweekly after-school meetings, and 3 full release days per year
COLLABORATION ENDED WITHOUT MEETING CHALLENGES			
Mimas High	Math Grades 9–12 Only bilingual teachers agreed to participate Four teachers participated in the first year and 2 continued in the second	The lead researcher had ties with two of the teachers when they were university students; this formed the basis for collaboration The collaboration at the school lasted for 2 years	Focused on understanding student thinking about algebra, using the Connected Math curriculum Meetings averaged once per month, usually after school
Janus Middle	Math Grades 6–8 Seven teachers participated in a brief summer collaboration	The lead researchers conducted teaching experiments in elementary schools and one middle school classroom The researchers then organized a workshop with seven different teachers, to initiate a new collaboration	Planned to develop a statistics unit to focus on student understanding Held one short summer workshop but the teachers put the project indefinitely on hold due to competing district pressures

the middle school groups drew teachers from single departments, while the elementary school groups drew teachers from across schools. The groups' goals also varied, in that Callisto did not focus on recruiting additional teachers, while Europa elementary participants continually invited new teachers to join, and the Mimas participants tried but were unable to recruit additional members.

Fifth, relationships between the researchers and the teachers differed across sites. All the design collaboratives were organized by one or two lead researchers from the National Center for Improving Student Learning and Achievement in Mathematics and Science (NCISLA), who were either university professors of mathematics or science education, or occupied senior-level positions at research centers. The remaining research staff comprised researchers who held doctorates in their fields and graduate students. Most of the researchers were former mathematics or science teachers. The greatest contrasts among sites involved the roles of teachers and researchers with respect to one another. At Oberon, one of the teachers had a doctorate in science education, held a part-time position at the research center, and had collaborated with the lead researcher for the decade prior to the design collaborative's formation. Similarly, the Europa elementary group grew out of a smaller teacher–researcher collaboration, and two of the Mimas teachers were former students of the lead researcher. The teachers in the other groups did not have the same types of external relationships to draw upon, and so relied on different combinations of resources to launch their collaborations. In Mimas, the lead researcher was also a member of the Organizational Capacity Study Group—our project—but in all other cases the NCISLA researchers who organized the design collaboratives were not members of our group.

Finally, some of the groups, such as at Europa and Callisto elementary and middle schools, used published curriculum packages, while others, such as the Oberon High School science department, wrote new curricula. These differences were tied to the specificity of the curricular development, in that the elementary groups spanned several grades and included teachers with a broad range of subject-area expertise, while the high school teachers had more specialized scientific or mathematical knowledge. Also, the teachers in some groups had stronger preexisting professional communities and more knowledge about teaching for understanding than those in other groups, and this affected the trajectories of the design collaboratives.

DATA COLLECTION

We collected the data for this project as members of the Organizational Capacity Study Group, which was part of the university-based NCISLA research center that housed the design collaboratives. We observed the collaboratives in order to understand the relationship among contexts, activities, and outcomes in each case. Our lead researchers included two sociologists, a math education professor, and a science education professor. Six graduate students and two other university faculty members participated for various lengths of time.

The timing and focus of data collection varied among the cases, primarily because our grant funding supported data collection during one 4-year period, but the design collaboratives formed at different times and were organized by different groups of researchers. Consequently, we sometimes began collecting data on a project that was underway, sometimes continued to observe a group after formal university collaboration had ended, and other times collected data during a group's inception but were unable to follow it over several years. While this variation did not allow the control that we would have had if every site was coordinated along the same time line, it lent a complexity to our analyses that suggests a range of possibilities for these types of groups.

There was more consistency in our methods for collecting information across these six sites. We gathered four types of data. One was direct observation of 102 design collaborative meetings. We also interviewed most of the teachers in the collaboratives, the majority at least twice, for a total of 155 teacher interviews. In addition, we conducted 42 interviews of school and district administrators, including principals, superintendents, curriculum specialists, and department chairs, many of whom also were interviewed twice. Finally, we surveyed design collaborative members as well as other teachers in those schools, so that we collected about 500 surveys, across multiple years, at a response rate of about 75%. The Appendix includes more details about the data collection.

INTRODUCING THE SIX CASES

In this section we depict the district and school context, and main activities, of each design collaborative.

Europa Elementary: Team-Building Across Schools

> Excellent teaching of math and science [is] I guess any teaching that focuses more on kids' understanding than just on what [the lead researcher] likes to call "factoids," [which are] just the pure memorization of facts. . . . And knowing how far you can push their thinking on a certain topic, I guess is a key . . . and something that I think that the SAMM [Science and Mathematics Modeling] project thinks a lot about. (Europa elementary teacher)

As in the statement above, teachers in the Europa elementary design collaborative often contrasted their approach to teaching with what they described as a more traditional focus on memorization of specific facts. A characteristic activity was for teachers to present examples from their classrooms so that they could receive feedback and others could adapt the ideas for their own classrooms. Participants frequently worked out answers to problems in small groups in order to anticipate their students' thought processes. They identified themselves as a teacher-driven team that spanned several schools and, ideally, would continue to expand.

In the spring of 2000, the Europa school district served a rapidly growing suburb of a mid-sized Wisconsin city. The district included four elementary schools, a middle school, and a high school, as well as two charter schools housed within the other schools. A self-selected group of teachers from the four elementary schools participated in the Science and Mathematics Modeling (SAMM) program, which was into its second year of work after the 3-year formal collaboration with the NCISLA researchers had ended. The central focus of this program was to develop elementary school children's thinking and representation of mathematical and scientific concepts through modeling.

The Europa School District. Europa has been growing and becoming more diverse. The district had fewer than 2,000 students in the late 1980s, but around 4,000 by 1999. From 1994 to 1999 the percentage of African American students grew from 3% to 6%, and the proportion of students who received free or reduced-price lunch increased from 4% in 1990 to over 9% in 1997. These students primarily attended the two most recently built of the four Europa elementary schools. Three geographic communities constituted the district. One began as a small town that grew 70% between 1980 and 1993, and another formed as a growing suburb of the adjacent city. The third, most recent addition was the least affluent neighborhood of the city and of the Europa district, which provided the smallest number of students.

Test scores consistently have hovered well above national and state averages. For example, over 90% of the Europa children who took the third-grade reading test were above standard, as opposed to 87% statewide. Likewise, on the eighth-grade state mathematics and science tests, district students ranked above the 80th percentile in math and above the 75th percentile in science (using a nationally normed instrument), whereas the state average was at the 65th percentile for both subjects.

The growth in the student population required new buildings, new teachers, and an enlarged administration. Between 1988 and 1996, taxpayers passed referenda to build two new elementary schools, a new middle school, a new high school, and an administration building. They also passed a technology referendum to reduce the ratio of students to networked computers to around 6:1. All of these referenda ultimately passed by margins of about 2:1. However, between 1997 and 1999, voters narrowly refused to increase tax funds for new construction. An informal analysis of letters to newspaper editors and observation of a public meeting to discuss space issues suggested that this opposition reflected not only tax issues, but also a reluctance to encourage further growth by allowing schools to expand.

The organization of the Europa district changed substantially in the decade before our study. The superintendent prior to 1988 had an "autocratic" style, but community members supported a devolution of authority to schools, which led to school-site councils. By the late 1990s, the instructional philosophy of the district administration had become more constructivist. Senior-level district administrators emphasized the importance of process over content, of reasoning over memorization. The district's overall administrative perspective was, as one district-level administrator put it, "a place where innovations are the norm and not the exception." They perpetuated this norm in their hiring by selecting people with the capacity for innovation and growth.

The district's philosophy of teacher learning was similar. The administrator quoted above explained that "where a shift is occurring in putting kids more in charge of their growth and learning, a shift was also occurring in the way in which teachers were engaged in their own improvement curve." This complemented the superintendent's view that teachers must create "circles of excellence" around them based on their own talents and skills. Teachers received this district support through coaching teams, flex days, and a technology academy. Coaching teams involved pairs of teachers who collaborated to improve their teaching. While coaching teams were optional, the district's 2 paid professional development days, called flex days, were mandatory. Teachers were encouraged to have a professional development plan on file with their principal, to use as a guide. Finally, the district ran a 6-day summer program to train teachers on using computer technology. This technology academy was unpaid, but teachers earned credits toward advancement on the salary schedule. The superintendent reported that response to this summer opportunity was overwhelmingly positive.

The belief that each teacher had unique strengths that should be developed was key to the district's teaching philosophy. Rather than require adherence to common pedagogical approaches and curricula, the district encouraged teachers to develop their talents in the classroom. The superintendent maintained that the district's overall framework prevented fragmentation, but that there was room within that framework for teachers to move in different directions.

The Europa Elementary Design Collaborative. This program originally began with a pilot project during the 1992–93 school year that involved 10 teachers and a group of university researchers. It included 75 hours of workshops during the school year and a week-long summer seminar. With renewed support from the district and outside grants, its current incarnation began in 1995–96 and participants inaugurated the group "SAMM." This phase of formal teacher–researcher collaboration lasted for 3 years, and teacher participation grew from 25 in year one to 34 at the end of year three. In addition, one school principal attended SAMM meetings regularly in 1996–97, and another was a regular participant during 1998–99. During this 3-year period, the group's activities included frequent workshops involving all of the participants and small-group meetings where two subgroups met separately. In addition, participants organized an intensive 1–2 week seminar each summer. After the 3-year collaboration, the researchers concluded their work, leaving a group of 20 teachers who continued to organize monthly full-day workshops with district financial support. These activities continued for at least 2 years beyond the researchers' involvement.

We found clear evidence of professional community that supported teaching for understanding within the SAMM group, in that participants shared many values and norms about teaching, collectively focused on student learning, collaborated with one another, shared details about their teaching practice so that it was "deprivatized," and engaged in reflective dialogue about their teaching. The core activity of SAMM was examination of student work as a means of understanding student thinking. Almost every monthly whole-group seminar had a component that featured student work. The group also pursued four focus areas. The first, and most central, involved persistent attention to student learning, through addressing questions such as, "what do students know," and "how do students represent their knowledge?" The second area was to encourage collaboration among teachers, in that the meetings and workshops included substantial time for planning classroom activities. Third, teachers developed a shared technical vocabulary. Finally, SAMM workshops became a forum for making teachers' work public, in that teachers talked directly about classroom scenarios, showed video clips of their teaching, and shared examples of students' work.

Our data collection began in the summer of 1996, as the second year of SAMM began, and continued through 1998–99, one school year after the researchers ended their formal involvement. This allowed us to follow the group's trajectory as it continued under the sole leadership of the teachers.

In sum, the organization of the district both constrained and facilitated the design collaborative's work. A multiplicity of reforms, committee work, and site council responsibilities competed for teachers' time and energy. Also, district growth and new school construction led to a reshuffling of staff among schools, sometimes involuntarily. This created challenges for the teachers in this project and required them to refashion their working groups, although it also presented opportunities to disseminate SAMM. However, in addition to substantial university grant support, the group received steady funding from the district that was supplemented by outside grants that the teachers obtained. In general, the district context aided the group's efforts, in that teachers had substantial professional development time from the district, and the principals and superintendent had a policy of staying "out of the way" so that teachers improved their practices according to their preferences.

Oberon High School: A Strong Departmental Team with a Long History of Collaboration with Researchers

> Really our best accomplishments are the actual physical curriculum that's come out of the collaborations. Just to have the time and the input of all these dynamic people working on one goal . . . to make science more

accessible and more engaging, more understandable for students, that's been wonderful. And it seems like we are accomplishing that further and further each time we meet. (Oberon teacher)

The Oberon design collaborative grew out of a long history of smaller-scale collaboration with researchers and an existing sense of teamwork in the science department. The group created a new series of curricular units that were organized around modeling activities. Participants researched potential topics, constructed classroom materials, experimented with the sequencing and timing of activities, and struggled to create assessments that demonstrated the depth of students' learning. Expertise was widely distributed within the group, and researchers and teachers shared leadership roles.

Oberon High School was located in a small, part-rural and part-suburban district in Wisconsin. Besides the one public high school of 650 students in grades 9–12, the district had one middle school and four elementary schools. In the summer of 2000, the design collaborative was 2 years old and included seven of the eight teachers in the science department and six NCISLA researchers. The two groups overlapped somewhat, in that one teacher held a half-time position at the research center and, for 1 year of the project, one of the graduate students on the research team taught half time in the department. The group's main goal involved developing original curricular units that emphasized modeling approaches in high school science. It addressed an increasing proportion of the school's science curriculum, in that it focused initially on creating only two units within one introductory course, but eventually rewrote several units across multiple grade levels.

The Oberon School and District Context. The Oberon district and high school were racially homogeneous and relatively affluent, as over 95% of its students were non-Hispanic White and the local tax expenditures per student were more than double the national average. During the period we observed, the community had shown mixed support for recent district initiatives; after extensive debate and three local referenda, it funded construction of a new high school building, which opened in the late 1990s. However, it defeated a referendum that would have provided more school computer technology.

The state and district implemented several initiatives related to standards and assessment that affected the high school science curriculum. First, all curriculum must correspond with the Wisconsin Model Academic Standards, which have a science component. All tenth graders must take the State Knowledge and Concepts examination, and in 1999 students at this school scored at around the 75th percentile nationwide in science. In addition, efforts at curriculum coordination were under way, as representatives from the high school science department collaborated with other district teachers to rewrite the K–12 science curriculum. Finally, the state High School Graduation Test, which had a science component, was being phased into the system so that it would be administered to the graduating class of 2004 beginning in fall 2002. This test would be a certification exam that drew from the state standards, although high school graduation would not rest entirely on exam success.

The science department included seven teachers in the 1998–99 school year and eight in 1999–2000. A receptiveness to innovation grew out of internal organizational conditions that had coalesced over a decade and through opportunities from the outside, such as building relationships with researchers and other professionals. For instance, the school provided regular professional development grants for teachers to attend conferences every year if they applied. In addition, the overall structure of the science curriculum was unusual in that it was organized around a core of integrated, multidisciplinary courses titled Science I through Science IV, instead of around the more traditional disciplines of biology, chemistry, geology, and physics. Related to this, the department voluntarily compiled packets of readings and other materials that teachers copied and distributed to students, instead of ordering textbooks. This required teachers to think continually about what the curriculum would include.

The department's solid, long-term professional community made it difficult to disentangle what was present prior to the university collaboration and what developed as a result of that relationship. The teachers had seen themselves as part of a department that they each supported and strengthened on a daily basis. For instance, they had daily "team meetings" before the lunch hour, which included all of the science teachers but not the researchers. Here, teachers talked about their classes and exchanged feedback. To maintain this cohesion, the department was proactive in its recruitment of new teachers by recommending those with similar approaches to collaboration and community. In essence, the department sought innovation, although primarily on the terms defined by the teachers and built into the department's structure.

The Oberon Design Collaborative. This design collaborative had an interesting history, in that it developed from collaboration of over a decade between a science education professor and one teacher who had a part-time appointment at the professor's research center. From the beginning, the focus of this work was to develop the curriculum for that teacher's upper-level genetics course, especially through incorporating a hands-on modeling approach. The graduate student researchers who worked with her spent a lot of time in her classroom, interacting with students and giving feedback.

In July 1998, all but one of the other teachers in the department became involved when a more formal design collaborative was organized. The group met regularly to discuss the teachers' work and cooperatively develop curriculum. The focus remained on integrating a modeling perspective into science teaching, and an important dimension involved talking about what that meant to participants and how it could be translated into classroom activities. Substantively, the group concentrated on developing the first 2 units of the ninth-grade integrated Science I course. This included about a month of material that explored the nature of science and norms of scientific inquiry, followed by a month-long astronomy unit. When the school year began and the teachers implemented the group's plans, the researchers spent substantial time in several classrooms, helping with instruction and collecting data on student thinking. The formal observations and teachers' perspectives provided a focus for after-school seminar meetings. Throughout the first year of the collaborative, the seminar meetings averaged 2 hours once every 2 weeks.

During the second year of the design collaborative, in the 1999–2000 school year, one of the researchers taught half time in the science department while maintaining her position as half-time researcher at NCISLA. This meant that two participants had a formal affiliation with both the university research center and the science department. Also, the scope of the curriculum development broadened so that some of the teachers and researchers continued to rework the Science I units from the previous year and others focused on integrated Science II and III courses. The after-school seminar continued, although much less frequently because subgroups met more informally to work on curriculum. So far, this group's flexibility and participants' desire to expand the project's scope allowed more crossover between the roles of researcher and teacher than exists in most professional development groups.

In sum, this group was built on long-term professional relationships, flexible leadership, multiple bases of expertise, and ample opportunity for communication. Solid financial support and material resources also made many of the other elements possible. The participants hoped that, with clearly demonstrable successes in student achievement, the department could gain more school and district commitment that would ensure the continuity of the teachers' curricular work when formal support from the research center had ended.

Europa Middle: Aligning Goals for Middle School Algebra

> The [design collaborative] project is about . . . trying to learn different ways to have kids learn . . . and also different ways to teach. . . . I was able to collaborate with some of my colleagues and I also received . . . much assistance with the technique of using the Math in Context materials. . . . One of the things that led me to involvement was that some of the other teachers had already been using . . . some of the materials the year previous to my joining and they were pretty satisfied with what was going on. . . . And the monetary support, also, the stipend, that helps. And . . . the assistance that I got last year . . . my first year in the program, was just excellent. (Europa Middle School teacher)

The Europa Middle School collaborative provided teachers with a forum to utilize a published mathematics curriculum that emphasized teaching for understanding. Many teachers saw it as a way to receive professional assistance and material resources to connect more effectively with their students. During group meetings they often shared examples of classroom activities and generated ideas for incorporating new curricular materials into their teaching.

Europa Middle was in the same suburban district as the Europa elementary schools, and it received students from the district's four regular elementary schools and two charter schools. In the spring of 2000, the Europa Middle design collaborative concluded its third year of formal teacher–researcher collaboration. The group officially formed in January 1998, and several of the teachers were familiar with the progress of the SAMM elementary school group. Although the program was designed for a dual math-science focus, and included teachers of both subjects, it actually focused predominantly on mathematics. This happened because the university researchers and the two strongest teacher-leaders had primary expertise in mathematics, and because the collaborative's focus coincided with school-wide discussions about how to make higher-level mathematics accessible to all students.

The Organizational Context of Europa Middle School. As in all of the other sites, the school's organizational structure framed the design collaborative's efforts. When the project began, the middle school was organized into 12 subunits called "houses." A team of two to four teachers led each house, which had a student-to-teacher ratio of approximately 25:1. Each teacher within a house took charge of one or two of the four core areas of math, science, language arts, and social studies, and students spent about two-thirds of their day within this grouping. The principal believed that teachers identified most with their houses, but departments also existed. The mathematics department was more unified than the science, although neither had a formal chair. All teachers had daily planning time with their house colleagues. As did other Europa teachers, they had two professional development days per year that they structured around their own objectives. Additionally, they could enter into district-sponsored coaching teams, which allocated paid time for teachers to observe one another's practice.

The Europa Middle School Design Collaborative. A grant acquired by the university researchers, along with district funds, provided support for the collaboration. Perhaps the most crucial funding allocation was to buy teachers' time for the project, which paid teachers to attend monthly after-school meetings and work a few days on the project each summer. The project also funded substitutes to cover teachers' classes for 4 half-day design collaborative meetings each year. An important part of this work involved creating connections between teachers' classroom activities and ideas that developed in the meetings. Teachers often brought samples of student work to discuss, so that the others could try similar things in their classrooms.

When this collaborative began in January 1998, it included five NCISLA researchers, four of the six teachers in the sixth-grade math department, and two teachers from seventh and eighth grades. These teachers also taught other subjects, most commonly science, because of the school's structure. By the end of this first year of collaboration, all of the sixth-grade math teachers voluntarily participated. Throughout the second and third years, the group expanded to include more of the seventh- and eighth-grade math teachers, to total 12 teachers. Substantial researcher turnover occurred during this time, including a change in the lead researcher. In spring 2000, the final year of university grant funding, the NCISLA team began to shift more control to the teachers. We collected data from the group's inception in 1998 until early summer 2000.

Over the course of this collaboration, the focus shifted to emphasize mathematics more than science and to formalize connections between the school and university. Toward the end of its second academic year, the math department detracked the curriculum to expose all students to pre-algebra and algebra in sixth through eighth grades, in preparation for ninth-grade geometry. This brought resolution to an ongoing departmental controversy, although tensions remained that surfaced in design collaborative meetings. However, the decision resulted in school-wide implementation of the Math in Context curricular package that the design collaborative used. This curriculum focused on equity among students and on algebra concepts as learning objectives, both key elements of the design collaborative's orientation. Since the university researchers helped the teachers follow this curriculum, five additional seventh-grade math teachers joined the collaborative at this time. During the third year, the two major areas of activity included (1) familiarizing teachers, particularly those new to the collaborative, with the Math in Context curriculum, and (2) finding multiple ways of assessing student knowledge. The Math in Context focus meant even more formal support from the researchers, since some of the NCISLA personnel also were paid to provide professional development support for that curricular package. This new arrangement between the math department and the university substantially overlapped with the design collaborative and reinforced the formal ties between the two groups. The focus of the meetings shifted from a pattern where teachers frequently discussed concerns and frustrations that were not on the agenda, to one where the teachers participated more actively and attended more to the formal agenda.

In sum, the Europa Middle collaborative revolved around the Math in Context curriculum, although it initially intended to focus on both mathematics and science. The group provided a space where participants could meet as mathematics teachers, a crucial function because most of their other interactions with colleagues were not subject-specific and involved broader school issues. A driving principle became the belief that all students should learn algebra, and that algebraic concepts should be integrated into the curriculum throughout middle school.

Callisto Elementary and Middle: A Haven for Bilingual Teachers in a District with Diverse and Crisscrossing Goals

> The [design collaborative] is very interesting because when we started 3 years ago, we were almost double the size that we are now. . . . And what happened is that as people have weeded themselves out, the core group [has] a lot in common to my ideas about teaching. . . . A number of them . . . have been involved in other projects with me, not just at Uhuru [name of design collabroative]. And a couple of years ago, [another teacher in the group] and I were taking a dance umbrella seminar . . . and then I have been doing another project in biotechnology with another participant . . . so there's been a number of people that have worked with some of the initiatives, in addition to the Uhuru. . . . And my assumption is that there is this group that [is] together because we share a decent attitude toward teaching. I don't see the same position with other teachers in my school as a whole. . . . I . . . share my style of teaching with . . . one . . . at the most, [where] we not only talk about what we are doing in teaching, we share ideas. The others I have no clue what they are doing. (Callisto teacher)

The Callisto design collaborative supported teaching for understanding within a district that housed dozens of programs and competing visions for teaching. This group included only bilingual and monolingual teachers of bilingual students. The organizers' approach, although emphasizing ongoing collaboration, was to help a small cadre of participants to teach science more effectively rather than to recruit additional teachers over the years.

The Callisto school system was an urban district in Massachusetts with one high school and 15 primary schools that spanned elementary and middle school grades. Six of the primary schools housed bilingual programs, and 23 separate educational programs existed in the district, with goals ranging from gifted to multicultural education. The design collaborative, called Uhuru (Swahili for "freedom"), drew teachers largely from four of the primary schools. Uhuru sought to improve science teaching by assisting teachers in becoming reflective in their practices.

The Callisto School District. Overall, the Callisto school district served over 6,000 students but was shrinking in size. Students came from a wide variety of sociolinguistic, socioeconomic, and racial/ethnic backgrounds. Equity and diversity were explicit goals, and the district implemented a school choice program while attempting to maintain diversity along racial/ethnic, sociolinguistic, and socioeconomic lines. Schools varied substantially, in that many classrooms were multigrade, school hours varied, and the schools were categorized as "traditional" or "alternative" based on their organizational and curricular emphasis. Five of the traditional schools were distinguished as "target" schools because of disproportionately large enrollments of students from low-income families, racial/ethnic minorities, students with limited English proficiency (LEP), and relatively lower standardized test scores. The three alternative schools, in contrast, had more abundant resources and above-average student performance on standardized tests and other achievement measures. The remaining seven schools had no distinctive mission, although several housed bilingual programs or academic programs such as "talented and gifted." The district supported several forms of bilingual education, and six schools each focused on one of five different language groups. Programs were designated as English as a second language, early-exit transitional, modified-transitional, or two-way bilingual. The language groups included Spanish, Chinese Mandarin, Korean, Haitian Creole, and Portuguese. The four Uhuru schools included two target and two alternative schools, each with at least one bilingual program.

According to some teachers and principals, changing laws and the district's shifting demography made the maintenance of socioeconomic diversity within schools the most difficult challenge. At the time of this study, a recent state decision to eliminate rent control had a tremendous impact on lower- and working-class families, particularly minority and immigrant families, many of whom had to leave the district. This meant that the school system disproportionately represented more affluent, White, native families. Related to this, during 1997–98 the new superintendent declared that the district's teaching staff soon would be reduced due to the already low student-to-teacher ratio.

The Callisto district explicitly encouraged curriculum design and content that focused on teaching for understanding, and this was evident in the administration's endorsements. However, no mechanisms existed to coordinate how teachers adapted the curricula for their classrooms. Patrons from local colleges and universities created "professional development sites," typically in alternative schools, that also supported this instructional approach. These efforts were separate from the Uhuru design collaborative, although based on similar underlying philosophies.

The district also directly sponsored teachers' professional development. Through the efforts of the district science coordinator, teachers received several release days each year to attend district-sponsored professional development opportunities. Also, a newly created position of district professional development coordinator ostensibly made additional curricular materials and staff development available to teachers, although during our observations many teachers were unaware of the position and had not yet received any benefits. Finally, each school's weekly grade-level "team" meetings combined with faculty meetings to promote collaboration among teachers and encourage a transformation in science teaching that had been underway in the Callisto district for the past 4 years.

The Callisto Design Collaborative. Funded by a federal grant and organized primarily by two NCISLA researchers from an educational development firm, the design collaborative was intended to increase the effectiveness of science teaching for students from non-English linguistic backgrounds and low-income families. In fact, the original collaboration among researchers and a few bilingual teachers began in 1988, and only in fall 1997, when we began observing it, did it expand to include monolingual teachers of bilingual students. In addition to three 6-hour "release days" per school year, the group met for two 2-hour sessions per month throughout the academic year and one full week each summer. Membership in the program was voluntary, and the project provided a stipend to compensate teachers for their time. In addition, teachers could elect to earn graduate credit. All of the Uhuru teachers had been in the district for some time, and the language-minority teachers constituted half of the participants.

The primary goal of Uhuru's two project directors was to help participants teach science for understanding, and they considered systemic change across the district as outside of their project's scope. They viewed success as dependent on the development of trust among participants and, to facilitate this interdependence, limited the group's size and asked teachers to make a 5-year commitment before joining. Since the lead researchers did not replace teachers who left the group, substantial attrition occurred, although a small number of teachers did join after the first year because of contacts with other teacher-participants. Overall, the project included 22 teachers in 1996–97, 16 in 1997–98, and 13 in 1998–99, the final year of our data collection.

Uhuru's collaborative work revolved around specific activities that focused on bilingual students' thinking about science. All of the meetings were videotaped and audiotaped. A central feature was that teachers were encouraged to videotape and transcribe, with the help of Uhuru staff, segments of classroom discussion that revolved around science. Then, the group viewed the videos collectively and read the transcripts in small groups. This generated discussions about student understanding and reflections on teaching, and provided specific feedback to the teachers whose videos were analyzed. The group also read and discussed academic articles that were relevant to classroom work.

In addition to these group activities, the teachers worked from a common curriculum that focused on teaching for understanding in elementary and middle school science. However, as we will discuss in a later chapter, the bilingual teachers experienced more difficulties than the monolingual teachers, since they often had to translate their materials from English into one of the five second languages in which they taught. Students came from many different backgrounds, so the bilingual teachers faced an additional challenge of making their newly developed science pedagogies accessible to the entire range of their students. These realities, as well as other social and structural differences in the working environments of monolingual and bilingual teachers, sometimes led subgroups to form within the collaborative.

In sum, Callisto was a very diverse and progressive school district with a national reputation for progress over the past decade. It had developed a culture wherein experimentation at both the institutional and classroom levels was common, although the dozens of ongoing projects and programs were largely uncoordinated. As part of this district culture, the administration encouraged teachers to participate in professional development that was endorsed by outside parties as well as the district. This supported the design collaborative's efforts, in that teachers were not limited to a tightly defined set of practices. However, the diversity of goals also meant that teachers had tremendous constraints on their time and energy as they balanced multiple commitments.

Mimas High School: A Department Split Against Itself, with Little Meeting Time for Bilingual Math Teachers

> Probably the community that I fit best with would be the bilingual math teachers . . . , those [are the] people I share the most values with. . . . I would say the biggest [similarity] would be relationship with the students. . . . I think we all three of us believe that that in some ways needs to come first. And sometimes it is more important to dedicate more of your time and more of your energy and more of your expertise to developing relationships with the students, sometimes even over developing curriculum. . . . If . . . we somehow had a free hour, we would probably be more likely to use that hour doing something . . . for the benefit of the students before we would use it for something directly related with the curriculum. (Mimas teacher)

The Mimas design collaborative provided the only time that the school's bilingual mathematics teachers could meet. Meetings frequently included discussions of the mathematics curriculum as the teachers began to coordinate across classes. The group also devoted substantial attention to creating, administering, and evaluating written assessments of students' knowledge of particular concepts. Although the collaboration strengthened these teachers' sense of professional community, a persistent challenge was to maintain a focus on curriculum and teaching rather than use meeting time to discuss individual students and organizational details.

Mimas was a large, central-city high school in Wisconsin. The school was bilingual, which meant that many—although not all—of its classes included instruction in Spanish and English. The design collaborative focused on student understanding in bilingual mathematics classrooms. It began in the middle of the 1997–98 school year but ended in the spring of 1999 because the teachers were diverging and the researchers could not recruit new teachers. The mathematics teachers barely functioned as a department because they did not meet frequently. Consequently, a major goal of the collaborative was to increase the sense of professional community among the subset of participating bilingual teachers.

The School and District Context of Mimas. Mimas was a diverse and relatively low-income school, whose student body represented a substantial range of racial/ethnic backgrounds. In 1997–98, approximately 60% of its over 1,600 students were Hispanic; 20% African American; 10% non-Hispanic White; and 10% Asian/Pacific Islander or American Indian/Alaskan. The faculty was also diverse, and included many Hispanic teachers. The majority of students came from low-income backgrounds; 66% were eligible for free or reduced-price lunch.

In some respects, the school had relatively ample resources. In 1996, the district launched a large-scale school restructuring effort that focused on helping more students to pass the district's graduation test. This was driven by a mandate from the state government to improve graduation, dropout, and attendance rates before the year 2000. If the goals for improvement were not met, the school would be removed from the control of the school board. A national project, Equity 2000, which focused on equal access to college preparatory mathematics, was also in progress at the school. Its purpose was to help more students become successful in algebra and to require all students to enroll in ninth-grade algebra. One result of these wide-ranging initiatives was that the administration was open to new ideas. For example, much of the school was organized into multidisciplinary groups called "families," some of the students created portfolios as alternative assessments, and several other collaborative projects with universities were underway.

Several levels of faculty organization directly affected the teachers in the design collaborative. These included the multidisciplinary families, the school faculty, and the mathematics department. The most striking feature of these groups was that none functioned as a strong professional community. The mathematics department, in particular, met approximately five times per school year and was not a community. Teachers in the design collaborative also were affected by the bilingual–monolingual differentiation. The bilingual teachers shared a greater sense of cohesion than the others, although issues relating to the bilingual aspect of their teaching did not appear to be a central focus for the design collaborative participants. Aside from the design collaborative meetings, the teachers reported that they had little discretionary time in common and usually could not communicate with each other much beyond talking across the hall between classes. In fact, before the design collaborative meetings began, the four participating teachers communicated primarily at faculty meetings and school-wide professional development days, called "banking days," that occurred every 1–2 months. (The term *banking days* referred to the fact that the school day was made slightly longer on other days to make up for them.)

As mentioned earlier, the restructuring efforts channeled teachers' collaborative energies into the multidisciplinary families that students affiliated with throughout their high school years. The school's five families were organized by topic, such as arts, geography, and so forth. They included two teachers from each subject area (one bilingual and one monolingual), and meetings did not feature much discussion of pedagogy or subject-specific material. Rather, meetings focused more on the circumstances of particular students. Aside from this, since the families had been in place for only 2 years when this research began, they existed only at the ninth- and tenth-grade levels. This meant that not all students and teachers in the school participated; only two of the four teacher-participants belonged to a family during the collaborative's first year.

The Mimas Design Collaborative. The Mimas design collaborative formed during the 1997–98 school year and met through 1998–99. Initially, it consisted of four teachers who taught bilingual classes and five university researchers from a nearby city. In the fall of the second year, two of the teachers chose not to rejoin the group for personal reasons, and the number of teacher-participants dropped to two.

During its first year of collaboration, the group did not have a clear focus, and this inhibited its cohesion. Its main activities included creating regular meeting time for the teachers, designing strategies for successful professional development, and exploring the school context and the topics that the four teachers found interesting. These topics included coordination of course curricula, curriculum development in algebra, and discussion about teaching methods and classroom practices.

Beginning in its second year of collaboration, the group focused more directly on students' understanding of algebra. This marked a significant turning point that changed the nature of the meetings. The shift grew from the researchers' efforts to introduce conversations about student understanding and demonstrate how to analyze student work. However, the small number of teachers limited the group's long-term momentum. When teachers began to drop out due to interpersonal tensions with one another and other personal reasons, there was no critical mass to maintain the group.

To a large extent, a lack of crucial resources and difficulties in activating others limited this collaborative's efforts. Partly, this appeared to be because, although the school had relatively high levels of resources, those resources were deployed in many varied, and sometimes contradictory, ways. Most important, the lack of a common planning period made it very difficult for teachers to find opportunities to communicate. Related to this, the multidisciplinary families made the design collaborative's task more challenging since the families were not centered on pedagogy or subject knowledge. At times, the teachers in the collaborative discussed the incompatibility between participating in a family and interacting more directly with other mathematics teachers. They reported that some of the other teachers saw them as involved in a special program that was separate from the departments, families, and the rest of the school. Indeed, most of the other teachers did not want to participate in the group or allow the researchers to observe them in their classrooms. Assessment requirements and standardized tests created additional structures that teachers sometimes struggled to accommodate. At times, teachers reported that the task of preparing their students specifically for college entrance exams detracted from their exploration of ideas developed within the collaborative.

An important basis for solidarity among this group of bilingual teachers was the belief that their colleagues who taught monolingual classes unjustly held lower expectations for Spanish-speaking students. The four design collaborative teachers emphasized their view that the majority of Mimas students could succeed, even if they were in bilingual classes and came from low-income and nonacademic backgrounds. Initially, this strengthened the group's cohesion, but eventually the oppositional orientation toward the other math teachers posed a barrier to recruiting more people. The division was only somewhat mitigated by the fact that the department chair participated in the collaborative during the first year.

While attempting to overcome such obstacles, the collaborative played a dual role in focusing existing resources and bringing additional resources to support its activities. These resources supported teaching for understanding through their effects on the group's development. Every 1 to 2 months, the design collaborative met during a school-wide professional development day through an arrangement where the participating teachers were able to forgo the meetings that the rest of the faculty attended. The remainder of the collaborative's meetings took place outside of regular school hours, and teachers received payment for their time through grant funding from the research project.

In sum, participants in the Mimas collaborative had many different ideas about what student understanding looks like. The group lacked the critical mass, joint meeting time, and institutional support to build a common vision from these disparate ideas. The school's organization created contradictory goals and time pressures. For instance, the visions of student learning held by the administration and the rest of the math department did not coincide with the researchers' ideas about teaching for understanding. In addition, both the district competency exam and the state exam obstructed the collaborative's goals. The teachers developed interesting ideas for their classrooms, but the effort remained small scale.

Janus Middle Schools: City Curriculum Framework Mandates and Misaligned Visions

> CCF [City Curriculum Framework] is, there are specific skills in all four of the basic subjects that must be taught within a given 6-week period. . . . But it's been difficult this year, that's been a frustration for me. I miss it, I miss it, . . . I lost some of the creativity and the real fun that will come when you can let up on the demands of some of the skills and let the students begin to kind of show you a different side. We're searching, we're hoping, and we're working but it will come. It definitely won't go out the window, and that's to me, an important [thing] to remember, and a benefit for them. If it's good for them, I'm not going to [say], oh, well, I'm just going to teach these [other things]. (Janus teacher)

The teachers and researchers who participated in the initial collaboration at Janus were enthusiastic about teaching for understanding and eager to include more teachers from the four middle schools that they represented. However, the district's newly mandated City Curriculum Framework (CCF) demanded much of their time and energy while offering little flexibility. As the group formed, the teachers were experiencing increased pressure from the district and quickly realized that they could not pursue two divergent directions. The teachers expressed frustration at their lack of classroom control, but also hoped that, in the future, they could incorporate more creative approaches.

Janus was an urban district in Tennessee, serving over 50,000 students. The design collaborative formed in the summer of 1999 to focus on middle school statistics. It included seven teachers from four middle schools and was led by two mathematics education researchers who had worked with teachers in the district for 2 years. However, the collaboration was short-lived. The school district recently had adopted a curriculum framework that sharply conflicted with the researchers' perspective of teaching for understanding. This framework rested on a definition of equity that required all students to learn the same knowledge and skills in the same sequence, and the approach relied on accountability and conformity within specific skill areas. In contrast, the NCISLA research team held a vision of equity that encouraged teachers to tailor experiences to students' development along a mathematical learning trajectory, so as to enable all students to achieve similar mathematical and cognitive outcomes. The team ultimately deemed the pursuit of innovations within a climate that stressed the standardization of inputs as an insurmountable challenge.

The Janus District and School Contexts. The Janus district's major emphasis was improvement and accountability. Students' test scores on standardized tests were consistently below national averages, although in recent years they had been rising. Overall, the district was relatively balanced along racial/ethnic lines, with just under half of its students African American and a similar number non-Hispanic White. Six percent were either Hispanic or Asian American, and less than 1% were American Indian. Large-scale organizational changes had been underway for several years, as evidenced by the new district-wide CCF, the opening of three new school buildings in 1999, and a proposal to rearrange the grade-level boundaries between elementary and middle schools.

The district math curriculum represented a codification of an initiative that began with teachers' support 20 years earlier. The scope and sequence were established in the late 1970s when the city school district received a federal planning grant. The district math coordinator, along with a team of teachers representing schools throughout the district, developed what was called the Math Scope and Sequence (MSS). Teachers determined the skills to be taught in each mathematical strand and then decided on skills for each grade level. Over the following 20 years, this local math curriculum had undergone five revisions. Stable curriculum leadership over this 20-plus-year history, as well as the teachers' continued participation in the multiple revisions, meant preservation of the MSS. In the early

1990s, a new superintendent decentralized decision making in the district. Some flexibility in implementation evolved during his tenure.

Throughout the 1990s, the district fell under increasing scrutiny from local business and government leadership. Toward the end of the decade, in return for a tax increase to benefit education, the school system adopted the new content-driven CCF. At the same time, the district reinvigorated its efforts to hold teachers accountable to the language arts and mathematics scope and sequence, establishing a strict sequence and time line for skills testing. As in the other CCF academic subjects, math content and skills for each 6-week reporting period were clearly articulated and closely monitored.

Teachers in Janus had limited professional development time, with few opportunities for genuine collaboration in developing curriculum. Beyond 5 half-days for planning around the CCF, each teacher was allotted 5 professional days per year for workshops, conferences, and so forth. Periodically, teachers were asked to commit these days to specific district tasks. Also, in unusual circumstances, district administrators could grant teachers release days for working on particular district issues.

Within the four middle schools in this project, subject-area departments were an important part of school organization. However, mathematics teachers did not necessarily have common planning periods. One school was organized into "teams" that brought together teachers of different subjects. In this case, when teachers met in the multidisciplinary teams, they tended to talk more about individual students than about subject-area pedagogy. The exception to this lack of communication was in one school that had more subject-focused mentoring. The teacher from that school interacted with her mathematics colleagues more often than did the other teachers.

As described above, the district committed tremendous energy in the years prior to the design collaborative's initiation to making its policy more defined and tied to practice. Earlier, teachers' and administrators' goals had been more vaguely stated and not explicitly addressed. That arrangement had given teachers more latitude for experimentation, even when they did not have full district support. When district goals became more explicit, more conflict arose within the community of educators, and it became more difficult for teachers to envision independent collaboration with outside researchers.

The Janus Design Collaborative. The design collaborative's lead researcher is a renowned mathematics educator. His method, in many school sites across the country, had been to conduct classroom teaching experiments in which a staff person would teach and the teacher would observe. This approach was very intensive and produced audio- and videotapes of all classroom activities. The experiments focused on helping students to learn what constituted a good mathematical argument and to develop norms for interacting in a mathematics classroom. This researcher had extensive experience in other districts before he began to work in the Janus elementary schools in the mid-1990s. After a couple of years, he and his collaborator—a former middle school teacher—became interested in expanding to the middle school grades. In the 1997–98 school year, they received a federal research grant to do a 2-year teaching experiment in a seventh-grade classroom. As the second year of this effort began, the CCF was established at the middle school level. Because of the additional constraints that this entailed, the project's focus shifted to follow-up with the same group of students—now in eighth grade—but during a flexible activity period instead of a regular math class. Around 13 students remained as voluntary participants during the second year.

Not surprisingly, the researchers' approach to math differed both from the CCF and from the conception of math held by many of the teachers in the district. Even before the CCF was established, many teachers believed that learning math centered on skill acquisition, and this diverged from teaching for understanding perspectives. As the researchers visited the schools, they noticed that teachers did not consistently focus on math ideas or on students' conceptual understanding, nor did they talk about issues like "math as discourse," or "norms of justification in mathematics," as the researchers did.

After the second year, the researchers obtained new funding to address the divergence of the teachers' and their own perspectives. The elementary teachers who had participated before had not necessarily altered their teaching methods, since they were not the ones who had been teaching the new material in the first place. A key goal of the new grant, then, was to involve teachers. The researchers planned to use the videos and other materials produced by the 2-year experimental program to start a design collaborative.

In the summer of 1999, the researchers held a workshop for seven teachers from four middle schools. This was intended to begin a new collaboration to foster in-depth understanding in statistics. Only one of the seven teacher-participants had a math background, which is common for the middle school level. Although initially planned to take 1 week, the workshop lasted only 2½ days, but the teachers were excited about collaborating after the first meetings. However, by the start of school in mid-August, they had reassessed the demands on their time and energy and decided that they could not participate. A middle school math text had been adopted that addressed neither the CCF nor the teaching for understanding approach, and the task of synthesizing a new curricular sequence and new text—which were at odds with one another—deflected energy from the design collaborative. Although the teachers continued to express interest in maintaining contact with the researchers, and at one point the researchers considered helping the teachers to map the new textbook to the Math Scope and Sequence, there were no more meetings after the first summer.

In sum, the Janus design collaborative emerged within a context where teachers felt too constrained by district mandates to experiment with instruction. Although the researchers had extensive experience collaborating with other teachers, they did not have prior relationships with this particular group. Even though the teachers wanted to develop a teaching for understanding approach, the immediacy of responding to the CCF requirements and new textbook series took priority, at least in the short term.

CONCLUSIONS

Each of these six cases involved teachers and researchers aiming for teaching for understanding in mathematics and science. Yet the design collaboratives were not fully autonomous, but were embedded in wider school and district contexts. How did the teachers, researchers, and their organizational environments interact in the effort to move toward teaching for understanding? What sorts of barriers were raised in the school and district contexts, and what supports were evident? The following chapters will address these questions, in order to help us understand how supports can be enhanced and barriers removed to aid such efforts in the future.

Responding to the Challenges

Now that we see the challenges of supporting teaching for understanding, what can we say about how schools and districts can respond? That is the task of Part II. Our analysis focuses on elements identified as important in our conceptual model. In Chapter 4, we explore the importance of access to resources for supporting change. We show how material, human, and social resources are involved in three different ways: Resources *support* professional development; they are *generated by* professional development; and they *enhance the impact of* professional development on classroom teaching. Chapter 5 takes the analysis of resources a step further by examining the role they play with regard to *equity* in support of teaching for understanding within and across districts. We identify particular difficulties faced by urban districts and districts with large numbers of language-minority children, and also show the special benefits that teacher–researcher collaboration can bring to these challenging contexts. In Chapter 6, we ask how school leadership will need to change to support teaching for understanding. Our data suggest that leadership will need to be responsive to teacher initiatives instead of directing teachers via resource allocation; and that leadership will need to be distributed among a variety of actors, including teachers, instead of resting solely among persons in positions of authority, such as principals. Chapter 7 takes up the popular concept of professional community and uses our data to show how material, human, and social resources are essential for developing community, and how community in turn provides essential resources to help stimulate and sustain teachers' efforts.

CHAPTER 4

Access to Resources

Adam Gamoran

It is commonplace these days to caution against "throwing money at schools," as if extra resources allocated to schools are invariably wasted. Some analysts go so far as to say that additional resources are irrelevant for student outcomes (Hanushek, 1994), although others disagree (Greenwald, Hedges, & Laine, 1996). In the meantime, families continue to act as if school resources do matter by choosing, if they can afford it, neighborhoods whose schools are relatively well off.

In our view, asking whether resources matter is the wrong question. Instead, we should ask *how* resources can be used in ways that benefit teaching and learning. As we focus on access to resources in the context of teacher change, we seek to identify ways that resources can be deployed strategically to enhance teachers' ability to teach for understanding. By resources, of course, we mean more than money, because what matters most is not the dollar amount, but how dollars are translated into the capacity to support teaching for understanding. How is time allocated? What tools and materials are available to teachers? How are teachers' knowledge and skills enhanced, and what activities lead to strong professional ties among teachers?

Posing the question of *how* resources matter takes for granted the notion that resources *do* matter, at least in some circumstances. As we explained in Chapter 2, the effects of resources on teaching have been documented in some cases; notably, increased time and more challenging curricular materials tend to enhance curricular coverage. There are other examples of resources that seem to matter in some situations and not others. For instance, smaller classes benefit achievement in the early grades. None of these examples touches on teaching for understanding, and the relation between resources and teaching for understanding has not been explored systematically. Consequently, in the context of answering the question of *how* resources matter, we also will have to demonstrate that, at least in some cases, resources *do* matter for teaching for understanding.

Administrators who support teaching for understanding use resources differently than those who go along with conventional teaching. To support conventional teaching, one may allocate time and materials to direct and constrain teachers, as explained by the nested-layers model of school organization (see Chapter 2). By contrast, supporting teaching for understanding calls on administrators to enhance schools' capacity for change by allocating substantial time for professional development, by offering autonomy to teachers in the content as well as methods of instruction, and, most important, by allocating resources in response to teachers' efforts instead of limiting their efforts through resource or structural constraints. As Peterson, McCarthey, and Elmore (1996) explained, teacher change is a result of teacher learning (i.e., professional development), not school organization. Our position takes this claim a step further, proposing that schools can support teacher change by *responding* to teacher learning.

This chapter is about access to resources, but that does not mean it responds only to the first challenge we identified in Chapter 1. In fact, access to resources is fundamental to all three challenges. First, resources help teachers begin the process of change, and how schools meet the first challenge—providing resources—is a central concern of this chapter. Second, a teacher's ability to benefit from resources is closely related to whether educators in a school share common purposes and commitments. So, resources are also relevant for the second challenge—aligning commitments. Third, resources are needed over the long term, so they also bear on the third challenge—sustaining change.

HOW RESOURCES MATTER: APPLYING THE DYNAMIC MODEL

In our conception of school organization, teaching for understanding does not follow directly from resources allocated to classroom teachers, because it is not a practice that emerges in isolation, but an approach that develops in a learning community. Teaching for understanding occurs when teachers develop new habits of practice through sustained, cohesive professional development, and when they have access to resources and structures that allow those insights to flourish. At the same time, professional development that emphasizes teaching for understanding may help create resources, particularly human and social resources, as teachers gain knowledge and skills and strengthen their relationships with other educators. These new resources, along with additional resources from outside venues, make it possible for activities of a professional development group to affect teachers' classroom activities. Thus, supporting teaching for understanding involves resources in three different ways:

- Material, human, and social resources may establish and sustain professional development with a focus on student thinking.

- Professional development may generate new resources that support teaching for understanding.
- Newly created and externally provided resources make it possible for teachers to implement in their classrooms what they have learned in professional development.

According to this model, resources are not the responsibility of schools and districts alone. Two other sources of resources are especially important: First, external groups such as the university-based researchers in our study bring resources that allow professional development to occur. In our research, all the cases of supporting teaching for understanding involved teacher–researcher collaboratives that provided such external support. Consequently, we will not contrast the presence and absence of outside resources, but trace the role of resources in stimulating professional development and teaching for understanding in the cases we studied. Second, the professional development groups themselves generate new resources. This is extremely important because it means that a moderate quantity of resources, when applied to teacher learning, can be multiplied into a greater quantity over time. Commonly, resources are conceived as a constant, unchanging flow. By contrast, our conception of resources as human and social as well as material allows us to observe how professional development transforms a small amount of resources into a larger amount. As we will demonstrate, this process is primarily one of material resources being transformed into human and social resources through professional development.

Our conception also distinguishes among different applications of resources in support of teaching for understanding. In our dynamic model, resources are applied to initiate professional development where teachers gain new knowledge and skills. Resources used for this purpose may come from outside the school, or they may be allocated internally. Professional development may be a necessary stimulus for teaching for understanding, but even with the knowledge teachers gain, professional development may not be sufficient to foster teaching for understanding. This is because teachers may need additional resources, such as materials, consultation, and collaboration, to implement in their classrooms what they have learned in professional development. Consequently, another application of resources we examine is their use in enabling or enhancing the impact of professional development on teaching for understanding. These resources, too, may have external or internal sources, but we are especially interested in the possibility that professional development that results from external resources may generate resources that, in turn, support the classroom implementation of teaching for understanding. Note that evidence about the absence of resources coupled with a *lack* of support for teaching for understanding would be consistent with our conceptions, as would findings about the presence of resources that support teaching for understanding. (More information about our data and methods of coding and analysis may be found in the Appendix.)

RESOURCES THAT SUPPORT TEACHING
FOR UNDERSTANDING

According to the dynamic model we presented in Chapter 2, professional development that is sustained, coherent, and focused on student thinking is the primary stimulus to teachers who are changing their practice toward teaching for understanding in mathematics and science. We are not testing this assertion in the present study; rather, our purpose is to understand how districts and schools can assist in this process and support it when it is in progress. We found evidence of such support in material, human, and social resources.

Resources That Support Professional Development

What resources support professional development that focuses on student thinking? We found evidence for time and other material conditions, expertise from outsiders and insiders, and communities of teachers within schools that facilitated the professional development collaboratives.

Material Resources: Time and Curricular Materials. From the perspective of teachers, time is the most important material resource. Many teachers viewed the use of funds to provide time to work together on issues of student thinking as the most important contribution of the design collaboratives to their teaching practices. Over 60% of the teacher interviews mentioned time as a resource, and for the vast majority, the most precious use of time was for planning and learning with other teachers.

> INTERVIEWER: What resources do you think are necessary for you and
> your colleagues to maintain your efforts to improve your program and
> science teaching?
> OBERON TEACHER: Time. Time's the biggest one of all. Time to be
> together and talking and doing and interacting and . . . That's the
> biggest one of all. I mean money and verbal support from people
> around you is important, but I think in the long run if you don't have
> the time, you can't do it.

Conversely, the lack of meeting time engenders frustration.

> As a team [of same-grade teachers] . . . we feel frustrated. We do have time
> in our schedule that we're supposed to meet. It always seems when we're
> [at] our busiest time and really under the crunch . . . oh we've got to plan
> this and then one of us has to leave because we have to go down and cover
> the class and that gets us angry, and we've talked about our time being a
> little more sacred and not being interrupted so much. (Callisto teacher)

Another urban teacher, this one from Mimas High School in Wisconsin, expressed similar frustration during a professional development meeting: "We don't have the time. We don't have it now and we need more of it. And it's obvious if we had more time we could do a better job [as teachers] but we don't have it."

Lack of time for teachers to collaborate when they are not meeting with their classes is recognized increasingly as an important impediment to reform in American schools. Moreover, when American teachers do have time to meet, typically they devote their time to administrative matters, or to issues of student behavior, instead of focusing on teaching and learning. For this reason, teachers especially valued the professional development time afforded by the design collaboratives we observed, as they spent it working on their own learning of subject matter and pedagogical strategies. As Newmann and Associates (1996) argued, "authentic pedagogy" (their term for what we call teaching for understanding) occurs only when teachers focus on the intellectual quality of students' work. Supporting teaching for understanding, therefore, means providing time for teachers to work together on matters of teaching and learning.

Even when financial resources are available to provide time for teachers to work together, practical limitations made finding time to meet difficult. During the school day, funds could be allocated to hire substitutes so that teachers could work together during class time. However, in at least three of our sites, teachers were frustrated with the quality of their substitutes and found it difficult to miss class time on a regular basis. The other option, meeting after school, became a regular solution in four of the six contexts, but this solution had its own problems, particularly other projects and obligations that competed for teachers' after-school time.

In Mimas, teachers began meeting with their professional development collaborative in their regular common planning periods during the school day. This schedule avoided the problems associated with missing class time and competing responsibilities after school. However, it meant that common planning periods could not be used for other purposes. By contrast, professional development time at the other sites was paid time *added on* to the normal work schedules. This meant that regular planning periods and team meetings (i.e., grade-level meetings in the elementary sites, and department or house meetings in the middle and high school sites) could be devoted to other purposes. Often, we discovered, participants in the professional development collaboratives used these meetings to share what they were learning in the professional development collaboratives. This appeared most common in Europa, the Wisconsin suburban elementary and middle school sites, possibly because those cases had the most extensive time for teachers to meet aside from the professional development collaboratives. At the elementary schools, 2 half-days per month were devoted to professional development or other teacher meetings at each school, plus 1 hour per week of planning time, in contrast to about half that amount elsewhere. At the middle school, teachers had one daily period to meet with their team and another period for individual planning. With extra time for professional development, regular teacher meetings and school-sponsored activities for teachers became occasions for diffusion of ideas and materials drawn from professional development in the collaboratives. This process provided a basis for the longer-term sustainability of the reforms, creating a base of support that extended beyond the participants in the professional development seminars.

Overall, we found prepackaged curriculum materials less essential for supporting professional development than time to meet. At only one of our six sites, Europa Middle School, was a prepared curriculum central to the professional development program. In this case, teachers and researchers focused on the Math in Context curriculum as a teaching tool, and the Boxer computer software as an approach to integrating mathematics and science to study the physics of motion. Here, curricular materials were an essential resource for professional development, but the teachers had substantial freedom to select and modify the curricula to suit their needs and interests. At the other sites, the professional development seminars did not begin with a designed curriculum at all. For example, much of the activity in the Europa elementary collaborative focused on teachers designing their own curricula to encourage a greater focus on student thinking. At Oberon High School, rather than taking curriculum as a starting point, developing new curricula was the outcome of the collaborative process.

The advantage to commencing professional development *without* a prepared curriculum is that it allows teachers to match their own interests to their students' emerging thinking. Hence, teachers can proceed as they deem appropriate instead of following a script. The disadvantage, however, is that teachers must spend substantial time determining a direction. Thus, in the Europa elementary collaborative workshop, many hours were devoted to discussions of what projects teachers could design that would make students' thinking evident. This was especially true in the year we observed after the university researchers had pulled back from their leadership roles in the collaborative. Whereas some teachers appreciated the opportunity to determine the group's direction, others were frustrated at the time spent on administrative issues and wished for more decisive leadership.

Although time and curriculum may contribute to professional development that supports teaching for understanding, they do not bring it about in isolation. In Janus, the Tennessee urban site we studied, a group of teachers and researchers wanted to form a collaborative to work on middle school statistics. Resources to support new professional development efforts were available from both the school and the district, but nonetheless the collaborative did not go beyond the planning stage. We observed, here, that when sharp conflicts between district goals and the purpose of teacher–researcher collaboration are perceived, the collaboration is likely to be forestalled. By contrast, the Europa and Callisto collaboratives took full advantage of external resources, since the goals of participants in the professional development were consistent with district aims.

Human Resources: Expertise from Outside and Inside the Schools.

Precisely because the teachers' knowledge about student thinking was limited, expertise from outside the schools was essential to stimulating their investigations and learning. University researchers affiliated with the design collaboratives served as key resources at all six sites. This was acknowledged frequently by teachers. For example, when we asked them to whom they would go with questions about mathematics and science teaching, many indicated a member of the university research team. Europa elementary is an interesting case in point. In the first year we interviewed participants, 30% of the teachers listed at least one member of the research team as someone they would go to with a question. In the second year, the percentage more than doubled to 63%. In the third year of our data collection, when we monitored the professional development group after the researchers had pulled back from their leadership role, still one-third of the teachers we interviewed said they would call on a member of the research team when a question arose. The university staff saw themselves similarly, as resources upon whom the teachers could draw.

In addition to external expertise, human resources from within the district served as important stimuli for the professional development that followed. In the successful elementary and middle school cases in Wisconsin and Massachusetts, we identified a district official who played a key role in promoting the cause of the collaboratives. By contrast, the unsuccessful case in Tennessee had no district champion. In both of the Wisconsin high schools we studied, Oberon and Mimas, a department chair played a key role in accepting the teacher–researcher groups.

More important than this administrative leadership, however, was the substantive expertise of teachers who provided leadership in the professional development groups.

> INTERVIEWER: What resources have been helpful or important to you this year for supporting your science instruction?
>
> OBERON TEACHER: People that I work with. That resource is invaluable. I don't know what I would do in another situation where I didn't have the experience of the other teachers to draw on for ideas and things of that nature. So that resource for me is the one without which I would be floundering.

Whereas many teachers confirmed that their participation in the design collaboratives led to changes in their teaching practices, some teachers reported that their practices had changed in advance of the program. These teachers offered leadership for the group. The following Europa elementary teacher, for example, provided both administrative support and substantive guidance to other teachers in the project:

> I don't know if . . . participation in [the professional development collaborative] has changed the way [I] teach. I think the way I teach changed before the . . . project began and I think that the . . . project is just kind of continuation of that for me and it's [a] chance for me to collaborate with other people and to reach out more and to serve as a resource or to try to

push things that I had found to be very exciting and very powerful and very effective in terms of math instruction to try to help them spread further.

Four of our six sites included at least one teacher among the participants who had worked previously with the researchers, in some cases for many years. This local expertise served as an important resource for establishing the new professional development groups and fostering further exploration.

Social Resources: Communities and Catalysts. A community of teachers that is ripe for collaboration on a broader scale is especially conducive to establishing ongoing, intensive professional development. As a Callisto bilingual teacher recounted,

> The third-grade team . . . [had] been meeting over the last 3 years [to integrate science throughout the curriculum] . . . using content-area instruction in both Spanish and English. So that is what really pushed the whole thing of working together in collaboration . . . that's one of the reasons we got involved in the [professional development group]. 'Cause when it happened, it was a continuation of the work that we started the year before. So we were very enthusiastic about having not only additional support, but the opportunity to continue that interaction.

In this case, the professional development group offered an opportunity to extend collaboration from a colleague group that was already in place to a larger, cross-school group.

Similarly, the Oberon science department followed a team-oriented approach to planning, and, as one of the teachers reported, willingness to collaborate was a criterion of selection for this department.

> When we are interviewing people . . . one of the things we are looking for [is] somebody that fits in. I mean we like to have people bring different perspectives and experience but they have to be able and willing to work in that team environment. We can't have three of the Science II teachers who feel that it is important to teach a certain subject matter a certain way and somebody else who says, "No, you are wrong, I am going to do it this way." There is value in the team aspect.

In this case, the department as a whole—including all members but one—commenced a process of redesigning the science curriculum in collaboration with university researchers, to place more emphasis on student thinking. The university researchers served as catalysts for a process that was already in motion, led by members of the department. We found a similar pattern in the Europa Middle site, where years of collaboration within teams of two to four teachers had laid the foundation for the professional development group. At this site, teachers shaped the activities of the professional development program to suit a need they had already identified: integrating algebra throughout the middle school curriculum so as to eliminate the high-track, eighth-grade algebra class. Again, the collaboration with university researchers served as a catalyst for a process that was already underway in the school.

By contrast, Mimas High School did not have a community of teachers in place that could have embraced the professional development opportunity. Although subject-matter affiliations are extremely important for high school teachers, this school was organized into "families" that separated mathematics teachers from one another, making subject-matter collaboration difficult. The professional development opportunity in mathematics was especially attractive to some teachers because it gave them a chance to address subject-matter issues, but it also meant there was no ready-made community in which the professional development could be embedded. In addition, the school staff was divided between bilingual and monolingual teachers, and the two informal groups did not collaborate with one another. Consequently, the professional development group that was established in this school—originally with four teachers, reduced to two teachers in the second year—could not draw on social resources in the school that might have supported and sustained the professional development program.

Although a strong colleague group is an asset for professional development, it is not clear that such a group is essential for establishing an intensive program focused on teaching for understanding. At the Europa elementary site, teachers had been working for some time with the university researchers, at first individually and then in a small group. The teachers who formed the design collaborative, however, extended far beyond the small core of previous participants. In addition, the collaborative expanded during the period of university participation, from 25 Europa teachers the first year to 27 the second year and 34 in the third. (In the year following, when the university researchers were no longer centrally involved, the group's roster still listed 27 teacher-participants.) The teachers came from four elementary schools in the district, including eight to ten teachers from each of two schools, and two to six teachers (depending on the year) from the other two. An existing network was not a precondition for teachers' decisions to participate in professional development, at least in this district.

These findings suggest that material, human, and social resources all help bring about professional development that has the potential to transform teachers' practice. Clearly, material resources that expand the amount of teachers' meeting time are the most indispensable resource. Where human resources are lacking within the district, outside expertise such as that provided by the university researchers in our study can pave the way for success. Still, outside expertise can have an impact only if it is perceived to be consistent with, or at least not opposed to, other district initiatives that affect the same teachers. Human resources in the form of expertise and leadership from teachers as well as school and district administrators also can support a program of ongoing professional development. Finally, a strong existing colleague group enhances the likelihood that professional development for teaching for understanding can occur, if members of the group want to embrace that approach. In cases where such teacher networks do not exist, can they be created through professional development programs that begin with looser collections of teachers? That is a question for the next part of our analysis, which concerns the possible "feedback" effect from professional development to resources.

Resources Generated by Professional Development

Does professional development that focuses on teaching for understanding in mathematics and science generate new resources that may keep the process moving? Our findings suggest the answer is yes, particularly with respect to social and human resources.

Generating Social Resources: Toward a Professional Community.

Observations of workshops and interviews with teachers indicate that professional development helps create or strengthen social ties among the educators who participate. This claim, which is consistent with large-scale survey analysis (Grodsky & Gamoran, in press), could be supported with evidence from any of the five sites in which ongoing professional development occurred. Here we present an instance from the Europa elementary case. At this site, the core professional development activity was examining student work to understand student thinking. Almost every whole-group seminar had a major or minor component that featured student work. By examining student work collaboratively, teachers gained insight into what students were thinking and how their thinking was changing in response to classroom activities. The process of working together also engendered cohesiveness within the professional development group.

> For most of this period I [the observer] sat with the small group of Gloria, Sara, and Anita [Sara was a many-year veteran and Anita and Gloria were in their second years with the project]. . . . Their [first-grade] kids had done some problems for which they had received, on a piece of paper, a drawing of a jack-o'-lantern which included two eyes, one nose, and four holes for a mouth. The kids were supposed to figure out how many eyes, noses, and mouth holes there would be if there were 3, 5, or 13 jack-o'-lanterns. . . . In discussion with the small group it emerged that Sara had a lot more information about children's thinking than the other teachers because she had interviewed the children. Sara explained that she carried out this exercise by taking kids into small groups of 6 at a time while the other 2/3 of her class were with the teachers aide. . . . Sara was clearly a resource for the other teachers. She was advising them on whom to use the sheets with,

for example. . . . Sara also takes advice. She asked about first graders since some of the other teachers had more experience teaching first graders than she did. She was teaching first grade this year but had previously been a second-grade teacher. Sara maintains that experience with counting and modeling is important so it's not necessary to push advanced strategies on first graders. That can be pushed in second grade. In first grade it is important that children have a lot of experience with counting and direct modeling. (Field notes)

In this vignette, Sara and her fellow teachers are deeply engaged in figuring out what the children were thinking as they responded to the exercise. They listen attentively to one another and share thoughts and experiences. Not every small-group activity that occurred in this professional development group operated with such a high level of engagement, but we observed this type of interaction with great regularity.

This example illustrates how professional development of this nature builds social relationships among educators. Following Newmann and Associates (1996), we can identify the elements of a professional community within this group of teachers:

- They exhibit a *shared sense of purpose* in their attention to student thinking.
- They are *focusing collectively on student learning*, as opposed to teachers' more common conversations about administrative details and managing student behavior.
- They are *collaborating* on ways to improve their students' understanding of mathematics, in contrast to teachers' usual practice of working in isolation.
- They are engaged in *reflective dialogue*, a conversation about the nature and practice of teaching.
- They are *making their own teaching practices public*, instead of keeping their practices private and confined to the classroom.

Thus, professional community is constituted in the activities of the professional development group. If a cohesive network among educators does not predate the professional development program, the program may generate such ties subsequently, which could provide support for maintaining collaboration over a long period of time. The small group of Gloria, Sara, and Anita described above comprised teachers from the same grade level in three different elementary schools. This was not an instance of an existing community engaging in collective professional development, but rather the professional development activity provided the opportunity to establish and sustain professional relationships.

Much of the discussion about professional community in the research literature focuses on the school as the location of community, including Newmann and Associates' (1996) study of restructured schools and Grodsky and Gamoran's (in press) survey analysis, but the case of professional community we have exhibited here is not confined to the boundaries of a school, nor does it include all the members of any particular school. In the Europa Middle and Oberon High School sites, the professional development groups were located within single schools and contained almost all the members of the relevant subject-area departments. In these cases, the teacher–researcher collaboration may have enhanced professional community within the schools. In the other cases, the professional development groups either drew from several schools (Europa elementary, Callisto, and Janus) or included only a fraction of the teachers within a school (Mimas High School), and we did not observe any impact on school-wide professional community in these cases.

Effects on Human Resources: Teacher Learning Through Professional Development. It almost goes without saying that teachers increased their knowledge through the experiences of professional development; this finding would be entirely unremarkable were it not for earlier research showing that teachers often do *not* learn from professional development and consider it a waste of time (Fullan, 2001). Based on our observations of five sites (as explained in Chapter 3, ongoing professional development did not occur at Janus), teacher learning was clearly evident when professional development took place, and in the interviews teachers recognized their learning.

> INTERVIEWER: Has your participation in the project led to changes in the way your students think about science or how you think about student thinking in science?
>
> OBERON TEACHER: Probably just because I emphasize things better or differently than what I did maybe last year. Again it has to do with I have a better understanding of how to use model-based teaching and learning. I probably use those terms much better in more of context. Last year it was kind of thrown at me. Sometimes I heard it but I wasn't sure, like kids are going to model-build. Well, I just really didn't have a good understanding of what that was. They would use that word so I would incorporate [it] into my interpretation and use it. This year it was because I have heard more about [what] Sharon has done with her classes and her [model]-based approaches in her senior genetics class I have been able to use those, either ideas or teaching. The few times I do some modeling in class I have been able to use it a lot better I think.

Interestingly, teachers rarely articulated a contribution to their own subject-matter knowledge; even when we explicitly asked them what they had learned about science or mathematics, they responded in terms of the activities they carried out.

More important than the learning of individual teachers, however, is the increase in the collective level of expertise among teachers within a school or district. The more expert teachers in a school, the more likely it is that other teachers, even those who are not part of a professional development group, may benefit from the collective wisdom. According to this interpretation, professional development enhances human resources not only at the level of individuals but also at the organizational (school or district) level. Although we cannot demonstrate it with the present data, we speculate that increases in collective levels of expertise in a given subject area enhance teaching in that area on an organization-wide basis.

The selection above from the Europa elementary site also shows how the professional development program can generate leadership, another sort of human resource. Sara, the longtime veteran of the design collaborative, exhibits leadership as she helps the newer participants devise strategies for uncovering their students' thinking. Sara's leadership has emerged over time within the collaborative, and this was the first clear instance of her leadership in an observation of professional development. Another Europa teacher, who provided leadership for the collaborative over many years, had discussed Sara's emerging leadership in an interview during the previous summer.

> Sara in her own quiet way has come so far in the last couple of years and she is such a complement to my kind of leadership style. . . . Sara is the patient, calm one who tries some of it out, and when Sara says . . . , "I really like this, and I am learning a lot," . . . that kind of endorsement . . . gives all kinds of people faith then [that] "this will really work for me, too."

Sara's leadership is based on recognition of her knowledge and experience. Her projects often are cited among those that influenced other teachers, as one of her colleagues explained: "Sara wrote [a paper] on place value, and it is part of my resource file and I refer to it." In this way, the professional development group has created not only individual knowledge, but collective expertise that other teachers can draw upon, and relationships among teachers that provide access to such expertise.

Material Resources That Result from Professional Development.

Although most of the association between material resources and professional development runs from the former to the latter, we found some cases where professional development generated material resources. First, in three of the sites we studied (Oberon, Europa elementary, and Callisto), the teachers produced tangible curricula that could be implemented not only in their own classrooms but also in those of others. In Europa, teachers were responsible for writing up a project they did with their classes, and some of the papers were compiled into books that served as material resources for other teachers in later years of the project. In Callisto, teachers wrote papers and developed curricula that they used in bilingual classes.

Second, professional development creates incentives for the allocation of material resources to support continued collaboration. These resources may be external supplements to existing support, or they may be internal reallocations of currently available resources. For instance, we observed the teachers and researchers at Mimas discussing the possibility of leveraging their current work to obtain additional resources.

At the initial professional development session, the teachers are asking for more time to meet than the resources of the grant will allow. The researchers and teachers then discuss ways of obtaining additional resources for meeting time.

RESEARCHER: Is it possible to leverage? To get additional time? I mean, are there resources even within the school to try to find some of that or Eisenhower monies available for the district to try to get some of this? I know there's the—what's this thing called—the [a local reform with national ties]. Do they have monies for something like this? Should we try to approach them for more release time for you?

TEACHER: I'm not sure how much monies—how much money—they're willing to put into this type of—a different project itself but I know that a lot of the money goes into the "families" [unit of school organization] so the families do get a certain amount to meet and plan. That might be a good question for [a school administrator]. He's very open-minded about it and I'm sure he's willing to—I'm sure he's willing to give out some money. How much, that I don't know . . . because we're talking about teacher collaboration here. (Field notes)

Taken as a whole, our findings about how professional development generates social, human, and material resources indicate that the relation between professional development and resources is a two-way process. Time to meet is fundamental, but beyond that a cohesive program of professional development can generate the resources it needs to affect practice and sustain itself—particularly collective human and social resources.

We can raise two important caveats to this conclusion. First, high levels of human and social resources can be decimated through administrative changes and turnover within the school district. The collaboratives we observed in the Europa elementary and middle schools had great success in generating resources, but these gains were tempered by the departure of key teachers from the elementary site, and by administrative decisions to shift teachers across schools at both sites. Due to rapid growth in the student population of this district, new schools opened repeatedly. Each time new schools opened, teachers moved. These moves threatened to fragment social networks that had been established (or enhanced) through years of teacher–researcher collaboration.

Second, even when the professional development group succeeds in creating new resources, that may not be enough to change classrooms directly. Teaching for understanding requires new kinds of materials and new relationships, so the impact of professional development on teaching for understanding depends in part on the availability of resources for implementation.

Resources That Enhance the Impact of Professional Development

Even cohesive, sustained, collaborative professional development is no guarantee of classroom changes, because the human resources created by professional development are necessary but not sufficient to support teaching for understanding in practice. The importance of material resources for taking what one has learned in professional development, and applying it in the classroom, cannot be overstated. This point epitomizes the claim that what matters about resources is not how much there is, but how they are used. We find that resources deployed in the service of teacher learning can have an impact. For example, teachers at Europa elementary were enthusiastic about curricular materials produced by TERC, an educational research and design group in Massachusetts whose curricular programs were conducive to the types of classroom activities they were seeking to implement. Funds from their district and from the university research grant permitted them to purchase books and supplies to help them investigate student thinking in their classrooms. In Callisto, we found that a *lack* of materials from the district and schools impaired teachers' ability to carry new ideas to their classrooms, but the teacher–researcher collaborative funds made implementation possible.

> TEACHER: I asked the science teacher at [her school], the upper-grade science teacher, if we could borrow a bank of lights . . . for the fast plants. She said she'd been asking for years for a bank of lights and had never got one.
> INTERVIEWER: Where does a resource like that come from?
> TEACHER: From the [district] science department.

> *Later in the interview, in response to a question about resources:*

> TEACHER: Right, well if you want to, if you want to grow fast plants . . . you've got to have lights. . . . The bank of lights is very expensive, so what [the design collaborative] gave me was more single lights and . . . those are very expensive so they're working on having them built.

Generally, we found in this district that teachers of language-minority students had more difficulty obtaining materials than did regular classroom teachers (see further discussion in Chapter 5). First, language-minority teachers lacked access to special district resources set aside for teaching for understanding in science, because of their roles as teachers in bilingual education (as opposed to science) classrooms.

Second, innovative curricular materials for bilingual education are simply less available, leaving teachers the difficult and burdensome task of translating English materials for use in bilingual classrooms. These challenges were compounded by the usual problems of obtaining basic supplies in a large urban district, resulting in perceptions of isolation for bilingual teachers. This district placed great weight on entrepreneurship, an approach that is gaining currency in educational reform circles. Our study reveals problems associated with relying on entrepreneurship to generate resources for teachers: Those who tend to be less successful entrepreneurs, such as novice teachers or teachers outside of the networks that open doors, fail to obtain the resources they need to activate their commitments to teaching for understanding.

There are also limits to the resources that professional development groups can provide. While the Europa elementary site may be viewed as a model of success in light of its continuous expansion and wide impact in the district, such growth also engenders problems. In this case, the researchers were overburdened by the opportunities for collaboration with teachers and were unable to extend themselves to all teachers who wished for support. As one Europa elementary teacher who felt neglected explained:

> I was interested in one of the projects in the beginning on portraits and . . . how kids develop their . . . self-portraits and the house project. [This was a project on how children think about classification, an important concept in both mathematics and scientific inquiry.] I really thought that was cool. I wanted to get in on that because I hadn't heard about it from the year before. So, one night we went, one of the first or second meetings, went into a different room from everybody else. . . . We separated portraits and I thought that we were going to get in on the project right then and there. That was my understanding. . . . I requested . . . the materials to do the project twice, and never got it. And I had that same problem the year before with requesting some help and some materials for something. . . . So to me, that was a waste of my time, cause what I basically did was, I went and sorted out things. And yeah I did understand, okay, kids in kindergarten think about drawing this way . . . but I didn't get anything out of it after that because I never got the materials. . . . I feel like I was ignored.

Participation in professional development stimulated and nurtured this teacher's interest in teaching for understanding in her fifth-grade classroom. As her statement indicates, however, professional development was not sufficient in itself for her to carry out the approach with her students. Because she lacked access to the material and human resources she needed to activate the learning and commitment she had obtained from professional development, her interest in teaching for understanding remained unfulfilled in the classroom.

Since the outside agents are limited in their capacity to provide assistance, a better solution to the challenge of providing widespread assistance would seem to be to use professional development to create new resources, as explained earlier, and then use those resources to enhance implementation. That is, in fact, what we observed above in the case of Sara, the teacher who provided leadership—that is, lent her human resources—to other teachers and in this way made the professional development experience more effective for her colleagues. Similarly, the Europa Middle School teachers described the benefits of having a researcher in their classroom as a source of specialized knowledge that helped them teach for understanding in mathematics, but they recognized that access to the researchers was not unlimited. In a design collaborative workshop, the teachers proposed an alternative approach for drawing on human resources to enhance the impact of professional development on their teaching: lending expertise to one another.

TEACHER 1: I want to make a comment before we leave. It's about the type of feedback we get. I was hoping we could have a chat after the classroom observation so that we could get some feedback. Otherwise, it seems like we're not learning anything.

TEACHER 2: I don't want that.

TEACHER 1: There's some emotional drain when you're being watched.

TEACHER 3: Or videotaped for 15 days (laughs).

RESEARCHER: We can try and do that more and adjust it on an individual basis. After winter break, we're planning to spend some time going over observations and scheduling time to talk to each of you. We can certainly try to give you more feedback.

TEACHER 3: Looking over it all, it seems really intimidating.

RESEARCHER: But having multiple observations helps filter out the bad day. We can try to be more in touch.

TEACHER 1: That's the main thing that you miss [from] student teaching. Bouncing ideas off of other people. It helps me to think about things.

TEACHER 4: Last year, [the lead researcher] shared a lot with me. One of the biggest advantages of being in the project is having an extra adult and being able to share observations on what you did.

TEACHER 5: Last year, there seemed to be a better balance. With a bigger group it's harder.

RESEARCHER: Last year, the number of teachers was equal to the number of researchers. With everyone doing teaching experiments, there are more teachers than researchers.

TEACHER 5: Would it be possible to work together *without* researchers? [Teacher 3] and I observing each other would in some ways be more valuable.

RESEARCHER: I agree wholeheartedly. (Field notes)

At the end of this discussion, the teachers come to the realization that there are not enough researchers to go around, so they will have to work with one another. This seems to be an instance not only of human but of social resources—that is, the existing relationships among the educators—serving as a potential resource for enhancing the impact of professional development. Note that Teacher 5 says that "observing each other would in some ways be *more* valuable" than having a researcher in the classroom [emphasis added]. This suggests that human and social resources together (i.e., drawing on the expertise of colleagues) may be more powerful than external expertise alone.

Consider two models of professional development aimed at changing teaching. In one model, teachers attend professional development sessions, learn new ideas (i.e., increase their individual human resources), and enact the ideas in their classrooms. In the other model, teachers attend professional development, learn new ideas, and collaborate with others (i.e., establish social resources) in enacting the ideas in their classrooms. The latter model was envisioned by the teacher–researcher collaboratives we studied, and the researchers have documented that teachers who applied new knowledge did so in collaboration with colleagues (Berman & Giles, 2000). In addition to providing essential knowledge, effective professional development secures the commitment of teachers to higher standards of practice and generates social support networks for this more demanding practice. Unlike conventional teaching, in which teachers avoid uncertainty by following a scripted lesson plan, teaching for understanding forces teachers to confront uncertainties as they struggle to uncover their students' thinking. Collaboration offers a forum for developing ideas that respond to the uncertainties of teaching for understanding. Several teachers recognized and articulated the value of such collegiality.

> I think [collaboration has] affected my classroom a great deal. I think writing curriculum with other people is very good, because no matter how much energy and creativity and background you put into it, other people always have other ideas as well. And that's what I love about working on a team, because you end up coming up with something better than, none of the people could have done on their own. None of them. Sometimes I think people, and I guess I've never felt this way, think that if you're working on a team like that in a collaboration that if you've got some really great ideas, maybe they're stifled because you are working on a team. But I think overall, if they're that good and you feel that strongly about them, they're gonna hang on there and so I think overall I think working on a team in a collaboration is without comparison. (Oberon teacher)

Colleagues engaged in the same effort are an important resource for engaging in teaching for understanding; we speculate that it is an essential resource, but we cannot test that claim because all of the cases in which we observed ongoing professional development resulted in collaborative implementation.

This exploration shows that resources are important not only to begin the process of teacher learning, but to take advantage of teacher learning in the classroom. Whereas Peterson and colleagues (1996) concluded that changes in teaching followed from teacher learning, our analysis adds an important caveat to this claim: Changes in teaching are dependent not only on teacher learning, but on the material, human, and social resources that make it possible for teachers to act on their own new knowledge and commitments.

One potential objection to our claims is that we have largely ignored the direct effect of resources on teaching for understanding. Obviously, human resources at the individual level are an essential resource for teaching: If teachers do not know or understand the reform they are attempting to implement, they will not succeed (Gamoran, 1996a). Material resources also may have a direct impact on teaching— that is, given new materials, a teacher may begin to teach in a new way—but our sense is that most of the impact of new materials is mediated by professional development. We are unable to test this interpretation, however, because we did not study any cases of teachers who obtained materials that would support teaching for understanding in the absence of corresponding professional development.

In the case of social resources, also, we speculate but cannot confirm that their chief impact on teaching for understanding is to enable professional development and enhance its impact on teaching, rather than affecting teaching directly. Hence, we cannot fully reject the nested-layers model, which claims that material resources constrain teaching by directing and limiting teachers' classroom practice. On the contrary, we should acknowledge that at least in the case of the Europa elementary site, the hands-on materials that became available through the teacher–researcher collaborative had a substantial impact on classroom activities, just as the nested-layers model would predict. Of course, even if this conclusion about nested layers were fully confirmed, it would not indicate a rejection of the dynamic, multidirectional model we introduced in Chapter 2, but simply would specify another element in the causal chain, which our evidence does not address well enough to confirm or deny.

CONCLUSIONS

This chapter illustrates the critical role that district and school capacity play in supporting teacher change. We found evidence for material, human, and social resources in all three of the aspects that we anticipated: creating opportunities for professional development, being generated by professional development, and enhancing the impact of professional development on teaching for understanding. Within these findings, several points stand out as particularly important.

First, time to meet with other teachers is an essential ingredient for teacher change, at least as it occurs through the process of collective growth we observed. The cases we studied adopted different approaches to providing time—some groups met during the school day while substitutes handled their classes, others met during regularly scheduled planning periods, and still others met after school—but each of these approaches had limitations. To build the capacity for change, schools and districts would do better to set aside substantial time for teachers to collaborate as part of the regular working schedule. This would avoid the problems of finding substitutes and competing for after-school time. It would reflect an increase from current allocations of planning periods because, as we have seen, those allocations are barely enough for teachers to handle routine administrative matters and typically do not allow time for teacher learning. Even in the case of the Europa elementary group, which had the most regular time available for teacher meetings, the time added on by the teacher–researcher collaborative was essential for professional development, and the regular meeting time was an opportunity for the diffusion of ideas beyond the professional development group. Thus, increasing the capacity for change means, first and foremost, building in more time for teachers to work together on matters of teaching and learning.

Second, expertise from outside the school district can be an important source of stimulation—an infusion of human resources—but the more important point is that through that process, the district and schools can "grow" their own, internal human resources, as teachers increase their knowledge and change their commitments through professional development. This process requires room to experiment, to try out new ideas and reflect on them with colleagues. It also seems to require sufficient autonomy for teachers to follow their own notions of enhancing student understanding, because the decisions about teaching for understanding occur when teachers examine their own students' thinking. Social relationships established in the course of professional development constitute another element of the capacity for change that cannot be provided from the outside, but must develop internally. In the cases we studied, these relations were constituted in professional development, but they also could be weakened by teacher turnover and changes in teaching assignments (changing grade levels, subjects, and schools).

Third, implementing what teachers have learned from professional development requires resources, particularly the materials that teachers need in order to embark on innovative projects. Professional development seems necessary for stimulating and nurturing teachers' intentions to teach for understanding, but additional resources are necessary to put these intentions into practice. Whether it is a bank of lights for growing "fast plants," or a block of time to work longer with students, districts and schools are an important source of these resources, but teachers often struggle to obtain what they need. This was particularly the case in the urban districts we studied, and it was especially true for the teachers of language-minority students. In part, the resources that enhance implementation also emerge in professional development—in particular, professional development generates social resources that teachers can draw upon to resolve questions or problems they may have during implementation. Teachers who are involved in professional development with others in the same school may have better access to these social resources than those who participate mainly with teachers from other schools, because the day-to-day contact with same-school colleagues offers better opportunities for collaboration and advice seeking. The teachers we interviewed perceived that collaborating with other teachers helped them explore new approaches to teaching, and the scope of changes in teaching appeared broader in the sites in which collaboration was most extensive.

Some of the new resource allocations we have described may be quite costly. The districts we observed were not paying for the time of the university researchers who worked with their teachers; were they to bring in outside experts with similar levels of intensity devoted to the professional development groups, the cost would run in the tens of thousands of dollars, or more (see Herman, 1999, for estimated costs of comprehensive school reform programs). Building substantial time for teachers to meet regularly during the school day is another potentially costly innovation. In considering the costs of these reforms, however, it is important to bear in mind that allocating resources to professional development that focuses on students' understanding of powerful mathematical and scientific ideas is likely to have a "multiplier" effect—that is, resources from the school and district will generate new resources that will help the professional development group sustain itself. We will discuss the issue of sustainability at greater length in Chapter 9, but the findings in this chapter show how successful professional development creates new resources in the form of individual and collective expertise, leadership, new curricular materials, and social relationships among teachers that provide a supportive context for teaching for understanding.

What did we learn in this chapter about how *not* to use resources? First, we learned that resources may be wasted if there are conflicts about basic purposes and approaches to teaching. In Janus, we found a university research group ready to work with teachers, and several teachers who devoted many hours to planning meetings, considering a collaborative project on teaching middle school statistics for understanding. Yet these preparation efforts came to naught, because ultimately the teachers decided that the core curriculum mandated by the school system did not provide room for an in-depth study of statistics. Similarly, 2 years of professional development workshops in Mimas were a stimulating opportunity for a few teachers to reflect on their teaching, but did not result in fundamental changes because of fragmentation within the school staff. A corollary to this finding is that allocating resources for teacher change in the absence of visionary leadership that contributes to a guiding purpose may fail to produce the anticipated benefits. We explore the topic of leadership more fully in Chapter 6.

Second, this chapter suggests that the payoff from resources allocated is less than optimal when only a few teachers within a given school participate in the program to which resources are devoted. Allocating resources in this case may still be deemed worthwhile—the program may help individual teachers, and there may be some diffusion of new ideas to others—but the potential for a multiplier effect, in which resources are not depleted but instead generate new material, human, and social resources, is greater when a substantial number of teachers from the same school participate in the same program focusing on understanding student thinking.

Districts and schools with the capacity for change use their resources strategically to create new resources that foster change. Districts and schools that wish to enhance their capacity for change would do well to increase teachers' opportunities to meet together, provide an infusion of human resources by bringing in outside expertise, and allow teachers the autonomy to try out new approaches in a supportive environment.

CHAPTER 5

Responding to Diversity

Pamela Anne Quiroz and Walter G. Secada

As we move into the twenty-first century, profound demographic changes are shifting our expectations for schools. About 35% of current U.S. students are members of racial/ethnic minority groups, and this number is expected to increase substantially over the next 50 years, presenting us with the most racially/ethnically diverse student population in our nation's history. While this diversity is geographically focused (i.e., primarily in metropolitan areas) and poses new challenges for school systems, there are other challenges as well. Not only are schools expected to provide a variety of services for students and communities, but they are also expected to educate everyone. These expectations are simultaneously being coupled with demands from different ethnic/racial, linguistic, and gender groups. Racial/ethnic groups are no longer content to accept a strictly Western European education designed to produce a melting pot culture, but rather are demanding a more inclusive and multicultural education that includes their histories, values, and cultural traditions (Olneck, 1993). Consequently, two types of diversity mark student populations: diversity of background (e.g., race, culture) and diversity of expectations regarding the educational content offered to students. Serious reform efforts, including teaching for understanding, must respond not only to the increasing demographic diversity of the U.S. student population but also to the diversity of its demands in order to transform public schools into places where all children can learn.

Many educational researchers have argued that current reform efforts fail to assist particular populations of students in their academic achievement and may exacerbate existing inequalities. A few researchers even go so far as to suggest that such reform practices intentionally exclude culturally diverse and disadvantaged groups in order to maintain the existing inequities to access and opportunity between groups (Apple, 2001; Giroux, 1992; McLaren, 1994; Walsh, 1996).

As part of the response to changes in their student populations, teachers are being trained to address diversity issues, yet teachers are still not part of reform planning. Although professional development is now regarded as a necessary component of reform, teachers remain largely defined as recipients of professional development rather than as partners who bring knowledge, skills, and experience to this process. With teachers in general treated in this fashion, it is no surprise to find this situation exacerbated for some teachers. For example, bilingual teachers traditionally have been omitted from discussion of systemic reform. Indeed, research on effective teaching typically has ignored the instructional strategies of language-minority teachers, with the focus for bilingual education on students' development and English language proficiency rather than subject-matter content. Bilingual teachers as a source of educational change have been neglected, and their professional development in academic subjects has been left largely unattended.

In previous chapters, we have seen that resource distribution is critical to teaching for understanding, and the question we have asked is how resources are distributed among districts, within schools, and, more specifically, to participants in our design collaboratives. We also have examined how these resources are used to generate additional resources that enable teachers and students to engage in science and math activities. In this chapter, we begin by revisiting our discussion of how resources matter, by focusing on how the social contexts of the school and district shape the allocation of resources and affect teachers with diverse student populations. Recognizing that the U.S. education system is characterized by its diversity of constituents, forms, and settings, this chapter uses the sites to help us understand the challenges of teaching for understanding facing teachers who work in diverse settings. We attend to these teachers as they address the challenges of acquiring/using classroom resources, of dealing with conflicting preferences and commitments, and of generating and sustaining change. We examine the significance of diversity as a purpose for joining professional development groups, along with why certain forms of professional development are appealing and others are not. Finally, we address how diversity fundamentally affects the nature of the social relationships that are created within these groups.

For teachers in these sites, teaching for understanding was situated within the intersecting contexts of the school, the cultural frameworks of their students, and the professional development workshops. School contexts also shaped issues of diversity and equity, with teachers defining the issues in terms of their particular experiences and the problems of their particular student populations. Teachers negotiated and integrated resources as they tried to fulfill a variety of goals and expectations, expand their affiliations with colleagues, and generate additional resources to assist students in sustaining identities as racial/ethnic group members as well as science/math learners. In this chapter, we explore the distinctive challenges of attending to diversity and equity as an integral part of teaching for understanding.

DEFINING AND INTERPRETING DIVERSITY AND EQUITY

Diversity is understood as the condition where students from different racial/ethnic, language, and economic backgrounds or ability coexist within the same educational environment. Conversely, homogeneity is understood as the condition where these background characteristics do not vary substantially among students in the school or district. Educational equity is understood as the organization of policies, resources, and opportunities to enable students to utilize their cognitive and social abilities in order to become upwardly mobile (Hallinan, 2001). Three of our six sites were located in urban areas (Janus, in Tennessee; Mimas, in Wisconsin; and Callisto, in Massachusetts) and can be characterized as having racially/ethnically, linguistically, culturally, and economically diverse student populations. The Oberon and the two Europa sites were located in suburban Wisconsin areas with relatively homogeneous student populations.

Teachers at each site were asked whether their school or district struggled with issues of diversity and equity. While interviewers tried to clarify what was meant by "diversity" and "equity" (i.e., differences in characteristics of student populations and opportunities for learning), responses varied among teachers in the design collaboratives.

In Oberon High, issues such as bilingual education and multicultural education were not salient. Since most students had similar backgrounds, the demands upon the school were not as variable nor were the resources required in order to meet the needs of the science community as great as in more diverse settings. Indeed, concerns of equity for science teachers at Oberon revolved around ability grouping of their students, as two teachers explain.

> I think because Oberon is fairly homogeneous in terms of ethnic groups, although it is changing . . . But you still would say that by far the typical student at Oberon is middle class White. (Laughter) So that, you know, unfortunately it [diversity] doesn't come into our thinking a lot, but I think considering what different abilities students have, I mean, that is one of the reasons we have them working in groups, and we try to make the groups heterogeneous.

> In terms of equity, the biggest thing I think about this research or this collaborative is that this kind of science learning is really, it brings kids under equal footing. In other words, the kids that are considered the smartest frequently do not do the best in this kind of collaborative, problem-solving mode. . . . And those kids who really thrived, I mean, in ways that I can see now, they are not thriving anymore when we return to the more traditional. . . . And so that kind of success is so rewarding to them, that was just a huge thing about this curriculum than any others in terms of, not so much gender or ethnic equity, it is just sort of intellectual equity.

Although the Europa elementary and middle school sites were also relatively homogeneous ethnically and racially, recent demographic changes resulted in significant increases in the district's racial/ethnic student population and in its low-income population. Thus, the issue of multicultural education was becoming relevant to staff. Europa teachers and administrators were cognizant of resource distribution, and discussions of equity revolved around how to handle the newcomers and how to make math and science accessible to all students.

> You know, algebra is an equity issue that we want all kids to be exposed [to] and in particular Sherry Clawson raised the issue about, she said it is sad that we don't have more African American kids taking algebra. . . . This is a system that we think can address . . . that is, expose all kids in our systems who are not transient. We are talking about the kids who are here through the 3 years who can be exposed to it, and hopefully we would see kids, kids of color, more kids taking advantage of and being involved in those kinds of programs and getting exposure to the algebra and the geometry. . . . Diversity is an issue. We have more minority kids than we have ever had before. When I started here I think it was 1%, and that is 9 years ago. Now we are at 9, 10, 11% of our school. And so, hiring of staff of color, we have, this year we have hired a multicultural, cultural liaison, an African American gentleman who works at the high school and middle school full time and who is working with kids of color and minority students in trying to help the kids. The key is, helping the child feel connected in part of this system and not disjointed in looking at this as a White school. So it is as much creating that feeling. We have a diversity committee [the Diversity Action Team] that is taking a look at the specific initiative of involving parents of minority students in a more proactive way. (Europa Middle School administrator)

For the most part, however, Europa teachers—like those at Oberon—interpreted "diversity" and "equity" as focusing explicitly on ability.

Perhaps not surprisingly, bilingual and multicultural education, along with access and use of resources, were more problematic in urban settings. A variety of cultural, language, and racial/ethnic educational policy issues emerged. For example, in Mimas, a large central-city and bilingual high school, many classes included instruction in both Spanish and English. There, as at Callisto where bilingual education was an explicit aim, the design collaborative and the attendant resources needed for its success had to incorporate student understanding in bilingual classrooms. Although diversity and equity were equally relevant for teachers in the Mimas and Callisto collaboratives, teachers in Janus (also an urban site with racial/ethnic and economic diversity) tended to focus on equity mainly in terms of student access to the newly adopted city curriculum. Both Janus and Mimas teachers contended with district attempts to modify student performance, increased accountability measures that included evaluation of their work, and diverse student populations that created challenges for teaching math and science. However, discussions of multicultural education or socioeconomic diversity did not emerge among Janus staff as they did at Mimas.

Although racial/ethnic, socioeconomic, cultural, or linguistic diversity characterized each of our urban sites, discussions of diversity and equity predominated in the Callisto, Mimas, and Europa cases. Moreover, teachers across sites had strikingly different interpretations of the issues. Despite the fact that diversity and equity are inextricably linked in discussions of educational opportunity, each of these terms took on different meaning for teachers depending on where they worked. When discussing diversity and equity, Mimas and Callisto teachers and administrators placed more emphasis on familiar group attributes such as socioeconomic background, race and ethnicity, culture, and language. For the most part, issues of diversity were embedded within the contexts of bilingual programs and the dilemmas of teaching for understanding within these programs, since so many of the teachers at these sites were bilingual teachers. Europa teachers emphasized learning styles and ability grouping. Some teachers in Europa interpreted issues of equity on an individual level, viewing equity from their own vantage point or noting individual student differences.

> Well, in terms of my building, I think equity is always a concern. What are other people getting. What are other classes doing, projects people are associated with, grants, how people are sharing the resources. I think that is always an issue.

> There's diversity in all kids, and I can't pinpoint anything exactly because every child is an individual and every child is different. As far as issue problems [on a school-wide or district-wide basis], there's none that I know of.

> I think that a more diverse math and science program allows for equity and learning style differences definitely. I have kids who will say, "Oh, good, this is something I'm really good at." I have kids who will say to one another, "I knew you were gonna say something smart." There's the one boy in particular that I've heard commented to a couple of times, and he is a very poor reader and writer and I think that he will go out of here feeling like a smart kid, even though he is by far the lowest second-grade reader that has left my classroom. I think that it helps, you know, kids, because we're touching on more learning styles.

Unlike Europa teachers who concentrated their responses on personal equity or "intellectual" equity, Mimas and Callisto teachers described diversity and equity as involving a set of structural inequalities regarding learning opportunities by virtue of group memberships among students (i.e., economic class, linguistic, gender, or cultural memberships). Discussions with teachers in these schools frequently linked dilemmas of teaching for understanding to how these different characteristics affect student involvement with schooling, either directly or indirectly.

> Any urban school is a challenge. Any school is a challenging place to be. But our particular challenge is that we have some of the children who are as needy as any child in this district. We don't have a whole school of kids who are enormously needy. We have probably 25% of our school's students who are on reduced lunch. Now that doesn't necessarily translate to being needy, but it may say economics to you, you know. . . . First of all, your student population affects many of the components of your teaching. Lower-class schools with less involved parents get less money. (Callisto teacher)

> Bilingual teachers have unique situations, and in some ways I think that they have a harder job than English-speaking teachers. They not only have to deal with kids from different socioeconomic backgrounds, which every teacher has to deal with in this district. You know, every kid who speaks Spanish here is not from a poor home. We have the poor Spanish speakers, and then we have the wealthy kids from Latin American backgrounds, but we also have to deal with tremendous sociolinguistic differences. Bilingual teachers have to handle that. They not only have to handle socioeconomic differences, they have to handle cultural differences too. They have to acculturate kids. They have to teach them the ways here. We have to teach the culture, even though it's not our culture, and get the kid to understand it if he is to be successful. But we also have to teach math and science. It's very hard. (Callisto teacher)

> I think it [student engagement with teaching for understanding] depends on their social/cultural background. I can say Latino and you can say culture, but I have a lot of kids who have been here for a long time. A couple have been here for a couple of years. I have kids that just, I got a brand-new student yesterday from Puerto Rico that has never been in the United States. So how do you fit, I can't . . . they are all Latinos but they are so different. (Mimas teacher)

> We have bilingual children that are mainstreamed. There are children from Haiti; many of them never went to school before coming to this country. I have middle-class [students]. I had Rockefeller's grandson in my class for 2 years. There is quite a range of stuff that comes into my classroom. There are children from Bangladesh. All kinds of kids. I have kids who may go home to a shelter. I have kids who may go home behind the Peabody

Museum. There is a very big range of children . . . so clearly, there are some children who are at a greater advantage to do well on standardized tests. (Callisto teacher)

There was also some apparent confusion about "equity" and "diversity," with several Europa teachers either prompting the interviewer to explain what he or she meant by the terms, and some indicating reluctance to acknowledge these "social issues" as a factor in their school. Callisto teachers, on the other hand, discussed the challenges of diversity openly, frequently interjecting the topic into general discussions on teaching. Both Callisto and Europa teachers recognized the importance of social class in affecting learning opportunities.

Every school in Callisto is pretty amazingly diverse. Some schools have 70% or 60% or 80% [minority students]. I think the average is somewhere around 45%–55%. Every school is balanced racially so you know that you've got that but I think the key factor is social economic background because middle-class families have access to more educational resources in general. But if you are going to be a good school, you have to teach to all of the children in your school. You can't teach to the middle and leave out the kids in both ends. I think that is an enormous challenge in any school. So we have a lot of needy kids. We have kids who I can barely get to school, whose lives make you wonder how they can get there. That is just a huge challenge; at the same point a child who could probably do your income tax in fourth grade is in the same class. So it is really interesting, and I love the mix of kids. (Callisto teacher)

I think that any time you have kids who come from a more enriched background you got an advantage. However, I believe in the constructivist approaches and one of the reasons I'm so interested in them is that they're much more likely to lead to success for those who don't come from those enriched backgrounds because they provide that enriched experience for the kids. (Europa elementary teacher)

Whereas teachers in Callisto and Europa discussed the significance of social class, teachers in Mimas emphasized culture.

I think culturally, depending upon, I am thinking of Mexico where they were raised. Like in the city or in the small towns. And even, so even just being raised in different places, you are exposed to different things. . . . And it seems like in the city it is more, maybe more like it is here in the city, whereas in the small towns sometimes they only go up to like either elementary or eighth grade. . . . I think it does affect how they reason mathematically because I think, maybe I am stereotyping here, but I think

like if they were raised in the small town where, not that they don't value
education, but sometimes they have to do the labor first, then the education next. Schooling doesn't go that high. When they come here they might
not feel so confident, so secure in their work. And so that affects them to
ask questions or to clarify because they are not sure what they want to
clarify . . . it is kind of like, they might not be sure where they are lost.
(Mimas teacher)

Responses from teachers in Europa, Callisto, and Mimas indicated that two
important factors associated with equity and diversity were the distribution and
type of resources available. These two factors often resulted in educational practices and experiences that were inequitable for some students. This became obvious when teachers in all three sites discussed their acquisition and use of resources
in efforts to enhance their instructional practice. Therefore, we return to our earlier discussion of resources in order to understand how teachers engaged professional development, not only to enhance their instructional practices (i.e., teaching
for understanding), but also to sustain their motivation in their work.

Many factors contributed to the complexity of resource allocation in the cases
we observed, especially at the urban sites. Administrative rhetoric typically promoted the equitable distribution of students between and within schools (i.e., economically, racially/ethnically, and by ability). Nevertheless, many communities
lacked a practical awareness regarding the influence of economic class on educational opportunity, and few measures were taken to remedy segregation by economic class. In Callisto, however, generating equity among students included a
genuine attempt to maintain not only racial/ethnic balance both within and across
schools, but linguistic and socioeconomic diversity as well.

As our sites illustrate, schools in different demographic contexts face disparate challenges in their efforts to adopt teaching for understanding, and the more
factors to be considered in a district or school (e.g., economics, language, race/
ethnicity, ability), the more problematic access to resources and resource allocation become. We discovered in these sites that access to resources, as well as how
resources were used to benefit teaching and learning, were especially critical. In
general, resources often were not allocated evenly within schools, let alone across
school districts, and the impact on professional development of teachers was significant. Interviews with teachers in these sites illustrate that resources did matter
very much, perhaps for some groups more than for others.

NEGOTIATING RESOURCES

It would be misleading to suggest that any of our collaboratives were resource poor,
since even teachers in the urban sites had relatively good access to resources and
their schools participated in multiple collaborative projects with external partners.

However, we refer to our earlier typology of resources (i.e., material, human, and social) to highlight how similar resource needs often affect teachers in diverse settings differently. Like all teachers, teachers in our urban sites described the need for added time, professional development, input from external partners, and clarity of curricular policies.

Material Resources: Time and Curricula

The use of material resources as they interact with student needs was qualitatively different for teachers in the design collaboratives at Callisto and Mimas (urban sites) as compared with teachers at Oberon and Europa (suburban sites). For example, most teachers prioritized the need for additional time as the critical resource that could augment teaching practices through discussions and planning with other teachers.

> I mean all of this stuff is nice, but I think the number one problem is that we don't have time to meet together. That's why once a month, I'm thinking, is that going to be enough? And then, we are kind of segregated also in different families [interdepartmental units]. We also try to do projects with our science [colleagues] and our families. So, I think the bottom line is we don't have time to meet together. (Mimas teacher)

Nevertheless, teachers in Mimas and Callisto projected use of this resource differently. Undoubtedly this was largely because several of them were bilingual teachers who felt it necessary to address the multiple needs of their students, needs that added layers to how time was best used.

> I think we, all three of us [participants in the design collaborative], believe that [relationships with students] in some ways need to come first. And sometimes it is more important to dedicate more of your time and more of your energy and more of your expertise to developing relationships with the students, sometimes even over developing curriculum. (Mimas teacher)

> I try support. I try to understand their problems and try to say, my mother works right here. I went through what you are going through. You will make it. School is the way. (Mimas teacher)

Because bilingual education so often is tied to language acquisition, even in progressive school districts like Callisto, time was spent largely on issues ancillary to subject-matter acquisition.

> We had bilingual meetings every other week, the whole team in the school, but we dealt more with the structure of the program, not with the sub-

stance. The year before last we were trying a transitional bilingual program that was 25/50/75 [i.e., the percentage of time spent on English in order to transition from Spanish to English]. Last year we tried a 50/50 program because we realized that just doesn't work. I mean a lot of the meetings are over that. (Callisto teacher)

In the case of bilingual teachers, the use of time was closely tied to curricular materials. And while curricular materials may not be as important to teachers in general, for some of our teachers they were as critical as time.

It's not easy. Like for example, the AP, they have translated everything into Spanish. The science, or whatever unit I choose to do, I make sure it's in Spanish before I even choose it. Because that's the worst thing to have to do, you know, not only to have to teach the unit but also have to translate everything to kids, having the worksheet in English and then have to translate it into Spanish. I mean to me that doesn't work. (Callisto teacher)

Unfortunately, this problem was even more pronounced for teachers in other bilingual programs. Frequent policy changes compounded translation problems, so that attempts to standardize translation of adopted math and science curricula failed to keep up with the ever-changing adoption of new materials. One Callisto teacher who had translated for the Haitian Creole bilingual program found himself caught by a change in curricular policy (an experience common to all teachers and particularly important to bilingual teachers; see Chapter 9).

I was translating the Algebra Project for the past 3 or 4 years. But they came to me and said, "Oh, everybody in the system now is doing Connected Math." They said, "Well, you don't have to do it. But everybody else is doing it." And I said, "Well, you made me translate the Algebra Project and now it's clear, and all that time I went for 2 years in a row to seminars that would help me do that. I was very invested in that." So I won't do that anymore. She's [the District Bilingual Coordinator] presenting it as if I had a choice, but in fact, I didn't have a choice. I now have to translate Connected Math too. The Connected Math is very difficult, so much language that kids don't understand. They have the book, but they don't understand. So when I get to crucial points in the book, I do it at home, translate it and then give it to them. It takes extra time. This is the problem with a bilingual education classroom. Math is a language that is already difficult to understand, but now it has to be presented in a foreign language, so now in class I have to translate what is in the book and to make them understand and help them to reflect upon it. It's very difficult. Of course it affects how much I can cover in the class.

The time used for translating a lesson was time not used to teach the subject, to establish relationships with students, or to interact with colleagues. However, time needed for these latter pursuits became irrelevant when teachers failed to receive the assistance necessary to engage teaching for understanding. Without being included in professional development that is geared toward subject-matter comprehension (as opposed to only language acquisition), those who teach linguistically diverse students are at a disadvantage.

> We cannot afford to wait, which is the district's traditional stance on this issue, until students have "mastered" English until we teach them science. Nor can we afford to think that just because they don't know English that they don't know science or anything else. They do. (Callisto teacher)

Human Resources: Outside Expertise and Support Staff

Teachers in both Mimas and Callisto acknowledged a change in their districts' policies, particularly toward inclusion of bilingual teachers in math and science development, with both districts providing resource staff to assist in science or math teaching.

> Our bilingual teachers receive the same training that anyone in the district would receive. However, there was a time when they didn't. If it were a release day [for professional development], then the bilingual teachers would all have to get together and we could do whatever. (Callisto teacher)

> We also have the resource teacher initiative. She also helps us to integrate math and science or use the calculator. She is here every Monday and Tuesday. She also provides us with inservices for everyone to sign up again. The project at [a nearby university] which is how we basically met each other for this program. (Mimas teacher)

However, only in Callisto was teaching for understanding adopted as a district-wide policy, with several science staff positions created as a district resource for teachers and one staff position designated for bilingual teachers. In Mimas, the commitment to teaching for understanding was based on individual teachers; it was not a departmental, school, or district-wide commitment. Moreover, this commitment is one line along which the mathematics department was split.

> I think the difference, as far as us and the other monolingual teachers . . . is their philosophy of teaching. . . . I am teaching with two geometry monolingual classes, and just the comments that I have heard from the students about their monolingual teachers, how, in the classes not many students went or the teacher would just, I guess, just teach, teach, teach

[i.e., didactic presentation of the material without attention to student understanding]. And it was not really, you know, if you get it fine, if you don't, that's fine too. (Mimas teacher)

An even more distinctive example of how human resources affected teaching for understanding was in Janus, where teaching for understanding was virtually precluded by a mandated curriculum.

I'm kind of insulted [by] the City Curriculum Framework. I feel like I'm being dictated to and I feel like I'm a professional and I want to feel professional. And I feel with the City Curriculum Framework situation, I'm being told when, where, what to do, and it's just like a dictator kind of thing. Sometimes there are times when I want to spend more time on something or I may want to do it in a different order than what it has on the city curriculum, and I'm hindered with that kind of situation and so I have to decide, well, okay, either I know, and sometimes it's really things that I know that work . . . but I can't do it because it's not in the right order, the appropriate order of things to do. Or it may mean that I have to spend a little extra time in doing it and then that would put me off something else. And so I think, you know, for me, [the] City Curriculum Framework has been more of a hindrance than anything. (Janus teacher)

Each site encompassed multiple professional development efforts in addition to the design collaborative, and some teachers participated in more than one of these projects. Callisto reminds us that within districts, and even within the same school, education is not a single enterprise. Rather, it takes various organizational forms that reflect and dictate distinctive goals. For example, as mentioned in Chapter 3, the controlled-choice district of Callisto included both alternative and target schools. Two of the three alternative schools, including one with design collaborative participants, had been adopted by local colleges and universities as professional development sites. Collaborations with these universities resulted in added staff, student teachers, and graduate courses that presumably enhanced the collaborative efforts of teachers, a necessary component in teaching for understanding. These practices, however, did not necessarily include the schools' bilingual programs. One explanation is that it was undoubtedly more difficult to find student teachers or paraprofessionals knowledgeable in particular language groups (e.g., Haitian Creole). Of all the bilingual programs in this district, the Spanish programs received the most support with regard to paraprofessionals and teacher interns.

Such experiences often forced teachers to improvise in the face of these challenges, and what resulted was a collaborative effort that was conducive to teaching for understanding.

That is what I am saying, starting today the majority, a lot of, almost half of the students were failing geography and algebra so we were thinking of a way to help them not flunk semester 1 and semester 2. So we said, okay, how can we give them more attention? So first of all they remove my paraprofessional. So I don't have anyone for that third hour. So we figured, let's all switch them to one hour, try to make up for semester 1 and at the same time advance to semester 2 and see if we can at the end give them a test for semester 1 and see if we can give them credit and pass them. (Callisto teacher)

Actually, I had to teach four through eight science, and being one teacher, it was almost impossible for me to do it alone, so I did basically the four through eight, which I taught with Liza and the six through eight which I taught with Renee and Liza. The reason we decided to do community teaching that way was because Renee was in charge of the seventh-grade curriculum, while I was in charge of the sixth-grade curriculum, and since we couldn't teach science 10 times a week, we decided to come together as a group and do more of the unit type of science. (Callisto teacher)

For teachers who worked with diverse student populations, collaboration around subject-matter teaching was often an unintended consequence of negotiating multiple demands with limited resources. This was especially true for teachers in bilingual programs where the formal goals of the program (namely, to teach English as well as subject matter) often did not align with the informal goals dictated by student needs. Teachers with culturally and linguistically different students had to reconcile conflicting policies and commitments in order to accomplish their goals.

Clearly, teaching for understanding is not just an individual construction but also a social one, with teachers engaged in professional development groups and developing teacher communities. Through their participation in these design collaboratives, teachers gathered information, sorted information into systems of ideas, and shared their ideas with one another, thereby interpreting and generating this pedagogical approach to learning. Also in these contexts, teachers obtained access to and used resources in their practice.

We found that teaching for understanding is an instructional style that resonated with these teachers, whose own experiences made them sympathetic to issues of "voice" and experience in learning. Like most teachers who engage teaching for understanding, teachers in our sites who taught diverse student populations paid particular attention to student voice, or rather to who speaks and who listens. Which students have the power to present "scientific" or "mathematical" meaning and shape other students' perceptions? How do teachers manage children seen as purveyors of information by other children? How do teachers help children who are math/science "outsiders" to become "insiders"? They innovated, sometimes collaborated, and tried to bridge the educational, social, and cultural isolation experienced by their students.

> If a student has a question, I have that student explain to me what they are trying to do or what they are seeing in that problem before I try and give explanations. So whether the explanations are just quick explanations with an individual student at a desk or up in front of the class, if I have an idea of how students are viewing something like slope or something like trying to find the coordinates of a point or trying to find the rate of change in a table, I will try and give the explanation, using words from the perspective of the student. I don't water it down or use the correct vocabulary, because a lot of times if the student were to explain something to another student, you would never hear them say words that the teacher would use. But I think that some of that is necessary. I mean, I guess my explanations are geared toward what I know the perspective of the student is. (Mimas teacher)

Unfortunately, the effort to engage an instructional style embedded in collaborative energy was often difficult for bilingual teachers and monolingual teachers in diverse student classrooms. Without access to the human resources that so many monolingual teachers take for granted (e.g., paraprofessionals and staff development personnel), bilingual teachers frequently found themselves at odds with colleagues and administrators who they believed did not support their efforts.

> My class just finished geometry, . . . measuring art links and making an architectural theater. And so . . . the drawings that are coming out with calculations, they had put in a little parking lot, made it handicapped accessible. So there were a lot of social issues involved in it. And then [the other teachers] were saying, "Oh, that is good because they will do their math, how does it relate to English or social studies?" And I am saying . . . , "Well, everything, they enter in a proposal, they have to write this up, they had to present in class," blah, blah, blah. And they didn't support it. They wouldn't. They were just like, "Okay." They didn't want to integrate it among the other teachers. (Mimas teacher)

As part of the high school's organizational structure of interdisciplinary "families," this teacher was still left to convince his fellow "family" teachers that geometry did intersect with the other subjects. In this case, the subject-matter divide generated difficulties negotiating human resources in cross-disciplinary instruction (i.e., math, social studies, and English).

Oddly enough, in a period of increasing support for English immersion programs, bilingual teachers also mentioned resistance from colleagues and parents when attempting to mainstream their students. This resistance was perceived as the fear that integrating classrooms would retard the instructional process. In essence, it could be regarded as the lack of colleague and family networks necessary for a successful transitional bilingual program. One outcome was that mainstreamed bilingual students in Callisto automatically were placed in low-ability groups. An elementary school teacher admitted suggesting that parents of her bilingual students remove their children from the school rather than mainstream them, using the reasoning that, once mainstreamed, these children would be ignored by their monolingual classroom teachers.

> They don't even know where the kids are. They don't even know what these kids are learning, what level the kid is. They are just put in the lower group. And this teacher goes to you and says, "This child doesn't know anything." It hurts the child and it hurts you because the child does know things. They [certain monolingual teachers] don't care. I want to say to people, "Look closer. Listen to a bilingual child. He has a lot to say. He has a *lot* to say." If I could say that to all teachers, I think it would make a big difference in the way they treated the kids when they go to them from the bilingual program.

In her frustration, one Callisto teacher pointed to the lack of recognition (by colleagues, administrators, and parents) not only of her students' abilities but of her own, and her colleagues' knowledge as well.

> Just because we speak with an accent, it does not mean that our brains have an accent. I am as smart and as knowledgeable as anyone else in this job. I know science, I specialize in science, but I speak with an accent, and therefore people often treat me as if I'm not [as knowledgeable]. And because these kids have an accent, they assume that the kids cannot know science or math. They do.

Ironically, it was this perceived isolation and nonacceptance, combined with the necessity of negotiating limited material and human resources, that prompted teachers to form communities of like-minded colleagues and to seek them out in the design collaboratives.

Social Resources: Professional Isolation, Professional Development, and the Possibilities for Sustaining Change

In addition to the challenges for bilingual teachers generated by school organization, social and professional isolation are added obstacles. In the lexicon of modern-day reforms, Callisto illustrates the fact that bilingual programs can be regarded as a school within a school (SWS), given that most such programs are self-contained. Unfortunately, this type of SWS exists in a status hierarchy of students and teachers who often receive unequal access to resources and whose professional and social isolation is even more pronounced than that of their peers. Most teachers articulated feelings of isolation emerging from the structure of their work (i.e., working alone in a classroom with few opportunities for discussion with colleagues). However, the isolation characterized by teachers who worked with linguistically and culturally diverse children had a different tenor. Comments from teachers in both Callisto and Mimas reflect this alienation from their colleagues.

> I feel that some teachers feel that we watered down the curriculum or they see us as, I don't know, that we are not good enough . . . as they are. (Callisto teacher)

> I think for example, in terms of academics, maybe like in Advanced Math, the only people I would talk to would be Isabel, Gustavo [two other teachers]. But if I have questions about like if I am not clear about certain concepts . . . but those are just very brief, maybe once a month that I will talk to him about a concept, but other than that, academically I don't talk. I don't get along with the other teachers. Not that I don't get along, I just don't like the teachers. (Mimas teacher)

Given the conflicts built into their workplace structure, it is no surprise to find that teachers, particularly bilingual teachers in these districts, were drawn to collaboratives external to district-sponsored opportunities. This is precisely what made the Mimas and Callisto design collaboratives so appealing and valuable to all of the participating teachers.

In the case of Mimas, the four participating teachers were Latinos who taught bilingual math classes and who shared, however loosely, similar teaching philosophies and attitudes toward their students. These teachers also felt isolated from their monolingual colleagues and sought a means for engaging in reflective dialogue regarding their pedagogy and subject matter. The Callisto collaborative, also unique in its character, augmented the ties that had already formed among several of its participants prior to their participation. Similar to the Mimas collaborative, this program provided additional material, human, and social support for science teaching to both monolingual and bilingual teachers.

The opportunities to cross linguistic boundaries with monolingual teachers were equally important. All teachers experience a degree of professional isolation, particularly those who do not have teacher interns or other paraprofessionals assisting them in the classroom. However, the isolation described by bilingual teachers differed from the isolation precipitated by structural conditions of the profession (i.e., classroom teaching). This isolation was one of a more personal nature. Certainly it was structurally induced, but it was an interpersonal isolation from monolingual colleagues and from administrators, and was grounded in cultural or linguistic differences. This is yet another reason why the Callisto design collaborative was so valuable. It brought bilingual and monolingual teachers who often dealt with similar problems into communication with one another.

As a subject-oriented collaborative created explicitly for bilingual teachers, the Callisto collaborative legitimated teachers' efforts to teach for understanding and afforded them a safe environment in which to engage new science ideas. It also supported bilingual teachers as they built associations not only with other bilingual teachers but also across the linguistic boundaries that often separated them from monolingual teachers within the contexts of their schools. These newly forged relationships expanded a community of colleagues, several of whom used this newfound social capital in their schools. One bilingual Callisto elementary school teacher described how he established greater contact with a monolingual colleague in his school through participation in the collaborative.

> She is a science teacher at the junior high level but before, she used to teach a few years ago. She used to teach grades 5 and 6 too. Then she used to come to my class and we shared things. And she was a teacher in the design collaborative too. And then there were some projects that we taped together since we had to, we studied other things, for instance, ants. We studied mold, so we had a chance to work together. We have been doing that less in the past year but we still communicate because I have some of my students, when they are mainstreamed, they go to her class.

The ties between teachers in these collaboratives took some time to evolve and to produce social resources, which continued to be utilized idiosyncratically outside of the design collaboratives. Although these collaboratives served as conduits for pedagogical transformation, the benefits of the workshops sometimes were cited as the costs. For example, the emphasis on reflective dialogue in both the Mimas and Callisto collaboratives initially generated uncertainty for teachers. Indeed, teachers constantly commented on the fact that participation in the seminars made them reflect on what they *thought* they knew, consequently generating uncertainty regarding math or science. This was characterized as both liberating and anxiety-producing. With the resources provided by the design collaboratives and the deprivatized practice of sharing their work, their frustrations, and their questions with one another, an environment was created where teachers came to trust, to rely on, and ultimately to prefer the collective or collaborative experience over the individual one.

CONCLUSIONS

Teachers in our design collaboratives wrestled with issues of diversity and equity in various ways. For those who worked in homogeneous or changing student environments (Oberon and Europa), equity revolved around ability grouping and creating opportunities for students at different levels of understanding to learn math and science both experientially and conceptually. Issues of resource allocation and use were not yet problematic for these teachers, and they could concentrate on how to make science and math accessible to their students. Teachers who worked in classrooms/schools with diverse student populations also worked in structurally complex and politically charged environments with numerous competing demands. Consequently, equity and the resources, whether time, curriculum, knowledge, or staff assistance, needed to achieve it had multiple and competing uses. For example, the Callisto collaborative existed in a district with controlled school choice. While the district had organized schools in a way that facilitated use of resources in similar ways (e.g., three school schedules were coordinated to facilitate busing of students to schools outside of their neighborhoods), individual schools varied with respect to both their access to resources and how they organized resources (e.g., alternative schools were known to have more resources than did target schools).

The countervailing forces that undermined such collaborative efforts at Mimas (school structuring and multiple collaboratives with assessments driving teacher goals) or Janus (a curriculum that directed efforts toward performance on the district's assessment) point to the difficulties in meeting the challenges so prevalent in urban environments.

We believe that nothing in the school has greater impact on student academic and social development than the personal and professional development of teachers. Design collaboratives provide a resource to build relations among teachers, serving as a bridge to expand human resources and to support sustained efforts at change. To be effective, however, professional development must attend to teachers' unique circumstances, particularly in those contexts where social justice and educational equity are most needed. Indeed, this chapter shows that teacher professional development groups may be especially valuable and effective for teachers of diverse backgrounds and for those teaching diverse students.

CHAPTER 6

Leadership for Change

Adam Gamoran, Charles W. Anderson, and Scott Ashmann

What is the role of school leadership in supporting teaching for understanding? In Chapters 4 and 5, we showed that providing access to resources and creating conditions that encourage new resources to emerge are crucial. Are school leaders up to this challenge? How important is their role in forging a common vision for their district and school? What outside assistance do they need? And by school leaders, whom do we mean? Chapter 4 also portrayed teachers in leadership roles in the professional development groups. How does their leadership contribute to teaching for understanding, and what can traditional school leaders (such as principals) do to support it? In Chapter 2, we argued that a one-way model of resource allocation is not sufficient to understand the role of resources in school systems. In this chapter, we consider whether leadership means allocating resources *in response to change* as well as to direct activity.

NEW CONCEPTIONS OF LEADERSHIP

It has long been recognized that leadership in educational organizations encompasses a variety of roles, ranging from decisions about allocating resources, to supervision and guidance of instruction, to articulating a clear vision that rallies colleagues around a common enterprise. Two important insights recently have elaborated this vision. First, the nature of effective leadership is partially contingent on the character of the core technology—that is, teaching and learning—in the educational organization. Different approaches to teaching exert different pressures on leadership (Rowan, 1990). This is important for our study because as teachers change their teaching to focus more on student understanding, what they need from school leaders is likely to change as well. Second, the multiple and complex roles of leadership need not be vested in a single individual or small number of individuals in positions of authority (e.g., the principal), but may be distributed among colleagues at a variety of levels within an educational organization (Smylie & Hart, 1999).

Bureaucratic Versus Organic Management

Teaching is inherently an uncertain activity, because relations of cause and effect are poorly understood, and teaching that is effective with one group of students may be less successful with another (Weick, 1976). Commonly, teachers avoid this uncertainty by adopting scripts, or predictable patterns of practice, that allow them to carry on as if teaching were a routine activity with predictable consequences (Jackson, 1968). Rowan (1990) explained that when teaching is conceived as a routine activity, it is supported by bureaucratic management, in which the key leadership activities are allocating adequate resources to classrooms and buffering classrooms from external disturbances. Teaching for understanding, however, cannot rely on routine practice, because the emphasis on student thinking forces teachers to examine their assumptions and respond to students' ideas in their daily work. Consequently, leadership in a context of teaching for understanding must nurture new mechanisms (other than predictable routines) for responding to the uncertainties of teaching. In Rowan's (1990) view, this situation calls for a more organic approach to management, in which leadership responds to the technical core rather than solely constraining it through resource allocation. As in our dynamic model of school organization, decisions about resources and decisions about teaching may be reciprocally related. Organic management offers teachers the opportunity to respond to the uncertainties of teaching for understanding, not by following routines, but by collaborating with colleagues on developing insights about student thinking and by learning habits of practice that encourage understanding of powerful academic concepts among all students (Gamoran, Secada, & Marrett, 2000).

Distributed Leadership

In addition to the challenge of providing opportunities for ongoing teacher learning, leaders of schools working toward teaching for understanding are pressed to balance the need for teachers' autonomy to work out innovations, with the need for a coherent focus within a professional community in which teachers support one another with new ideas and tools. Synthesizing a large literature on leadership for instructional innovation, Spillane, Halverson, and Diamond (2001) identified at least four leadership tasks that are essential in such a context:

- Constructing and selling an instructional vision
- Building norms of trust, collaboration, and academic press among staff

- Supporting teacher development
- Monitoring instruction and innovation (p. 24)

In Gamoran and colleagues' (2000) terms, leaders who wish to support teaching for understanding must not only allocate resources, but also foster new ways of generating resources; and they must deal with not only material resources (time, materials, and compensation), but also human resources (teachers' knowledge, skills, and dispositions) and social resources (relations of trust and collaboration among educators). Although educators in positions of authority (e.g., principals and curriculum coordinators) have special roles to play in responding to these tasks (Goldring & Rallis, 1993), they cannot provide all the leadership necessary. Instead, leadership must be distributed throughout the organization, including teachers who take on leadership roles that support their learning and that of their colleagues (Smylie & Hart, 1999; Spillane et al., 2001). Developing capacity to support teaching for understanding involves recognizing new leadership demands and engaging in a distributed response.

Early in the past century, Max Weber (1922/1978) recognized that the management of modern organizations rested primarily on two foundations: authority of "office," or position, and authority of expertise. Weber explained that positions of authority and expert knowledge provided a rational basis for management because they are stable and efficient, in contrast to earlier ways of organizing that relied on age-old traditions or the charisma of unique individuals, which tended to be inefficient, unstable, or both. In the bureaucratic management style that characterizes most of today's schools, authority of position tends to serve as the main basis for leadership: Persons in formal authority positions—such as administrators and specialists—have most of the responsibility for decisions that concern the school. While administrators may be selected for their competence, they cannot be experts in everything, yet the typical school system allows little room for the professional knowledge of individual teachers to make a difference in the school beyond their own classrooms.

Schools that aim to support teaching for understanding may need more balance between position and expertise as bases for leadership. Authoritative positions are still essential for fulfilling management tasks that make the organization run, such as scheduling, class assignments, recruitment, and so on, but in these more complex schools it may be impossible for a single administrative leader to carry out all the necessary leadership tasks. We anticipate that schools that support teaching for understanding will be places that allow expert knowledge developed by teachers to stimulate leadership that helps guide the vision and practices in the school. In this conception, leadership may be *distributed* among a wide range of individuals within the school system, including not only those in formal authority positions, but also teachers and outside experts. If distributed leadership is to be sustained over time, we suspect it will rely neither on a formal structure of authority nor on the charisma of unique individuals, but on professional knowledge that is stimulated by contact with outsiders and developed and nurtured within communities of practitioners.

To explore these notions, we ask, What sort of leadership supports teachers' efforts to focus on student thinking, to emphasize powerful mathematical and scientific content, and to do so in an equitable fashion for all students? We address this question by considering supports and barriers posed by district and school administrators and specialists, leadership from outside school districts, and the emergence of new, distributed leadership within schools. To what extent does leadership rest on authority positions, and when does it draw more on expertise? What conditions foster distributed leadership, and does that support teaching for understanding, as our conception holds?

Our analysis relies mainly on qualitative evidence from administrator and teacher interviews and observations of professional development. To provide a broader picture, we also draw on surveys administered to all teachers in the schools of the two largest cases we studied. The survey evidence addresses teachers' perceptions of leadership and support in comparison to teacher responses to the same questions on a national survey. The Appendix provides details on the survey samples and questions.

SCHOOL LEADERSHIP AND TEACHING FOR UNDERSTANDING

In our study, we did not find any schools where one person carried out all the leadership tasks. Instead, these tasks were distributed among school administrators, researchers, and teachers. The collaborative partnerships provided a context in which teachers could develop their own expertise and use that as the basis for taking on leadership in particular instructional areas. Fundamentally, we found, educational administrators encouraged support for teaching for understanding in their districts and schools by allowing such distributed leadership to emerge. In this section we examine leadership roles of administrators, researchers, and teachers.

Positional Leadership: Administrative Barriers and Support

Since time is a teacher's most precious material resource (see Chapter 4), it is not surprising that teachers' views of administrative barriers to teaching for understanding focused on time—either time that they were required to devote to other tasks, or time that was denied to them when they wanted to focus on understanding student thinking. At one site, for example, teachers wanted to devote a school-wide professional development day to a workshop with a nationally known expert on science education. The expert's travel and time would be paid for by the research team that was leading the design collaborative; all the school needed to contribute was the teachers' time on a day that had already been designated for professional development. Yet the principal refused to allow teachers in the collaborative to skip the school-wide workshop, finally compromising by allowing them 2 hours to meet with the national expert. The principal's decision in this case reflected bureaucratic rather than organic management, giving higher priority to a centrally planned program than to a subgroup of teachers' pursuit of their own interests in professional growth. Many principals we spoke with recognized this issue as a dilemma and felt compelled to use professional development time for school-wide issues such as classroom management, inclusion of students with disabilities, curricular links across grades, and so on. When they allocated time for issues of concern to the design collaboratives, they regarded it as an important sacrifice. Some principals, however, recognized the potential payoff from this investment of resources.

> What I try and do is to provide opportunities for [ideas] to come forward from the staff and the parents who are also part of our site-based planning team. The main thing is . . . just making sure I am not a roadblock. The other thing that I try to do is not overload our staff then with other types of responsibilities. That has been a little bit frustrating for me because I haven't brought in other types of staff development that I might have been interested in because I think that it would just be overload for people. So I would have certainly been interested the last 2 or 3 years to do a lot with multiple intelligences and providing a variety of intelligence opportunities if you will, for learning within the classroom. (Europa elementary principal)

Although she has restrained herself from directing her staff in a direction she feels is important (appreciation of multiple intelligences), she views it as a worthwhile trade-off since her teachers have been pursuing other, meaningful opportunities for growth.

In the same comment, this principal also expressed a common claim among administrators about how they supported teacher development: She does not want to be a "roadblock" and tries not to "overload our staff . . . with other types of responsibilities." From the perspective of teachers, simply staying out of the way was one of the most important contributions that administrators made to their work in the collaboratives.

> INTERVIEWER: How well did your principal, learning resource coordinator, and the district office support your efforts to teach math and science?
> EUROPA ELEMENTARY TEACHER: Our resource person doesn't tend to get too involved . . . and the district office and our principal are certainly supportive but they aren't a part of our group. It is teacher run. And that is not all bad. So they don't put up any barriers for us.

Teachers viewed the absence of barriers as a form of support even when they claimed their principal had little idea of what they were doing in their design collaboratives.

INTERVIEWER: How well would you say the school administration and the
district office support your efforts to teach science?
OBERON TEACHER: I guess supportive. They don't really get in the way
(laughs).

*The teacher also recognizes financial support for professional development.
Later in the interview:*

INTERVIEWER: So have they expressed any concerns about what you are
doing with your science curriculum?
TEACHER: No, they really don't. I don't think they really know (laughs)
what goes on.

Although it may not have seemed so to some teachers, principals who supported teaching for understanding did more than just get out of the way. They
provided opportunities for teachers to take on leadership roles, allocated resources in response to needs, and helped establish productive relationships among
teachers. For example, an urban principal in Callisto, Massachusetts, explained,
"I look at myself as [taking] a facilitator, cheerleader role, not an expert role."
His comments were echoed by a suburban principal in Europa, Wisconsin, who
said, "I see my role as a facilitator, someone who creates the environment where
good teaching can take place and where decisions can be made in the best interests of kids." For these and other supportive principals, the key to leadership is
creating an environment in which teachers can pursue new knowledge. They
allocated resources in response to new directions that teachers identified, instead
of allocating resources to direct teachers' activities toward one instructional approach or another. They served as linkages, helping teachers with common approaches to find one another, rather than pushing a particular approach. In
Europa, the tone for this type of leadership was set by the district office. A senior
district administrator explained:

Our model of governance is not just shared decision making, it's shared
leadership. . . . What is the role of principal then? The role changes to
coordinator/facilitator/lead by model, not by directive . . . coach, partner,
creating learning opportunities for people [so they can create] circles of
excellence.

A principal in the same district described her experience with this type of leadership.

You go into administration with the idea that you'll be able to control and
have an effect on what happens with that school. And the biggest lesson
for me in all of this is the best way to control it is . . . you stand on the
sidelines and you say, "That's great! Good job! Would you like to try this

next? Here's something else you can do. Did you know so and so was doing this?" As opposed to saying, "This is how it's going to be done. You've got until Friday to turn this in." That way doesn't work. If you want people to behave as professionals, you have to treat them as professionals. And that means they make the majority of the decisions and they listen to each other, work things out.

By referring to herself as "stand[ing] on the sidelines," the principal was not saying she was uninvolved or inactive. Although she did not impose a decision on her staff, her suggestions and encouragement clearly helped the teachers work toward solutions to their problems and questions. Through this activity, the principal played a role in aligning commitments of her staff toward an emergent vision.

Visions. Perhaps surprisingly, we found little evidence that articulating a vision for mathematics and science teaching and learning was a major task for principals, even among those whom teachers regarded as supportive in their efforts to teach for understanding. Principals *did* play a role in fostering school visions, but these visions were more general, such as "all children can learn," and were not specific to mathematics or science. This pattern provided an opening for groups of teachers to develop, as the administrator quoted above called it, "circles of excellence" where colleagues engaged in deep study of students' scientific and mathematical reasoning. Supportive principals helped teachers work toward common visions, but in our cases they did not provide specific content for the visions themselves.

We found more administrative involvement in setting content-specific visions at the district level, primarily from specialists in curriculum and instruction who were charged with addressing subject areas. Two different models among the cases we studied led to three different outcomes for supporting teaching for understanding. In one sort of model, a district-wide vision of mathematics and/or science was reflected in a specific curriculum that teachers were expected to follow. Whether or not this approach supported teaching for understanding depended on the nature of the vision. In Callisto, a district science director developed a curriculum that was geared toward teaching for understanding. Consequently, teachers who joined the design collaborative, which emphasized scientific reasoning among students of diverse backgrounds, could participate and remain fully consistent with the district's direction. By contrast, Janus, the Tennessee urban district, had mandated a city-wide curriculum that was not compatible with the design collaborative's emphasis on in-depth understanding of mathematical ideas. Instead, the district curriculum centered on specific, measurable goals and required teachers to follow a prescribed sequence of instruction and testing.

> Curriculum changes, it just won't happen this year. We've got too many people looking at us, you know, coming from the district, they're going to

come out, check our records, what we're doing to see that we are implementing core curriculum and it's not just, "Oh, yeah, we've got it," you
know, that we are (really) doing it. So curriculum changes are, I just don't
perceive that happening. Everybody's got to follow the little [district]
guidelines. (Janus teacher)

In this case, not only was teaching for understanding unsupported, but teachers
felt the district mandate did not leave room for the explorations offered by the
design collaborative.

Europa exhibited an entirely different model of district-wide vision, where
administrators emphasized the need for each teacher to pursue his or her own
passions, developing circles of excellence around particular practices. This approach
highlighted differences among teachers, and created problems of inconsistent approaches across the district and even within the same schools. At the same time, it
provided motivation and opportunity and, when complemented by material and
human resources from inside and outside the district, strong support for a teacher-
led approach that emphasized teaching for understanding. District administrators
claimed they personally favored "constructivist" teaching approaches, but their
broader commitment was to allow teachers to identify their own sense of what
constituted excellent teaching, and to pursue that with vigor.

Trade-offs. District and school officials who lead by responding to teacher initiatives face two important trade-offs. First, strengthening teacher autonomy makes
it difficult to establish a coherent direction for curriculum and instruction within
the district and school. The Europa elementary site, where autonomy was emphasized through development of circles of excellence around teachers' commitment
to particular instructional approaches, was faced with striking differences in the
approaches that different groups of teachers wished to take. In some schools, a
student might encounter a teacher with a strong constructivist approach to mathematics in one year, and a teacher who placed greater emphasis on drill and practice in the next. One way of dealing with this problem is through the selection of
staff. A Europa elementary principal explained it this way:

> INTERVIEWER: Well, how does teachers' freedom and autonomy mesh
> with a widely shared vision? One can imagine that those might work
> against one another.
> PRINCIPAL: We have a lot of control over the hiring policy within the
> building. So, our interviews are structured to find people who have a
> similar philosophy. It's a real benefit in a growing district where you
> have new [staff] coming in to be able to shape a more coherent
> philosophy. It might be much more difficult in a system where you
> have people who got into this business [with] a whole different
> philosophy and view of education and are unwilling to let go of that.

Because the school district was growing, the principal and her staff had the opportunity to hire new teachers whose approach to teaching was consistent with that of others in the school. Extensive hiring opportunities are not often a viable option for creating coherence in established schools. In that case, promoting a common approach across the district may help create more coherence. Indeed, the decision in Callisto to promote a district-wide approach to teaching science came in response to lack of coherence at an earlier period. Whether a district-wide approach supports or inhibits teaching for understanding depends on the content of the district's vision, as is evident in the contrast between the Callisto and Janus urban sites.

A second important trade-off is between the desire to allow teachers to provide their own leadership, and the need to see that routine administrative tasks, such as calling meetings, preparing an agenda, and ordering supplies, are carried out. The literature on organic management, whether by sociologists or experts in educational administration, pays scant attention to the fact that bureaucratic tasks need to be accomplished, even when administrators would rather respond to teacher initiatives than push teachers in a particular direction. The design collaboratives responded to this dilemma in different ways. A response that was common across our sites was to rely on outside experts to serve as the agenda setters and logistical managers, at least in the beginning. This is a short-term strategy, however, when one is interested in an initiative that will last beyond the involvement of the outside experts. A second approach was to provide resources for a teacher-participant to serve in a formal authority position. This approach exhibited some success, and we will explore it in greater detail when we examine teacher leadership more closely below. Other sites made little or no allowance for carrying out routine administrative tasks. This led teachers to complain about time wasted figuring out what they were going to do, even as they expressed appreciation for opportunities to set their own direction.

Our analysis of the trade-offs that arise under organic management is supported by results of the teacher surveys. In Table 6.1, we compare the responses of teachers in the Europa elementary and middle school sites and teachers in the four K–8 Callisto schools with responses from a nationally representative sample of elementary and middle school teachers in the Schools and Staffing Survey. The teachers we surveyed reported high levels of classroom autonomy, approaching the maximum of 5 for "a great deal of influence" on these items. Teachers in Europa also exhibited extraordinary influence over school policies, whereas the Callisto teachers were more comparable to the national averages. This pattern was consistent with interview responses from teachers, principals, and district staff about shared leadership in Europa. At the same time, most perceptions of administrative leadership and support were *below* national norms in these districts. This was particularly true for survey items regarding principal leadership. Both the Callisto and the Europa teachers less often regarded their principals as setting clear expectations, knowing what type of school they wanted, and communicating that to the staff, compared with national averages. This pattern is consistent with our interpretation that opening opportunities for autonomy means less vision setting in the principal's role.

Table 6.1. Teachers' Perceptions of Autonomy, Influence, Support, and Principal's Leadership (mean ratings)

Indicator	Europa Elementary/ Middle	Callisto Elementary/ Middle	National Sample [a]
Classroom autonomy: How much control do you feel you have in your classroom over each of the following areas of your planning and teaching? [b]			
Select textbooks and other materials	4.12[*]	3.85[*]	2.30
Select content, topics, skills taught	3.54[*]	3.30[*]	3.16
Select teaching techniques	4.52[*]	4.20	4.21
Influence on school policy: At this school how much actual influence do you think teachers have over school policy in each of the following areas? [b]			
Determine inservice content	3.08[*]	2.17[*]	2.64
Hire new teachers	3.62[*]	2.54[*]	1.08
Decide how budget spent	3.37[*]	1.50[*]	1.43
Establishing curriculum	3.58[*]	3.11[*]	2.55
Administrative support: To what extent has each of the following people helped you improve your teaching or solve an instructional or class management problem? [c]			
Principal/head of school	3.78[*]	3.96[*]	4.07
School curriculum specialist	3.35	3.50	—
District curriculum specialist	2.81	3.05	—
Other teachers	—	—	4.63
Other teachers at this school	5.18	4.39	—
Other teachers in this district	3.18	3.25	—
Principal's leadership: Please indicate how strongly you agree or disagree with each of the following statements about your school. [d]			
Principal lets staff know expectations	3.03[*]	3.05[*]	3.34
Principal does poor job getting resources	1.79[*]	1.89[*]	1.64
Principal knows goals and communicates to staff	3.00[*]	2.98[*]	3.25

Notes. Values are mean responses on teacher surveys. Asterisk indicates that Europa or Callisto mean is outside the 95% confidence interval that we constructed around each SASS mean. Dash indicates that question was not asked.

[a] Data from elementary and middle schools in the Schools and Staffing Survey (SASS) 1987–88 (administrative support) and 1993–94 (other items), with SASS weights used.

[b] Scale from 0 = no influence to 5 = great deal of influence.

[c] Scale from 1 = no help to 6 = extremely helpful.

[d] Scale from 1 = strongly disagree to 4 = strongly agree.

If the principal is not setting a direction for teacher development in mathematics and science, who is? As noted above, in some cases district specialists provided guidance. A more salient contribution in our cases, however, came from the outside experts who served as leaders for the professional development groups.

Expert Leadership: Professional Developers and Emergent Visions

If organic management means responding to teacher initiatives rather than setting constraints, where do teacher initiatives come from, and how do they find a guiding vision? In the design collaboratives we studied, mathematics and science education researchers from outside the districts filled these catalytic roles. In all six cases, the researchers brought a conception of teaching for understanding, attracting teachers who sought professional development that would allow them to pursue an interest in student thinking about powerful mathematical and/or scientific ideas. In Janus, the researcher's vision was incompatible with the district curriculum framework, so the collaborative did not go forward even though, in principle, the teachers were interested. At the other five sites, teachers and researchers began working together to help the teachers focus on student thinking.

Although teachers brought a general interest in teaching for understanding, the researchers played a key role in stimulating a vision of what that might mean. We observed researchers in the five active groups leading teachers through activities that focused on student thinking. Frequently, the researchers were the ones who asked, "What is the 'big idea' here?" By "big idea," they meant the important mathematical or scientific concept that underlay the professional development activity. Whereas both the school districts and the researchers provided material resources that supported professional development, human resources—new ideas, knowledge, and commitments—came from the researchers and from the teachers themselves.

The researchers came with visions, but they did not specify how those visions would be enacted in classrooms. Rather, programs for teaching for understanding emerged through collaboration with teachers, particularly in viewing and discussing teachers' classroom practices and student work. Thus, the professional development groups developed their own visions of what teaching for understanding meant in their particular settings.

In developing the vision, an important behind-the-scenes role for the researchers was that of working with teachers to schedule meetings, establish agendas, and so on. Despite the teachers' commitment to the collaboratives, they often left it to the researchers to plan the meetings. As one Oberon teacher explained:

> You need somebody who can figure out what it is that you want to accomplish. So somebody should at least have an agenda. For us that has been coming from the [research] Center in that they are the ones who are

funding it, so do we want to address what their desires are, what research they want to see. . . . [On] our end of things, what do we think freshman science students should learn from a certain unit? So I guess we negotiated that and made sure both parties (researchers and teachers) were satisfied.

At the meetings, the researchers played a variety of roles, from guiding teachers through activities to remaining more on the sidelines, but they invariably appeared ready to jump in when the teachers had questions or needed focus. In interviews, teachers expressed appreciation for this approach to leadership, commending the researchers for validating teachers' ideas and actions, and appreciating their openness in asking and answering questions.

What [the research team] does is they model, you know, those [researchers] are really the leaders if you want to know who the leaders are and they're the models. This is how I learned. They ask questions as well. (Callisto teacher)

[The lead researcher] is certainly no one you would guess is [the leader] by just necessarily walking into one of those meetings, hardly ever. But when he says something, you'll notice that he may be very self-effacing on many occasions, but you'll notice that people really listen to what he says. And he doesn't waste what he says, but he's also very supportive of people's strengths. (Oberon teacher)

Ultimately, the researchers transferred leadership of the professional development activities more and more to the teachers themselves. Encouraging teacher leadership involved the professional developers in providing not only material and human resources, but social resources: an environment of trust and collaboration in which teachers work together to develop their new initiatives.

Distributed Leadership: Teachers Leading Their Own Learning

As Max Weber might have predicted, teachers' experience, knowledge, and skills served as the basis for leadership that emerged within the collaboratives. We asked teachers whom they regarded as leaders in mathematics and science education in their schools and districts, and why. The teachers frequently identified their colleagues, and attributed leadership to experience, knowledge, and skills. These characteristics were cited at all five of the active collaboratives. Here are some examples:

There is a teacher in my school. . . . She has been teaching for a long time . . . and a lot of people like what she has to say because she is doing a terrific job, you know, in her classroom. And she . . . has been very respected particularly, you know, in the [professional development group]. . . . I could give her the title of leader in that sense. . . . Her name is Maureen Simmons. (Callisto teacher)

INTERVIEWER: Why do you think of these two [teachers], Carol and Lloyd, as leaders in the school? What is it about them or what do they do?

EUROPA ELEMENTARY TEACHER: Well, Carol, I think, really has . . . brought [the professional development collaborative] to our building. . . . What about her? I think it is the way she teaches. The way she has her students doing these incredibly great, interesting kinds of projects with math and science that are open-ended and take kids that can go as far as they want. . . . And just her technique and questioning, asking really good questions to me as I was learning it, I know she does it all the time with her students. And Lloyd is just always, you know, putting [out] a new idea or a question that I never thought of. . . . He also has his students thinking of really good questions. And I want to know how to get kids to ask good questions. I think he is really good at that.

INTERVIEWER: Why do you think of Michelle [a teacher colleague] as a leader in this area?

EUROPA MIDDLE SCHOOL TEACHER: It seems like she's the person who was led to the university and then led the university back here. And spread the word. And she is so good at what she does. And people here know that and respect her for that. . . . A lot of people look up to her.

Some teachers emphasized social resources—the ability to share with colleagues— in addition to the human resources noted above.

INTERVIEWER: Why do you think of Sherry [a teacher colleague] as a leader?

EUROPA MIDDLE SCHOOL TEACHER: Well, her experience and her willingness to talk with me and support me and then give me ideas.

Teacher-leaders preferred to lead "by example" rather than by exercising authority, even when they held official leadership positions. The creation of such positions of responsibility was essential, however, so that *management* tasks such as scheduling, disbursing funds, maintaining contacts with district administrators, and setting agendas for meetings could be accomplished, especially in the cases in which the researchers were trying to turn "ownership" of the collaboratives over to the teachers. These new positions, which embodied management as well as leadership in the collaboratives, required an investment of resources from the research group and ultimately from the school district, since teachers expect to be paid for taking on administrative tasks.

Although attributes such as knowledge and skills supported teacher leadership across sites, we also observed differences among the cases. Sustaining and diffusing teaching for understanding was an explicit goal at the Wisconsin suburban sites, but not at any of the urban sites. Not surprisingly, therefore, there was more emphasis on teacher leadership at the suburban sites. Still, important aspects of distributed leadership involving teachers were evident at two of the urban sites. In Callisto, a few teachers consistently were identified as leaders by their peers. In this case, a combination of strong district support and relatively weak school-level involvement allowed teachers to be entrepreneurs, acquiring resources through internal and external grants to support their efforts beyond the resources provided by the design collaborative research team. Moreover, leadership opportunities offered within the collaborative may have been particularly important for bilingual teachers, who generally saw themselves as isolated within their schools. At Mimas, teachers used the collaborative to pursue an agenda that was important to them. Although the collaborative was short-lived, it did not end due to lack of leadership from participants. Rather, the school's division into families and the social divisions between bilingual and monolingual teachers prevented intradepartmental ties that would have made a sustained program possible. Thus, conditions that are not directly about mathematics and science can influence efforts to transform those subjects. Both of these cases contrasted with Janus, the only case in which we found no evidence of distributed leadership in support of teaching for understanding. Teachers were held strictly accountable for a mandated curriculum, and principals were constantly aware of central office supervision. This bureaucratic approach to leadership may well have suited the district curriculum's emphasis on facts and skills, but it could not have supported teaching for understanding as we have defined it.

Meanwhile, all three of the suburban Wisconsin sites demonstrated stable teacher leadership, consistent with the researchers' aims of contributing to long-lasting change. Interview responses to questions about leadership were corroborated by observations of professional development, in which teachers played leading roles even early on, by showcasing their work with students to provide subject matter for probing student understanding. At Oberon, the boundary between teacher and researcher was blurred, as one of the teachers held a part-time position in the research institute and one of the researchers took a part-time job in the school. In Europa Middle School, established teacher-leaders used the design collaborative to pursue their purpose of creating heterogeneous mathematics classes in grades 6 to 8. At Europa elementary, leadership in the professional development group was widely distributed among teachers from four different schools. We observed at least 10 different teachers displaying students' work to the group, and even more were named as leaders by their colleagues in the interviews.

Activities Versus Structure. In our conception of schools as organizations, relationships among actors are not always reflected in formal structure. In studying leadership, we focus on activities and relationships such as constructing and selling an instructional vision and building norms of trust, collaboration, and academic press among staff. Following our dynamic model, we view these practices not as one-way mechanisms of organizational control, but as potentially distributed among a variety of committed actors. This conception weaves together the distributed leadership perspective of Spillane and his colleagues with Rowan's notion of organic management.

Spillane and colleagues (2001) described leadership practice as the interaction of leaders and their social and material situations. They focused on tasks such as interactions with others; the "moves" made by leaders; the role of artifacts, tools, and organizational structures; and what leaders know and do together (Spillane, Diamond, Walker, Halverson, & Jita, in press). Many of these tasks are organic in nature, meaning that the task originated as an idea or from an experience by a nonleader. The tasks may include rewriting curriculum, sharing teaching practices with colleagues, establishing norms to promote collaboration and continuous improvement, and creating a shared sense of purpose among community members (Rowan, 1990).

For example, in the Europa elementary collaborative, making teaching practices public was an important activity. Teachers often shared their students' work and reported on their activities, and this "deprivatization" enabled teachers to share ideas for teaching and receive feedback from their peers. One way teachers shared their practice was by watching a videotape of one of the teachers leading a lesson in her classroom.

> And we watched her . . . on a videotape doing a measurement area kind of a lesson. So she is somebody we get a chance to observe teach, and the reality is we don't very often get a chance to watch one another teach. And when we get to watch Carol, that is an important opportunity, and it is always very convincing. (Europa elementary teacher)

In this scenario, Carol acted as a leader. She displayed her teaching practice to other teachers through the use of a videotape and opened it up to comments and criticisms. The power behind this activity was not so much the viewing of the tape, but the discussion that ensued afterward. By analyzing Carol's actions during the lesson, the students' input, and the direction the lesson took, participants in this discussion glimpsed the decision-making processes used by Carol. By skillfully guiding the discussion and creatively utilizing material resources, Carol developed an understanding of her teaching practice in these teachers in much the same way she nurtured mathematical understandings in her students.

In some analyses of this professional development opportunity, the material artifacts, tools, and organizational structures would be treated as a backdrop for

Carol's presentation of her lesson. In our analysis, however, these components help define Carol's leadership practice. The organizational structure of the meetings, the time set aside for professional development, the videotape, the discussion of the lesson that ensued after viewing the tape, and her responses to questions and comments from the audience, all played key roles in the task of deprivatizing Carol's teaching. The setting and props did not simply *affect* what Carol did during her presentation; they were *constitutive of her practice* (Spillane et al., 2001).

Several of the leaders we observed, like Carol, were already regarded as leaders before their experiences with the design collaboratives. They were already attempting to teach for understanding and saw the professional development community as a supportive environment in which to pursue goals they already held. Other teachers came to the professional development group with less clearly defined goals, but stepped into leading roles as a direct result of their experiences. To illustrate these different sources of leadership, we profile two teacher-leaders: one who was already a leader prior to her involvement with the design collaborative, and another whose leadership emerged in the context of the design collaborative.

A Case of Established Teacher Leadership. Maureen Simmons had taught elementary school in the Callisto district for over 20 years when the Uhuru design collaborative began. She was highly respected by her peers, who viewed her as a leader in her school and in the design collaborative. A White woman herself, Maureen had many years of experience teaching children from diverse ethnic and linguistic backgrounds, a key focus of Uhuru. In the late 1970s, Maureen participated in a professional development program at a prestigious local university, and that experience had a transformative effect on her teaching and on her self-concept as a lifelong learner. Although her classroom was already oriented toward teaching for understanding, she embraced the opportunity to focus on science when Uhuru researchers first approached her to participate in a project 5 years earlier.

> But having had that [earlier professional development] experience, I already was teaching in an alternative program. I already was realizing that I needed to understand what I wanted from my kids in order to help them learn. Already my classroom was structured differently than the traditional classroom. . . . So I came to [the research project] because it seemed to me a way that I might be able to focus on science alone, with all this stuff inside of me already.

By the time the design collaborative we studied began, Maureen had already developed expertise in teaching science for understanding and a relationship with the researchers. Uhuru offered her a chance to further her goals of teaching science for understanding within a professional development community.

In her science teaching, Maureen emphasized the *meaning* in a curriculum—students should not just memorize facts, but develop deep meanings of the content. One of the design collaborative members related a story in which another teacher took pride in his students' abilities to answer specific questions on a standardized test. "Maureen did not feel this was knowledge or that this is what learning is about." Some of the collaborative's members described statements like these as part of Maureen's vision of science teaching. This vision led many teachers to identify Maureen as a leader. She "just stands out. I would not say she is better than the rest of the teachers, but I must say she is more impressive and more articulate." According to this colleague, Maureen is a leader not because she is a better teacher than her colleagues, but because she can express and defend a coherent vision of teaching science for understanding.

During many of the design collaborative meetings, Maureen performed a leadership role. She teaches science once a week and videotapes the lesson, which she views later to reflect upon it. This analysis of her teaching and students' interaction with the subject matter led Maureen to develop a sophisticated understanding of student learning. The design collaborative meetings became a place where Maureen could share some of her expertise with others. However, she did not always *tell* others her thoughts. Instead, she *created situations* where other teachers could develop a rich understanding.

For example, during one meeting three teachers (Maureen included) were involved in a discussion of how each interpreted a math problem that dealt with the slope of a line.

> What occurred was a discussion where Maureen, Simone, and Mei-ling interpreted the results. Each came to the same conclusion, but each solved the problem differently. Mei-ling, a [former] math major at [a prestigious university], conducted some quick calculations and made her interpretations rather easily. Simone and Maureen arrived at a similar solution to the answer. They used different techniques. At this point the process for them was . . . slower. . . . Mei-ling came in with the solution prepared and well understood. Simone and Maureen worked through it during this time and Maureen had really already worked through it, but did not profess to having done so. In addition, she indicated that to really look at the graph, she was not able to understand it. She had to sit down and calculate for herself in her own fashion. . . . At this point Mei-ling intervened and attempted to, in a sense, draw both Simone and Maureen into her procedure for answering the question. And a sort of positive tension occurred at this point, positive in the sense they were discussing and learning and at the same time Maureen became a bit defensive. I thought [she] displayed a bit of irritation with Mei-ling because she did not want to work the problem in the way that Mei-ling suggested. Mei-ling suggested that Maureen was being resistant to accepting certain ideas, and Maureen, who is not a

reticent individual, argued with her and was very adamant that she was not being resistant, but she simply couldn't understand and address the question in the manner in which Mei-ling addressed it, for that matter was not willing to address the question in the manner that Mei-ling addressed it. Mei-ling needed to be more understanding that there are a variety of interpretations and methods for solving a problem. (Field notes)

This scenario highlights three different leadership practices. First, Maureen was supporting teacher development. She was helping a less experienced colleague develop a more sophisticated understanding of teaching and learning processes by expressing her deeply held point of view that mathematics can be learned using different approaches. A significant strand of the work in this design collaborative was to learn together in an effort to help teachers understand what it means to be a learner of subject matter. Mei-ling had been schooled in the most efficient ways of solving a math problem dealing with slope. Maureen shared her expertise of student learning by articulating an alternative approach. Her point to Mei-ling was that just because students do not use the most direct means for solving a problem, does not mean their thinking is faulty.

Second, the exchange between Maureen and Mei-ling reflects the construction of an instructional vision. Maureen was raising the question, "What is good mathematics?" Does good mathematics mean that a student learns how to solve problems using the most efficient means possible? Or does good mathematics mean that the student makes sense of the problem, using whatever methods seem appropriate? Another of Maureen's questions concerned the treatment of members of a learning community whose sense making led to alternative solution paths. Should these students be required to learn the most efficient means? Should their reasoning go unchallenged by the teacher?

The third of Maureen's leadership practices was building norms in this community. In response to Mei-ling's effort to help her see the most efficient way of solving the slope problem, Maureen proposed and defended an alternative approach, just as a student might do in a classroom. Through their exchange, Maureen conveyed the message that a norm of this group was not to try to get others to change their solution to a math problem. Instead, one was to look for the reasoning used by the problem solver and develop ideas for future teaching moves that support learning, which is a goal of teaching for understanding.

Another effective leadership practice Maureen used was to expose her thought processes during a presentation. In the following example, the discussion topic was student performance on standardized tests:

Maureen was describing sitting around worrying about the particular mode of teaching, her instructional style right now, and having these kids in groups and spending the time on distance exercises and trip narrative, and so forth, with a test coming up. Will they be expected to have a certain kind

> of knowledge, [which] she is afraid they won't have? Or is she sacrificing one kind for another kind? While she clearly believes in what she is doing and thinks this is an important task in front of her to get these kids to understand distance, to think, to expect [a] level of confusion, to engage in critical thinking, and so on, she worries that this isn't going to move them along fast enough, given the current structure, the current testing system and the current expectations of students. (Field notes)

By sharing her concerns, Maureen helped others realize that, even though she has many years of experience, she never stops asking herself questions about her teaching practice. Therefore, she never stops learning. This example contradicts a commonly held belief about leadership—that leaders possess solutions to problems. Even though Maureen's peers identified her as a leader, she openly shared her questions about teaching. Once again, the perspective that leadership is distributed among several individuals rather than vested in persons in particular positions leads us to attend to the tasks that occur (e.g., asking important questions) more than to the personal attributes of individuals (e.g., "possessing" solutions).

A Case of Emerging Teacher Leadership. A fifth-grade teacher, Lloyd Green, had been teaching in the Europa district for 4 years when the design collaborative formed, and although his peers already regarded him as an excellent teacher, his relationship with the researchers did not predate the design collaborative. Many of his colleagues were already involved, and he found the project interesting at the outset, but he also revealed his skepticism on a number of occasions. In the first year of our observations, he was bothered by difficulties in responding to student questions, he was critical of a document from the research group about assessment, and he expressed reluctance about some activities. One such activity involved classifying houses and self-portraits as a way of understanding children's concepts of classification.

> [The researcher leading the workshop] asked, Is this activity worthwhile? Does this give people ideas for their classrooms? Lloyd responded, he hesitated to get involved in this type of classification work in his classroom. He would feel more comfortable with it if he thought the content of the classification were more important. . . . He didn't think that [classifying] self-portraits or houses was a good use of time, although he thought the classification idea was OK, he'd be more interested if they were classifying something that was [worth classifying]. (Field notes)

At this time, Lloyd tended to sit back during workshop sessions, as if leaning away from the action, and the observer noted that he and other male teachers seemed most ready to express skepticism about activities. Yet he continued to attend the professional development sessions with unfailing regularity, and over time became one of the most prominent presenters of classroom work. Through the experience of presenting and discussing his students' work with researchers and fellow teachers, Lloyd became deeply engaged in the collaborative. Although still skeptical and ambivalent at times (to the frequent frustration of the professional development leaders), Lloyd recommitted each year.

In the third year of the collaborative, Lloyd carried out an exercise in understanding proportion with his students that his colleagues described in year-end interviews as one of the year's highlights. The following year, after the researchers at this site had pulled back from leading the collaborative and the teachers held all the responsibility, Lloyd expressed much frustration with the amount of time spent figuring out what task would be undertaken, as opposed to actually doing the work. He also complained that the teachers—himself included—did not do enough work between meetings to make them as valuable as they could have been. Ultimately, however, he played a leading role in the activity that came to dominate his small group's professional development for the year: a cross-grade study of children's conceptions of growth and change, focusing on differences from kindergarten to fifth grade in how children understood the growth of a fast-growing plant. With Lloyd's leadership, a group of six teachers from five grades collected data on their children's thinking and shared their analysis with one another, with the larger collaborative group, and in a written paper that became part of the group's archive. Recognizing Lloyd's role, several teachers identified him in year-end interviews as one of the leaders in mathematics and science in their school and district. Charlotte, a kindergarten teacher new to the collaborative, was most expressive about Lloyd's leadership.

> I think of Lloyd Green in fifth grade as very much working in the direction that I think is really important with kids. He does a lot of inquiry. He does a lot of research. His children are conducting research. I think he has really perfected a means of that fitting very well into his curriculum. . . . The first time I met him . . . I remember him saying, "Oh, we teach so much alike." And I said, "I teach nothing like you." And we had this big debate. And I said, "How can you compare [fifth grade] and kindergarten?" And he said, "No, because there . . . are common strands that we both meet or things we do." And I was very intrigued. . . . I think a good leader is somebody who will really take the time to explain what they are doing and the reasons for it. I think a good leader is someone who is genuinely interested. . . . In some ways he has almost become a little bit of a mentor for us [kindergarten teachers] because he has been in [the professional development group] for so many years and he got into this growth and change unit with all these folks that are brand-new [to the professional development group]. So we wanted him to sort of mentor us in the sense of how does this work or how does this meeting go or what is the goal or how did we get here? Or

like one of the other kindergarten teachers said in February, "I still don't know why I am in [the professional development group]." And he kept validating that. "Well, that is a really good question. And that is a really good way of getting to this answer," or "How are we going to answer that problem for you, Charlotte? How are we going to help you know why you are here, what the objective is?" . . . [With Lloyd's help] we moved forward [to] where we are [now].

That summer, a district administrator centrally involved with supporting the design collaborative asked Lloyd to take over the position of coordinating the group—a paid position that supported the management tasks necessary to keep the group going, especially now that the researchers no longer played a major role. In making this appointment, the district administrator and Lloyd himself recognized that essential bureaucratic tasks, such as scheduling meetings, setting agendas, and monitoring funds, were inescapable if the group was to be sustained. Lloyd was the third teacher in succession to take on this role, vesting leadership of expertise and position in one person. The group continued for another year under Lloyd's leadership.

Although Lloyd's case is particularly vivid, it is not an isolated example; many other teachers in this district demonstrated leadership at workshops and were identified as leaders by their peers. Teacher leadership was supported by a district environment that emphasized teachers developing their own circles of excellence and provided material resources to support those developments. Corroboration for the importance of the district context may be seen in the finding of a similar pattern at the Europa Middle School site, where recognized leaders were allowed to seek their own way and, with the help of the research group, developed a consensus on a new direction for the middle school mathematics curriculum.

Not all veteran teachers showed leadership as Lloyd did; observations revealed instances of new teachers floundering when veteran teachers were available to help, but did not. Moreover, some veteran teachers expressed reluctance to engage in any sort of mentoring, preferring to focus on their own development. Finally, staff turnover and transfers in a growing district frequently disrupted patterns of leadership and collaboration. Thus, a supportive district environment makes teacher leadership possible, but does not ensure it.

CONCLUSIONS

Our analysis suggests that leadership for change has three key characteristics. First, it builds on infusions of resources from inside and outside the district. On their own, both administrators and teachers lacked the expertise to foster a deep focus on student understanding, but opening their doors to mathematics and science educators brought in essential human resources. Material resources from both inside and outside the districts complemented and sustained the infusion of human resources. Moreover, the Europa elementary case suggests that if material resources can be maintained by the district, human and social resources developed in the context of the design collaborative can become self-generating even after the outsiders end their involvement.

Second, leadership for change meant that districts either (1) established a compelling vision in support of teaching for understanding, or (2) provided teachers with the autonomy to develop their own visions. It may seem surprising that the first approach was no more effective than the second on the path to supporting teaching for understanding, but this finding is actually consistent with other recent research. A study of highly restructured schools discovered that among the two most successful cases of promoting authentic pedagogy, one was a district like Callisto, in which educators subscribed to a common vision that supported inquiry and depth, but the other was more like Europa, where teachers were expected to develop their own circles of excellence (Newmann & Associates, 1996).

Third, we found that leadership for change meant that leadership was distributed beyond those in conventional authority positions. Teachers take on leadership roles by developing expertise; in a supportive context, their new knowledge, skills, and relationships with colleagues naturally find an outlet in mentoring and leading by example. Because bureaucratic tasks need to be fulfilled even in a context of distributed leadership, teachers whose expertise brings them into informal leadership may find themselves called upon to carry out formal leadership tasks as well. Only if both types of leadership are available—leading colleagues in inquiry and managing logistics—can a professional development group be sustained and diffused beyond its original participants.

CHAPTER 7

Seeking Community

Charles W. Anderson, Scott Ashmann, Walter G. Secada, and Tona Williams

This chapter focuses on the challenges of creating professional communities in which educators work together to create and sustain teaching for understanding. We examine resources that contribute to the development of viable professional communities and barriers that can keep such communities from developing. We further examine how professional communities can help teachers to create the resources they need to teach for understanding and how teachers' classroom experiences can, in turn, contribute to the development of professional communities.

DEFINING PROFESSIONAL COMMUNITIES

The widespread enthusiasm that educational reformers express for professional communities is based in part on the vagueness of the term. Everyone is in favor of communities of teachers working to address problems of practice. While we recognize the importance of professional communities, we also hope to engage in a finer-grained analysis of how they develop and of their costs and benefits. To that end, we need to establish more precise meanings for the terms that we use. In this section we discuss four aspects of professional communities that enter into our analyses of the project sites:

- The characteristics that distinguish a true professional community from a group of professionals who happen to be working together
- The importance of a focus on teaching for understanding for the communities that we studied
- The presence of multiple professional groups or communities within a school
- The relationship between local professional communities and larger communities associated with national reform movements

Professional Groups and Communities

In Chapter 2 we distinguished between professional groups and true professional communities. For us, professional *groups* include any collection of professionals who share activities through direct personal interaction. For the sake of this analysis, the cohesiveness of the group, significance of the shared activities, and nature of shared resources are descriptors of a group. Thus, groups can be distinguished from professional *communities*, which generally are bound together by shared jargons or technical language, values, and social norms.

Newmann and Associates (1996) suggest five key characteristics of professional communities in schools that support authentic achievement: (1) shared norms and values, (2) collective focus on student learning, (3) collaboration, (4) reflective dialogue, and (5) deprivatization of practice. As we will see in this chapter, professional communities that have these characteristics do not develop quickly, and when they do develop, they are bound by common social norms, goals and practices, and habits of speech. Thus, they are what Swales (1990) describes as discourse communities.

Focusing on Teaching for Understanding

Professional communities can form around many different aspects of teaching practice. Our focus is on professional communities whose members share a commitment to teaching for understanding for all students. In Chapter 1 we discussed teaching for understanding in science and mathematics as a powerful but demanding technology that requires new frameworks, tools, and techniques. Teaching for understanding for all requires (1) a focus on student thinking, (2) teaching powerful scientific and mathematical ideas, and (3) the development of equitable classroom learning communities.

In addition to technical demands, teaching for understanding makes personal demands on teachers. They must learn to manage risk and ambiguity rather than avoid them through curriculum scripts and related means of control. They must find ways to engage students around scientific and mathematical reasoning. This requires both a commitment to putting extra time and effort into teaching, and extensive professional and craft knowledge to make that effort pay off. We explore how professional communities can support (or fail to support) teachers as they respond to these demands.

Professional Groups Within a School

None of the schools that we studied had a single professional community that included all of the teachers in the school. Instead, each school included several overlapping professional groups. In Chapter 2 we distinguished between the *school professional group*, including all the teachers and administrators who work in the school, and the *professional development group*, including the researchers and the teachers working directly with them. Closer analyses show more complex patterns of relationships among teachers, researchers, and administrators, with many overlapping groups and subgroups. While we recognize the importance of these multiple groups, our focus is on whether, or how, the school organizations supported professional communities with the characteristics described above.

The professional development groups included people with different types of knowledge and expertise. The researchers were members of national communities devoted to science and mathematics content, national standards, and educational research with large-scale implications. The teachers brought localized craft knowledge about their schools and students. The professional development groups blended the two kinds of knowledge for the benefit of the teachers and their students (and also of the national communities of the researchers).

CREATING PROFESSIONAL COMMUNITIES

Our six sites reveal wide variation in the nature of the professional communities and in their success in supporting teaching for understanding. As Chapter 3 describes, in two sites the professional development groups never developed into professional communities. At Janus, the Tennessee urban middle school, teachers, administrators, and researchers could not negotiate space in the curriculum to focus on teaching for understanding. At Mimas, the Wisconsin urban high school, the group diminished from four teachers the first year, to two the second year, and none the third year. At the other four sites, the professional development groups showed at least some of the characteristics of professional communities as described above, although they varied in the size of the communities, their practices, and the nature of the support for teaching for understanding that members received.

In this section we compare our data on the histories and practices of these communities, to understand the key factors in the development of each professional community and how those factors influenced the nature of the communities. Our data suggest four factors that had a critical influence on the nature and success of the professional communities:

- Sufficient *time and other material resources*
- *Human resources*, including technical knowledge and expertise that supported the teachers' efforts to teach for understanding
- *Social resources*, including shared histories and purposes based on previous relationships among teachers, administrators, and researchers
- The development of *distributed leadership* in which administrators, researchers, and teacher-leaders all supported and sustained the professional community

Time and Other Material Resources

The professional communities that made the most progress emerged through substantial investments of material resources. The most important, and expensive, of these resources was time. In all of the communities that flourished, the process was time-consuming in several different senses; it required *calendar time, professional development time,* and *classroom time.*

Calendar Time. It took years for each of the thriving professional communities to begin to function effectively in supporting teaching for understanding. Each of the best-developed communities was built in part on long-standing relationships among key members (see the discussion of shared histories below), and new members came to understand the social norms of the communities only through slow and sometimes painful processes. For example, our records of meetings abound with incidents in which veterans in a group helped new members to understand when they transgressed social norms or failed to grasp the purposes of the group's activities (see, for example, the description of the interaction between Maureen and Mei-ling toward the end of Chapter 6). Given the complexity of the professional communities' purposes and activities, it is hard to see how they could operate without substantial group development and induction periods.

Professional Development Time. As explained in Chapter 4, each community had to find time for continuing professional development. Members spent substantial amounts of time together in summer courses, after-school meetings, or meetings using release time during school hours. These meetings often generated additional work for both teachers and researchers: developing complex teaching plans, analyzing students' work, planning meetings, writing about their work, and so forth. The participants generally recognized this professional development time as an essential resource, and time limitations as a critical constraint.

Overall, the professional development communities made large demands on funds to pay for professional development and substitutes, on participants' (not always paid) personal time, and on the scheduling flexibility of participants and administrators. Investments of this magnitude required both access to financial resources from outside the district and continuing commitment by participants and administrators to a burdensome, although potentially rewarding, process.

Classroom Time. The teachers had to make time in their classrooms to try the innovative teaching practices that they discussed with other members of their professional communities. Teaching for understanding often slowed the pace of content coverage, requiring teachers either to find more time for math or science teaching (sometimes possible for elementary teachers) or, more commonly, to negotiate with administrators and colleagues about expectations for content coverage. A focus on student thinking also required time-consuming methods of assessment, such as open-response tasks or interviews with individual students.

Thus, the professional communities were sustainable only in districts where administrators had flexible expectations about schedules and content coverage and could be supportive in other ways, such as providing classroom aides. In the Janus urban collaborative, lack of flexibility about classroom time was the immediate cause of the cessation of the project. The researchers gave up their attempts to form a professional development group when it became clear that the teachers would not be given time to carry out the practices of teaching for understanding in their classrooms.

Other Material Resources. In the successful professional communities, other material resources played important roles in professional development activities and classroom activities. For example, in a single meeting of teachers from Europa, the Wisconsin suburban elementary collaborative, teachers mentioned the following resources for life science classroom activities:

Fast plants
Tobacco hornworms
Teaching video
SimLife computer program
Daphnia
Algae
Frogs, tadpoles, butterflies
Aquarium
Quick quail

Some of these resources came from the school administrations and some from the research grants. In general, adequate material resources were necessary for the professional development communities to do their work, but the level of support was not substantially greater than in other well-equipped schools.

Human Resources: Technical Knowledge and Expertise

We have described teaching for understanding as a complex technology that requires detailed understanding of content, pedagogical strategies, and the students in each class. Each of the communities began in a situation where the knowledge was unevenly distributed, residing initially in one or two members of the communities. No single member of any community possessed all of the knowledge needed to teach for understanding. Researchers typically started with technical skills and knowledge of general principles associated with the national research community, including knowledge of science and mathematics content, developmental trends in student thinking, and strategies for assessing and promoting student understanding. Teachers typically started with local knowledge of their students and class-rooms. Some essential knowledge was possessed by no one in the community; it had to be imported or invented. Thus, the creation and distribution of technical knowledge was an essential problem that faced each community. The communities approached this problem in different ways and solved it to different degrees.

For example, in Callisto, the Massachusetts urban group, there was a strong emphasis on helping teachers to develop knowledge through their personal inquiries, with support and assistance from the project staff. This emphasis on personal construction of knowledge was sometimes frustrating, but also rewarding to participants. Here is an account from a Callisto elementary bilingual teacher.

> It was kind of frustrating when at first I wasn't getting [specific classroom activities]. But we had journal writing and my journal person was Barb [a researcher] and we'd write back and forth and, and I realized that it takes a while and [that] the language, knowing the science lingo gives you power in the science classroom [to help] children and that's why some of them are not so successful—'cause they don't understand the language. But what I also realized is in, in the Uhuru group, which is mostly elementary school teachers, that some of them by not knowing the science lingo are left out in science discussions or keep quiet.

One indicator of the importance of the technical knowledge brought by members of the communities was the disruption caused when people with important technical knowledge changed the nature of their participation. Here, for example, a teacher from the Europa elementary collaborative discusses the consequences when the university researchers began to spend less time with the professional development group.

> INTERVIEWER: Are there gaps in resources and support that you get for your science and mathematics teachers?
> EUROPA ELEMENTARY TEACHER: I would say probably the biggest gap is that there are not as many people from the university actually participating, and so this year I noticed we would sit down and we would talk about a lot of different things. And you really needed that one outside person to just, again, come in and just give another perspective and kind of looking outside and saying, "Have you tried this?" And I think that is still a piece that is missing.

In general, the ongoing communities depended on the leadership of knowledge-able individuals (both teachers and researchers) who devoted substantial amounts of energy and personal time to making the communities work. These human resources were essential to the success of the communities, and changes in the participation of these key people could precipitate crises.

Social Resources: Shared History and Purposes

One obvious difference between the two short-lived sites and the four sites where professional communities were sustained concerned members' history of involvement with one another. Both less successful sites were attempts to start communities more or less "from scratch." Although some of the teachers at Janus knew one another, and two of the Mimas teachers had known the lead researcher as students, they previously had not collaborated on issues of teaching and learning. In contrast, each of the four more sustained communities was rooted in professional relationships that had existed before the beginning of the projects. In three cases (Callisto, Europa elementary, and Oberon), these included preexisting relationships among teachers, administrators, and researchers; in one case (Europa Middle), professional relationships existed among teachers and administrators but not with researchers.

These prior relationships had several important consequences, including the following:

- The development of reservoirs of mutual trust and respect on which the members of the nascent communities could draw to sustain engagement and resolve conflicts
- A preexisting sense of shared purpose among the members of the communities
- The presence of, if not shared technical vocabularies, at least shared habits of talking and working together on issues of teaching and learning

In three of the ongoing communities there were long-standing prior relationships between teachers and researchers that provided the foundation for the professional community. For example, one of the Oberon teachers explained the origins of that professional community in the work of a teacher who had a longtime relationship with the university.

> I think that one of the reasons why we chose modeling [as a theme] was because Sharon was very much into it. She has kind of infused it into this district over a period of time and this was finally a chance to say let's do a whole unit on it. So I think that she worked really hard to bring the two groups together to sell it to us as a group to do it.

In the one sustained community not built on prior relationships between teachers and researchers, Europa Middle School, it was notable that the math portion of the project was more successful than the science portion, at least in part due to a long history of collaborative work by members of the math department. Here is an account of that history from a leading teacher.

> We hired people with the idea that they would be open to change in mathematics and the next step in the middle school math level. . . . We structured it so that each math teacher would teach more than one grade level so that we could see, how does this thing called mathematics go throughout the whole middle school curriculum. . . . And that really, I think, helped people see, how does this mathematics flow through the middle school rather than just in isolation. . . . As people joined us, then, we have hired, I think, good people in the math department. Whenever we have a math meeting I look around and I think, these are good people who are willing to try new things, first of all. . . . They also really care about kids and they really care about kids learning mathematics. And they want to do a good job. I feel very strongly about my colleagues.

Thus, the ongoing professional communities were all built in part on preexisting social resources: personal trust, a commitment to shared values related to teaching for understanding, and shared ways of communicating about teaching and learning. It may be possible to create viable professional communities without such a base of social resources, but it is clearly very difficult. The two attempts to do so that we studied were not successful in creating and sustaining professional communities.

Distributed Leadership

Each of the more sustained professional communities developed leadership patterns in which the leadership was distributed among teachers, administrators, and researchers, and was, in Rowan's (1990) terms, organic rather than bureaucratic (see Chapter 6). In the schools with the most vibrant professional communities, the principals were *not* instructional leaders. Instead, they accepted roles as facilitators and supporters, while the teachers and researchers developed curriculum and instruction. For example, here is one Europa elementary principal's account of his role in supporting the professional development community in his school.

> I think administrators in this district are becoming, more and more, managers. I've worked on the literacy, the language arts literacy task force, and so I've kept up pretty well with the work there but that has been a supreme effort on my part. In no way would I profess to know enough about the modeling in math and science. So my credibility is pretty weak and I think I would be foolhardy to think that I should claim that much weight in curriculum development. I think that's falling to people from the university, people from within the staff who take . . . on a particular area of interest, and learning resource coordinators.

The modesty of this principal about his own expertise was notable, as was his willingness to support the professional development community and to mediate the conflicts that inevitably arose within the school and with parents. The successful professional communities depended on such rare administrators.

PROFESSIONAL COMMUNITIES AS RESOURCES FOR SCHOOLS

Creating and sustaining professional communities required intense effort and sustained investments of resources from the school organizations that we studied. What did they get in return? We address that question here, organizing our discussion around the three challenges discussed in Chapter 1: providing resources to classroom teachers; aligning purposes, perceptions, and commitments; and sustaining teaching for understanding. We discuss below the ways that the four successful professional communities helped school organizations meet each of these challenges.

Providing Resources to Classroom Teachers

The first challenge that schools face as organizations is to provide adequate resources to classroom teachers. They must help teachers to develop or acquire the knowledge and tools necessary to teach for understanding for all. These may include new curricular materials, new skills in using curricula, enhanced content knowledge, and, most especially, knowledge of student thinking so teachers can anticipate student responses to instruction. Resources such as these help teachers develop strategies for managing the uncertainty made salient by teaching for understanding. Our data show that the thriving professional communities played an essential role in developing new resources and providing them to their members.

In Chapter 1 we described three essential characteristics of classroom communities where most students were learning with understanding: attention to student thinking, a focus on powerful scientific and mathematical ideas and practices, and equitable classroom communities. As we have discussed above, none of the participants in the design collaboratives began with all of the knowledge they needed to create classroom communities with these characteristics. The teachers had local knowledge of their students and schools, and the researchers had general knowledge of science and mathematics content, patterns of development in student thinking, and pedagogical principles. The members of the sustained professional communities worked together to create new knowledge that synthesized both local and general knowledge. With this new knowledge, teachers created classroom communities where students learned science and mathematics with understanding. In the remainder of this section we examine the practices of the professional communities that supported teaching for understanding in classrooms.

Attention to Student Thinking. The records of the professional development meetings in the ongoing communities are dominated by two kinds of activities: discussions of scientific and mathematical ideas, and discussions of students' reasoning about science and mathematics. These types of discussions were often so closely linked as to be inseparable, as teachers used examples of students' work or classroom videotapes to raise questions about their own understanding of science and mathematics. In the following quote, a Europa elementary teacher describes a typical activity and attests to her perception of its value:

> I might show them a student paper and say, "What do you think about this?" Or I might say, "Come and look at these ideas that we put on chart paper today. Where do you think we grew with this?" Or, we might just talk about math in general and say, "What were your kids thinking about when you did this?" or, "Where did you guys end up?" And it is usually not in the same place. It is so different. And I use Nanette, too, I mean, she is definitely one who points things out and says, "Did you think about this?" And I am like, "No, I didn't even think about that. I could do that." And really helping me see what my students are thinking. Looking at something and say[ing], "Do you think they might have been thinking about this or that?" And sometimes we don't even, we can't answer our own questions. But, it gives us kind of a sense of maybe where to go next.

The insights that teachers gained from these discussions were essential resources for teaching for understanding. In some cases, the insights resembled those already recorded in the research literature. In other cases, the insights were new and original. It seems clear, though, that the professional community's activities were essential for helping its members to achieve these insights.

Powerful Scientific Ideas and Practices. All of the ongoing communities spent a substantial portion of their time learning in depth about the scientific and mathematical ideas they were teaching. They often studied these ideas first in summer workshops and returned to them repeatedly during the year. The focus and extent of the activities devoted to content learning varied with grade level. The two elementary collaboratives held summer workshops where teachers engaged in sustained learning of science content. These workshops both helped the teachers understand scientific ideas and practices, and transformed their perceptions of themselves as scientific learners and thinkers. The following comment from a Callisto elementary teacher is typical:

> What it has clearly done for me is it has given me the courage to trust myself in science teaching. That I can maybe help my kids understand in third and fourth grade in a way that I understood when I was 30 years old through the work I did with [a prominent education researcher]. . . . I hadn't focused on science. I was probably afraid to try it, afraid of, I don't know, that it wasn't the right thing to do. But that would not have hap-

pened without Amy and Barb and David and Mary and Cindy [researchers in the professional development group], it would not have happened without their support.

The middle and high school collaboratives did not have summer workshops for the purpose of content learning, but they, too, often spent time clarifying their understanding of content issues. Discussions of classroom teaching often provided occasions to clarify important ideas, as in the following discussion during a meeting of the Oberon High School design collaborative.

SHARON: It is probably important to be really proactive and clear about language—also to show how language changes over time.
RICK: We've just latched onto the modeling terminology because it has significance within the scientific community. We all need to be comfortable with a language that we're going to engage ourselves and our kids with.

Later in the meeting:

SHARON: Are people comfortable with being up front about this definition: In common usage, a model equals a representation, but the scientific usage is that a model is an explanatory idea?
BECKY: There are mental, pictorial, and physical models.
SHARON: We are using scientific models that are mental models, because all our models are based on ideas.
NICK: What scientists are trying to build are conceptual structures. That's what we want students to work toward.

The deeper understanding of science and mathematics that came out of this and hundreds of other discussions and activities within the professional communities was clearly a resource for classroom teaching that participants valued highly. This proved essential for teaching for understanding as we defined it in Chapter 1.

Creating Equitable Classroom Learning Communities. Although there was more focus on equity across racial, ethnic, and language groups in the urban sites and more concern about student ability in the suburban sites (see Chapter 5), all the collaboratives shared a core concern for equity within classroom communities. In particular, this concern took the form of careful attention to the reasoning of every student and a determination to find ways to involve every student productively in mathematical and scientific sense making. This was evident whenever the groups analyzed classroom videotapes or examples of student work. Participants sought ways to recognize the resources that each student brought to class discussions and assignments, and the teachers were troubled by any evidence that they had failed to do so. The following field notes from the Callisto collaborative provides a typical example. One of the teachers was sharing a videotape of one of her class discussions with the group. She saw that during the discussion she had not fully understood and recognized what some of the students were saying.

> She was very conflicted about it. She felt that she had narrowed the discussion in a way which was necessary but then in the process had missed some of the students' comments. She felt that a couple of students who were more advanced had been sidetracked. Their initial understanding of the lesson was a more sophisticated understanding that she had inadvertently narrowed down or had simplified. And this was a concern and something she, in fact, said she values [about] these videotapes.

The Europa Middle School collaborative faced a special equity-related challenge because of participants' desire to replace the traditional tracked middle school curriculum (with some students taking general math and other students taking algebra in eighth grade) with an untracked curriculum that exposed all students to ideas about algebra throughout middle school. They wanted to make this change, even in the face of substantial parent resistance, because they believed that the traditional hierarchy of "mathematical ability" did not apply to classrooms where students used mathematics to make sense of the world. The "more advanced" students often had much to learn from the "less advanced." The following discussion is one of many that took place among the teachers in this group:

MARGARET: "How did you build that beam?" is a question that really makes them think. Students who get Cs and Ds in other subjects are teaching other students how to do it because they're able to see it.

TANYA: There is a different crew of students who rise to the top.

BOB: Students are asking parents how to do problems. If one of the parents is an engineer or something, they would give them the real formal explanation for how to do the problem. Then the kid will come to school the next day and explain this and others will ask him, "How did you get that?" and he would go, "Well, my dad. . . ." So I would say, "Let's find a way that we understand it."

JASON: Then the student can go home and say, "I've got a better way, that's easier." (Laughter) (Field notes)

Interconnected Resources. When the professional development communities were working well, they did not address student thinking, powerful ideas, and equity as separate issues. Rather, their members collaborated to create and support classroom communities that had these characteristics. The activities of the professional communities gave their members deeper insights into science and mathematics content and their students' perspectives. With the benefit of these insights, the teachers and researchers developed teaching materials and strategies that enacted teaching for understanding in their classrooms. In the following quote, a Europa sixth-grade mathematics teacher describes this process to members of the school's parent advisory group:

> I personally had to relearn math. Like most of you, I learned math by learning the algorithm. Math used to be about who had the best memory, who could spit out the formula. This math program gets at multiple strategies. Kids might not have a name for it at first. They might call it Bill's way or Mary's strategy. As the class progresses we begin to name these strategies. We're really working to infuse algebra across all the grades. Rather than group kids, we are trying to structure the curriculum so that by the end of eighth grade all our kids will have had algebra. We have two units we use in the sixth grade. I brought them with me and you are welcome to look at them. You have to understand that the whole vocabulary of mathematics has changed. These kids might not have the same language that you are used to, but they're doing incredible things and they're doing them naturally. It's very exciting to see. The other day, for example, my kids started adding and subtracting negative numbers. It's amazing. When you hear them talking about patterns, they are learning algebra. It's very exciting to see. This morning, for example, they were multiplying fractions.

Just as the focus on student thinking, powerful ideas, and equity are more potent in concert than alone, the resources that support these attributes are enhanced by their interconnections. This was particularly evident in the way professional development communities helped teachers manage uncertainty by developing technical knowledge. In many interviews, teachers talked about how discussions with their colleagues—both researchers and other teachers—from the professional development communities helped them follow and respond to students' thinking more effectively by improving their own knowledge on a variety of topics. For example, a Europa elementary teacher was unsure about her students' thought process. She relied on colleagues for help on the mathematics behind students' answers and for advice on how to interpret students' responses.

> I was looking at the kids' work and I was having trouble understanding if the kids were right, because I really wasn't understanding the rule that I was coming up with. . . . So I was asking Rob and Nora [two researchers] and a couple of other people and it was basically kind of an algebra formula. . . . And then I just kind of sat down and [they] helped me see the pattern, helped me understand the math behind it, and then I really needed to understand that before I could go further with my kids, because I can kind of teach something with kind of half knowing what it is, but when

they start talking to you . . . you really have to know it. You really have to understand the [ideas] underneath of it. And, I was blocked before in the past by not really understanding some of the stuff. And so it just kind of cleared itself up. And once I got that I was fine. I understood everything. It really helped me with that.

The professional development communities also provided forums where teachers could make their questions explicit and recognize how much more they had to learn. One teacher reported how, in spite of learning so much about assessing student understanding, she still had many questions.

I feel like I'm just starting to get a handle on how to assess student work and I still have a lot of questions about how to do that. If I think about what I learned in teaching math this year through the [design collaborative], it was getting a better handle at how I can make a student learn. So [at] some of our after-school sessions that we had I got some really good ideas from Jason [a researcher] about looking at homework. I'm still working at trying to decide how we write a good assessment and I think it was Daniel [a researcher] and Jason came in one day to talk about one of the assessments I had and I got a lot of feedback and that was really valuable to me. That's one I'm still struggling with and wish if we had more time that we could go in that direction . . . how do we write a good assessment, how can we best give parents the feedback saying, "These are the skills your students need to continue to work on, these are the skills they feel comfortable with, this is what they're doing." (Europa Middle School teacher)

The professional development communities presented opportunities for teachers to express their beliefs and inquire about the experiences and values that supported or disconfirmed those beliefs. Within the groups, teachers also could discuss how ideas that they tried out worked, or in some cases failed to work, in their classrooms. By addressing such issues of instructional uncertainty, the professional development communities provided an important social forum for creating and testing beliefs, and for transforming empirically and socially validated beliefs into new technical knowledge. Thus, material resources invested in professional development supported communities that helped teachers develop new knowledge and skills, which in turn made it possible for teachers to relieve somewhat the risk and ambiguity they encountered in their efforts to teach for understanding.

Aligning Purposes, Perceptions, and Commitments

Teachers engaged in the arduous work of teaching for understanding need not only technical resources, but also the social support that comes from being a respected member of a community working with other members toward a common goal. The members of all of the ongoing communities that we studied devoted substantial time and energy to working out their shared purposes and commitments and providing one another with social support. The teachers testified to the essential role that this support played in sustaining their engagement with the work. At the same time, the resources for teaching and social support produced by the professional communities were gained at the price of serious conflicts, both within and outside the professional communities. In this section we discuss the importance of social support and the internal and external conflicts experienced by the professional communities.

Importance of Social Support. Many teachers in the professional communities emphasized their reliance on their colleagues for personal and social as well as intellectual support. The hard work and uncertainty of making radical changes in teaching practice were made tolerable by their students' successes and by the help of their colleagues. For instance, a teacher in the Europa Middle School collaborative had this to say about her colleagues' contributions to her morale and emotional well-being.

> Oh, gosh. It has been a confidence builder. So it has been an incredible benefit in that way, just kind of feeling like I have some company in what I am doing and it has been, it has just been an emotional support, and I can just go to Lisa and say like, "What am I doing?" And she is like, "Okay, it feels that way in this part of the unit and then it gets better," or for her to come to me and say, "Man, what would you do if this kid did this?" And so it is just incredible emotional support, stress relief, just to be able to laugh with somebody and feel human, have someone that has been there and knows where you are at.

A bilingual teacher from Callisto expressed similar feelings, emphasizing how valuable she found the collegiality of the group, as well as the confidence she gained in her scientific knowledge.

> In my building we'd gone through the experience together, and it was about things that I valued deeply. We were ready to give it a go and could work together, and that's because they asked us to do this science experiment together as adults. They wanted to look at our classrooms and have us do some version of peer review, if only because we'd bring our videotape or our audiotape to the whole Uhuru group and share it. Those activities really did build a sense of collegiality. I liked how we had people from my own building, but it wasn't just us. We existed within a Callisto group, so that I knew there were other people from the science department that are in this and I can talk that language with them.

Struggle to Create and Sustain Internal Coherence. Although many teachers found their experience in the professional development groups rewarding, there were other teachers who did not. There were always tensions within the groups and people who felt marginalized or unrewarded by their participation. These people sometimes left the groups; in general, we were not able to interview them about their reasons for leaving. These comments from a Callisto teacher who did not leave, however, suggest the kinds of tensions that existed even within the more successful groups.

> So I honestly don't know why people left. I know there was one woman who just, she wanted a kit. She wanted curriculum. She wasn't used to this. She wanted a textbook. She wanted the answer. So she left early on. There was another young woman who was very—she was a minority person and she was very much into being a star. . . . I don't know how much she engaged in the process.

Collaborative activities that were essential to the groups' success also led to tensions among their participants. Here, for example, an Oberon teacher discusses the stresses that she felt when researchers or other teachers observed her teaching. The benefits of deprivatized practice did not come without a price.

> Teaching a new unit this fall was stressful. . . . Having people in other people's classrooms constantly observing, being observed, that's stressful. That's stressful, you know, because no matter how comfortable you are in your classroom, when someone is sitting in the back, you know, typing down what you do and what's happening and you know, you're a human being. At the end of every day you think, I should have done X differently, I should have done Y differently, Z worked OK but . . .

It appears that even the most sustained groups struggled constantly to maintain internal cohesion and develop patterns of activity that were satisfying to all members. None of the groups was entirely successful in this respect. There were always open or tacit expressions of dissatisfaction and members who left the group.

Struggle to Defend the Interests of the Professional Community. In virtually all of the schools that we studied, the teachers in the professional development group were a minority trying to teach in ways that were substantially different from those of most of their colleagues. In every collaborative but one, this led to visible and sometimes acrimonious conflicts between the members of the group and other teachers and administrators. (At the Oberon site, accommodating administrators and the near-unanimity of the science department combined to keep visible conflict to a minimum.) These conflicts took several forms and hinged on a variety of issues.

Perhaps the most common form of conflict involved *differences in ideas about appropriate curricula and teaching standards.* In the schools where the members of the professional development group were a small minority, conflicts arose when teachers defended their ideas about curriculum and instruction against other teachers and administrators who held different opinions about what and how they should teach. For example, one of the Callisto teachers gave this account of her encounter with the district's science curriculum director.

> She said, "Bam, you are going to teach this, this, this." I mean, we were told exactly what we were going to teach and when we were going to go on certain field trips and I was furious. I just felt like I had no flexibility about when things were going to happen.

In the schools where the members of the professional development community acquired significant influence, conflicts over curriculum and instruction took a different form. Rather than defending their right to teach differently from other teachers, they became increasingly frustrated with teachers who continued to practice in more traditional ways. For example, a Europa elementary principal gave this account of relationships between the two groups within his school.

> There have been tensions between SAMM people and non-SAMM people. And it is around teachers who have not jumped into it and . . . I think they feel a little pressure to look at it and they are feeling fairly comfortable with what they are doing. When we had SAMM people move up to a grade level, there was tension because the grade level assumed that they would do the same mathematics basically that had been done and they didn't want to do that. So that is a problem.

Similar problems arose at Europa Middle School, where the members of the professional development group wanted to change the mathematics curriculum from one that tracked students into algebra and general math at the eighth-grade level to one that was untracked at all grade levels. In one of the professional development meetings, there was a discussion of tensions in mixed-ability classes and dissension within the math department about grouping. Discussions about algebra consistently arise in departmental meetings. Barry, a teacher in the professional development group, summed it up this way.

> When I sit in the math [department] meeting, I feel like I'm pitted against others. We're a pretty good group. We've done this so many times though. And it's not working. I just want to move ahead. [Observer note: There is

genuine distress in Barry's tone of voice. Emotions surrounding the math meetings are clearly strong.] (Field notes)

These tensions extended beyond the school. Parents were concerned about the end of tracking. One group of parents formed a charter school offering an alternative, more traditional curriculum. Teachers and administrators found it necessary to defend their practices against questions like this one, which came from a parent in a public meeting.

This is exciting, but it sounds like there are conflicting objectives. That is, heterogeneous grouping and upleveling. Someone has to lose. It seems like one teacher can't take care of both high- and low-end kids in the same class. I know that in one class last year they didn't cover all the material they intended to cover. How does one teacher handle this range of abilities? (Field notes)

These conflicts over curriculum and instruction were not fully resolved in any of the schools we studied. In most districts, administrators who were in sympathy with the goals of the professional development groups managed the conflicts in ways that protected teachers' freedom to experiment and pursue their own goals. In the three Wisconsin suburban sites the professional development groups acquired considerable influence over school and district goal-setting and testing procedures. In no school, however, was the professional development group successful in recruiting all the teachers to join or in setting standards for curriculum and instruction that all teachers had to follow.

Other kinds of conflicts also arose between members of the professional development groups and other professional groups within the schools, including *conflicts over allocation of material and human resources*, including time. The professional development groups sometimes required the reallocation of resources that previously served other purposes. For example, teachers at Oberon demanded, and got, a common planning period for the entire science department. The rest of the high school schedule had to accommodate this common planning period. At Europa Middle School, there were conflicts between Betty, a researcher in the professional development group, and Bart, the manager of the computer lab.

Bart pulled Betty out of a class Betty was observing to confront Betty about issues related to computer use. He seemed to complain that Betty had cut him out of the loop on the upcoming Boxer unit on motion which Allison and Lisa are undertaking for their teaching experiment. Allison and Lisa were planning to use Boxer to have the kids learn about the software during keyboarding time; thus Boxer and the tutorial needed to be installed on the machines. He told Betty that the resources necessary for Allison and Lisa's work with Boxer would not be available until the motion unit began in November. He made it clear to Betty that, although Betty had communicated with Diane about this program, communicating with her was not the same as communicating with him. (Field notes)

Overt conflicts over material resources are recorded relatively infrequently in our data set. This may be, however, because of the special circumstances in these schools, where the activities and material needs of the professional development groups were supported largely by research grants. If the professional development groups had competed more directly with other groups for school resources, we could expect much more conflict about time and other material resources.

Another major source of conflict between professional development groups and other members of school professional groups involved *changes in social roles and relationships*. The professional development communities changed status hierarchies, leadership roles, or other aspects of the social and professional relationships within their schools. These changes were not popular with all the teachers or administrators in these schools. Often these conflicts were ostensibly about something else, such as curriculum and instruction or material resources, but much of their bite came from underlying resentments about status within school professional groups. Here, for example, a relatively new member of the Europa elementary collaborative recounts her impressions of the behavior of some of the veteran members during a meeting.

[We had] a numeracy task force that was working at Europa 3 or 4 years ago and they came to the building to present their ideas and there were questions about the standards that they were coming up with. And I remember this meeting specifically where people that had been attending SAMM made some of the teachers who hadn't been attending SAMM feel like they were, oh, . . . the ones. The impression that I got from SAMM was that they were superior to the other teachers that were not working in SAMM. And that really, it was a lot of negative talk after that meeting about that. Did these teachers do this on purpose? I doubt it. But it was just the way their body language and what they said to the people, was pretty blatant.

Conflicts involving changes in social roles and relationships were not limited to teachers. People in administrative and support roles also were affected by the presence and activities of the professional development groups. As the incidents described above illustrate, this could bring them into conflict with the professional development groups over a variety of issues. In this interview, a Europa elementary principal reflects on the underlying social reasons for these conflicts.

What I have seen, and this is an interesting little dynamic, is that the learning coordinators have enjoyed a leadership role, and they should, among the staff. . . . As teachers are becoming leaders or coordinators for their projects, their curriculum innovations, I'm seeing a little shifting of, or redefinition, and with that comes some anguish on the part of the learning coordinators, role confusion. . . . First comes the confusion then comes maybe the sense of territoriality and then comes the redefinition of it. We'll move into solution here but it's real interesting to see.

Summary. The data concerning the attempts of the school professional groups and other school professionals to achieve coherence suggest both good and bad news. The good news is that, with supportive administrators, the professional development groups could continue their work and become productive professional communities. The bad news is that conflict seemed to be an inevitable part of the process, and that those conflicts never were fully resolved. The professional development groups faced determined substantive and social opposition. Supportive administrators were successful in managing these conflicts so that schools could keep functioning, and in some districts the members of the professional development groups exerted considerable influence on policies and curricula. We saw no instances, though, where the professionals in a school were completely united in their commitment to teaching science and mathematics for understanding. A gap remains, then, between the professional communities that we observed and the ideal of professional communities that might support teaching for understanding for all.

Creating New Resources to Sustain Change

The final challenge discussed in Chapter 1 is that of sustaining change. In this chapter, we examine the ways that professional communities generate human and social resources that contribute to their survival and continued productivity. Chapter 9 discusses further issues connected with sustainability.

In this discussion we return full circle to the issues, discussed above, that are associated with creating professional communities. The resources needed to sustain professional communities are the same as those needed to create them. We discussed four types of resources necessary to create—and sustain—professional communities: time and other material resources, the human resources of technical knowledge and expertise, the social resources of shared history and purposes, and distributed leadership.

As the examples above and in Chapter 4 illustrate, the ongoing professional communities were able to generate resources in three of these categories. The professional communities created human resources; their members grew in knowledge and in confidence in their ability to use that knowledge. They generated social resources; their members came to trust and support one another and developed norms that supported the hard work of teaching for understanding. They generated leadership; teachers who previously had not been recognized as professional leaders emerged and took leadership roles (see also Chapter 6). Thus, the viable professional communities created many of the resources they needed to sustain and expand their work.

Two threats to the continuation of the professional communities could not be met solely with internally generated resources. One was loss of funding. The professional communities continued to need time and other material resources to function productively. Two of the communities—the Europa elementary and middle school collaboratives—made some progress toward shifting their funding sources from research funding to local sources. In general, though, the funding for the communities and their continued existence remained uncertain.

The other threat to continuation of the professional communities was loss of human resources as leaders or other key members withdrew or moved on to other projects. We have a sense that, in spite of their success and productivity, these professional communities remained fragile and crucially dependent on a few key members. This is a major threat to sustainability because the professional activities or personal lives of participants often led to their withdrawal or reduced roles in the collaboratives. Here, for example, a Callisto elementary teacher looks forward uneasily to changes that will result from internal movements of teachers within her district.

> It's gonna be hard I think because in our immediate school we really had a united group, a really united community. I mean we liked each other not only as colleagues but as human beings. You know, we were really, really a tight group and we even noticed that. I think out of all the groups there, we were like the tightest but now we're . . . being broken up and we're gonna be going to a new school and there are a couple from that new school that are in the [collaborative].

In general, our data show that the successful professional communities generated many, but not all, of the resources that they would need to sustain themselves. They created human resources in the form of leaders and people with important professional knowledge. They also created social norms and support systems that supported participants' efforts to teach for understanding and encouraged them to continue. On the other hand, the communities faced the challenges of maintaining the flow of material resources and recruiting new members when others were lost.

CONCLUSIONS

We have seen in this chapter that professional communities are difficult and time-consuming to create and sustain. In our sites, they were built on foundations of prior relationships among teachers, administrators, and/or researchers, and they required continuing investments of material and human resources. Furthermore, they contributed to conflicts within school professional groups, conflicts that were not fully resolved in any of the sites. It is hard to see how the communities can be sustained in an environment where quick gains on achievement test scores are the "coin of the realm."

And yet, these professional communities were essential for teaching for understanding. Without them, the teachers would never have developed the expertise they needed to teach for understanding in their classrooms, nor would they have sustained their high levels of engagement without the social support of their colleagues. So it appears that the problem of creating and sustaining professional communities, troublesome as they are, will be with us as long as we retain the goal of teaching for understanding for all.

Supporting Teaching for Understanding over the Long Term

Can teaching for understanding in mathematics and science, once it begins to emerge, be sustained over time? This is the central question addressed by Part III. In Chapter 8, we examine the district policy environment as a context for long-term change. In this time of competing preferences, how does alignment with other district goals and activities affect the sustainability of teaching for understanding? We show how teaching for understanding reforms were sometimes compatible and sometimes in conflict with the ubiquitous emphasis on standards and accountability.

In Chapter 9, the last chapter in the book, we argue that four conditions work in concert to affect the prospects for sustainability: integration of members within the professional development groups; linkages between members of the professional development groups and other actors; organizational integrity (coherence and competence) of the schools and districts in which the professional development groups are embedded; and synergy between the aims of teaching for understanding and other local goals and initiatives. We conclude Chapter 9 by identifying three essential steps for organizational support of teaching for understanding: commitment from the teaching profession, responsiveness from school systems, and improving the research base about how students understand powerful ideas in mathematics and science.

CHAPTER 8

District Policy and Teaching for Understanding

Pamela Anne Quiroz and Walter G. Secada

With current efforts to restructure and decentralize large school systems, educational policy makers have generated many forms of site-based management and educational market systems. British sociologist Geoff Whitty (2000) takes issue with the common assumption that two of the primary beneficiaries of these changes are disadvantaged populations and teachers:

> For those schools ill-placed to capitalize on their market position, the devolution of responsibility can often merely lead to the devolution of blame. And, particularly for schools in the inner city, there is a danger that too much emphasis upon the power of individual school faculty to seek their own salvation may only result in further damage to the morale of an increasingly exploited workforce. (p. 86)

Along with these changing school structures is the trend of merging educational reforms into "systemic change" processes, which have received widespread attention, particularly in the areas of science and math. These reforms, funded by the federal government and widely adopted by state and local school districts, are manifested in such policies as the creation of national standards and assessments with new curricular materials and instructional strategies for achieving these goals. How do such seemingly contradictory trends (i.e., decentralization and the plurality of types of educational systems, and the merging of reforms into systemic change efforts) play out in the arena of professional development? More important for our purposes, how can we make sense of these educational policies with respect to teaching for understanding, and how did other district/school policies interact with teaching for understanding in our six sites?

This chapter explores the special challenges of reforms geared toward teaching for understanding by providing a brief history of this policy and subsequently examining how each of the districts of our design collaboratives supports or constrains professional development in teaching for understanding. We also examine how other educational policies interact and align with teaching for understanding in each site, as well as how these policies make organizational resources available to teachers who engage in this instructional approach. Finally, we return to a discussion of how schools, particularly urban schools, engage in teaching for understanding within the current national climate of accountability demands for curriculum and achievement.

TEACHING FOR UNDERSTANDING POLICY

According to Vito Perrone (1998), teaching for understanding is not a new policy. Rather, from the common school movement of the 1840s through the progressive movement of the late 1800s and up through its current reincarnation, teaching for understanding has been a guiding principle of schools, if only rhetorically. However, this goal often was reserved for specific groups at certain historical periods (e.g., elite White males). Perrone argues that our current formulations of teaching for understanding are grounded in the ideas of such educational pioneers as Horace Mann, John D. Pierce, Francis Parker, and John Dewey, whose ideas and hopes for education as a liberating, democratizing, and progressive force also included notions of experientially based teaching and learning. Both Parker and Dewey emphasized the importance of teachers and students as active participants in the learning process. The curriculum was to be integrated so that students could take classroom learning and apply it in their daily lives. Thus, the idea of schools as producers of critical thinkers and problem solvers who could apply their knowledge outside of the classroom has a long history in educational philosophy.

The primary difference between these historical periods and our contemporary movement is that teaching for understanding has gained more attention with respect to its application in our public education systems. While the practice of what educators like Parker and Dewey advocated had become a common orientation in some schools, the increasing attention to teaching for understanding is a relatively new phenomenon in public education. Why is this the case? Perhaps the structure of most public schools has not been conducive to teaching for understanding; or, as critical theorists might suggest, perhaps we are still engaged in the struggle to liberate, democratize, and empower certain groups of people. In addition, students' academic performance has become subjected to increasing political attention from a variety of sources, including the media, politicians, academicians, parents, and the business world. Such varied interests in modifying our schools and in doing *whatever it takes* to produce critical thinkers who can adapt to an ever-changing world have generated a tolerance for a number of different approaches that include teaching for understanding.

A focus on teacher professional development toward teaching for understanding is just one of many policies used to support the reforms desired by so many constituents. However, teaching for understanding typically resides alongside numerous other policies, some of which are compatible and others of which impede it. In previous chapters, we identified necessary resources for teaching for understanding. In this chapter, we illustrate the multiple mismatches among educational policies. Any attempt to understand how district and school policies generate environments conducive to teaching for understanding must address the complex ways that policies push and pull at each other. Our sites are no exception to this, as they operate within larger district and state frameworks held accountable for math and science teaching and learning.

DISTRICT AND SCHOOL POLICIES IN OUR SIX SITES

Added to the challenges of teaching for understanding in each collaborative are the more general challenges faced by the district and the school. These include the expectations for schools to develop character and skills and serve as community centers, and teachers' various goals for their students, such as creative thinking, self-discipline, and cooperative learning. Just as students are not *tabulae rasae*, teachers and schools are not passive receptors of educational policies. To the contrary, teachers interact with policies, other teachers, and students to transform policy into practices that are meaningful and useful to their efforts—which themselves may be in tension. For example, one goal may be to promote a teaching for understanding approach to science or math, while a competing effort may involve developing skills that will enable students to excel on state assessments. While in the long run these two goals can be congruent, in the short term teachers feel forced to choose one or the other.

Table 8.1 lists those policies that were salient to teachers and administrators at each of our sites. It also suggests whether a particular district contained an environment supportive of teaching for understanding. This assessment is based on the alignment of district policies, whether policies act as incentives or constraints to teaching for understanding, and whether organizational resources facilitate or constrain teaching for understanding. To understand how district policies affect teaching for understanding, it is important to look at the interactions among policies and in particular how they affect the organizational resources that are available to teachers in the design collaborative. The way in which the different policies of a district relate to one another ultimately results in an environment that is more

Table 8.1. Support for Teaching for Understanding in Six Sites

Design Collaborative	Policy Alignment and District Support	District Policies
Europa Elementary	High support	"Circles of excellence—coaching teams" Technology academy Flex days Science and Mathematics Modeling (SAMM) Wisconsin Student Assessment System (WSAS)
Europa Middle	High support	"Houses" Math in Context "Circles of excellence—coaching teams" Flex days WSAS
Oberon High	High support	K–12 science curriculum Site-based management Leadership Eisenhower Fund WSAS
Callisto Elementary and Middle	High support	"Science kits" Bilingual education Controlled choice Equity Massachusetts Comprehensive Assessment System
Janus Middle	Low support	City Curriculum Framework (CCF) Mathematics Scope and Sequence (MSS) Professional development Tennessee Comprehensive Assessment Program
Mimas High	Low support	Equity 2000, Algebra for All Mathematics Urban Systemic Initiative (MUSI) Banking days Links project WSAS

or less supportive of teaching for understanding. We illustrate how our data speak to these issues, asking whether such policies as curriculum, assessment, professional development, language, and so on, create an environment conducive to teaching for understanding and consistent with the collaboratives' efforts. We also address the question of how district policies increase organizational resources or make resources available so that teachers can succeed at teaching for understanding.

Europa Elementary and Europa Middle

Perhaps nowhere in our study was the alignment of policies and resources to support teaching for understanding better represented than in the Europa suburban school district in Wisconsin. Initiated by the community when it replaced its autocratic superintendent with an administration that was sympathetic to constructivist teaching approaches, teaching for understanding received widespread district support from the superintendent, principals, school-site councils, and teachers. Recruitment policies even used teaching philosophy as a hiring criterion. Not all teachers were comfortable with constructivist approaches, however, and the district used choice policies to defuse tensions that stemmed from conflicting educational approaches among teachers and parents. Parents could choose to send their children to charter schools, and principals in the regular elementary schools allowed parents to choose the teachers with whose pedagogical approaches they felt most comfortable.

Similar to our other sites where teaching for understanding was promoted within a particular discipline (e.g., science) and adopted idiosyncratically, senior administrators in Europa encouraged teachers to build on their strengths (as opposed to making everyone adopt a specific pedagogical approach). The structure of Europa Middle School consisted of 12 "houses" where teacher teams were responsible for one or two of the core subject areas of math, science, language arts, and social studies. In this way, the philosophy of developing one's own strengths was combined with SAMM (in the elementary schools) and Math in Context (in the middle school) to support teaching for understanding across disciplines. A district administrator explained the district's approach in this way.

> We ask each individual in the district, I don't care if you're a secretary, superintendent, teacher, you know, custodian, what have you, we ask you to look in that framework and say what part of that trips your trigger. Where do you get excited? And it is your job to develop a circle of excellence around that area. And we'll help you. Now you might do it alone, you might do it in teams, however, it's your job to always be working on developing what we call the circle of excellence.

Europa also established a district framework within which organizational resources aligned with policies and supported programs, such as our design collaborative, to generate a movement among staff toward teaching math and science for understanding.

> We have established, now by policy, formal structures that engage all of the corners of the district in the conversation. And that's done with formal site councils that run each school, that have parents and teachers literally voting on very significant decisions, becoming knowledgeable. The principals become more facilitators of that process. It includes a structure on the

district level called the educational forum that engages these various corners in conversation about the big issues of the district to inform the board before the board can make decisions. It includes the development of major goals and direction in the district through the site councils up to the board rather than from the board down to the site councils. And through these structures, we create what we call the framework of the district. (Europa administrator)

In its efforts to create systemic change and coordinate teaching math for understanding, the Europa district supported a design collaborative in the middle school that aligned with the work in the elementary schools. In addition, middle school teachers adopted a curriculum (Math in Context) consistent with the orientation of their design collaborative and with the SAMM design collaborative in the elementary schools. These policies were accompanied by specific resources that could be used to support teaching for understanding in both the elementary and middle schools, such as professional development workshops, 9 early release days per school year, money to attend conferences, tuition reimbursement for teachers, coaching teams, flex days (i.e., 2 days a year for individual teachers' professional development plans), and daily planning time in the middle school. In Europa elementary, a summer technology academy trained teachers on the use of computer technology.

> And so, within a period of 3 years, from zero to now and now this is the fourth year, we have every classroom in the district fiber optic wired, we've got one network computer for every 5.3 kids. We got one computer as a whole for 3.3 kids and probably have the most extensive networking and most highly trained staff and technology in the state. (Europa administrator)

Both collaboratives had access to additional funds from the district beyond what was provided by the university research grants.

Even in this supportive environment, however, some resources and policies generated challenges for teachers in both design collaboratives. For example, teachers in the design collaboratives not only served on site councils, but also were expected to participate in committees. Although committee work competed for their time, teachers also saw it as a potentially empowering resource, since these committees created district policy.

One of the problems with progressive districts is that they often juggle multiple efforts to improve education. Europa was no exception, and teachers in both design collaboratives cited this as a problem in determining how to allocate their energies.

> Our school and the district are involved in many valuable things, but we have too many in progress at any one time. There is not recognition of the simple fact that we are too busy to be truly effective at many things that we attempt. (Europa elementary teacher)

For middle school teachers, tension existed between their attempts to engage in the design collaborative and to align the curriculum with state and district standards, one of which was to introduce students to algebra at an earlier age. They also had made a recent attempt to create heterogeneous classrooms.

> As the upleveling started, we decided in the sixth grade to stop grouping our students, to stop categorizing them. Our goal has been to meet the needs of all students in heterogeneous classrooms. Right now we are using Mathematics in Context. In the sixth grade, all the math teachers are on board and have been using the curriculum. It's incredible. I personally had to relearn math. (Europa Middle School teacher)

Another factor involved the district's changing demographics, necessitating the building of new elementary and middle schools and hence the movement of teachers away from their "teams" or "houses."

> The past 2 years have brought about many changes in our school. We became a primary K–2 building. Over 50% of our staff are new to the building. Our principal was new and is no longer with us. The school climate this year has ranged from mediocre to dissatisfaction among staff. Overall the district is very progressive; it offers teachers many learning opportunities. They are very supportive and continually encourage involvement of all staff. (Europa elementary teacher)

Despite the district's high expectations and the challenges facing teachers at all levels, the general consensus, at least among the middle and elementary school teachers in our collaboratives, was that the Europa curriculum was well aligned with the state assessment and with teaching for understanding. In fact, teachers used the Wisconsin Student Assessment System (WSAS) to guide their selection of math and science units to teach for understanding.

> Our goal is to have all children completing algebra by the end of eighth grade, completing geometry by the end of ninth grade, and completing algebra II by the end of tenth grade. This is big news; we have not shared this with anyone until tonight. . . . Our curriculum maps pretty well on to the WSAS, so we'll be watching that. (Europa Middle School teacher)

Working in an environment where policies were well aligned and the district, community, and design collaborative provided ongoing support, Europa teachers continued to weather the challenges and pursue systemic change in math and science education.

> We want to create students who are life-long learners. Creating students who expect to be part of their learning, who expect to find learning

interesting, who expect to see connections between, for lack of a better term, curricular areas. That social studies has math in it, math has some science in it. The goals of the district and of the school are not to teach math stuff. It is to guide them to be their own problem-solving source. And that is exactly what we worked on throughout the project and what we work on when we shuttle kids out the door and on to the next. Not to be dependent on someone else to tell you what you need to know as much as having the strategies and the wherewithal, the resources, to figure out what you want to know. And even more than that, to have the curiosity to want to know something. (Europa Middle School teacher)

Oberon High

Although a small rural-suburban district in Wisconsin, Oberon prides itself on being a progressive school system that consistently implements innovations. Relative to our other collaboratives, this group had the most comprehensive participation (seven of its eight high school science teachers); however, the effects of the collaborative on the science department are difficult to assess since the teachers had been engaged in teaching for understanding and had developed a professional community that preceded the design collaborative.

> I think that the science teachers at Oberon are a far more cohesive group than any group of teachers I have ever worked with before in terms of really talking about what is going on each day. And I think there are pros and cons to that, but it is a pretty tight-knit group. We eat lunch together. We have a common planning hour every day where everyone sits down together. (Oberon teacher)

> We share a commitment to having kids thinking and doing, not just filling out worksheets, not just busy work, like that is a common value we all share. We don't want them . . . we don't have a textbook. We don't want it to become this very rote kind of chug-away through the chapters kind of thing. I think that is something that everyone agrees on out there pretty strongly. And so, so then the goal is always that we are all trying to do and find the best things to bring in and get the students interested in doing things. (Oberon teacher)

The Oberon school district can be characterized as providing an environment hospitable to, if not directly or explicitly supportive of, teaching science for understanding. Teachers perceived the district as uninvolved in their department's efforts and attempted to bring attention to their work with the design collaborative.

Again, I, Lou, and Sharon are the ones who have approached administration and told them we were planning on doing this collaboration and funding was there and how great it was going to be developing some units, some new approaches to teaching and things. They made their case but the district still said, "There isn't any money," last year. Now, but they are saying; now we are going to start working on some more things. But we kind of laughed about it, saying, "Well, sure they didn't have any money because, well, if somebody else is going to pick up the tab [the design collaborative], why should we bother paying for it?" (Oberon teacher)

Although Oberon science teachers initiated their curriculum (which integrated disciplines and reading packets without using a text), the school and district facilitated organizational resources such as professional development grants, daily departmental meeting time, a budget larger than for the other high school departments, and an ongoing affiliation with university researchers.

At the time of our study, however, other policies were failing to interface with the Oberon science department's efforts to teach science for understanding. In fact, the shift in administrative leadership and the school's infrastructure was not only distracting to our teachers but also affected morale. The principal's newly adopted site-based management was presented as a resource that ultimately would be empowering for teachers, yet the effect of the implementation of this new system (which continued to be coupled with bureaucratic decision making) was to create interdepartmental tensions as departments vied for money and influence.

Gwendolyn's approach is that she wants site-based management. But she hasn't really put in place the structure to make it effective. So what is happening is, some of the decisions that she is having us make are decisions that are pitting departments against each other. Like budgetary things . . . I mean, that is just something that just needs to be a top-down decision because then you are not squabbling against each other. . . . You can be pissed at the administration for doing that but all of a sudden now you don't have collaboration amongst the departments because everyone is squabbling for the same money and knowing that you might have some influence over the decision, can cause some really bad things to happen. . . . So all of a sudden you start to conquer and divide and that is what is happening in the school right now. (Oberon teacher)

Because instead of us concentrating on what we really need to change in science, it is just easier to say, "Well, who is this coming from?" It is almost like you start to focus on, you become paranoid. It has just affected the total school mood which then affects everything you do because all of a sudden, you don't feel like being here any more. (Oberon teacher)

Problems with leadership and infrastructure were exacerbated by frequent changes in district administration and contract disputes, with the result that teachers predicted the dissolution of their science department community within a few years.

> I think there is a problem with the fact that the administration in the district changes so frequently. . . . Like when we first set this up for the design collaborative to work with Oberon, it was with Pat as administrator and superintendent. And we had a meeting. And Lou came and I came, and we presented this pretty thick compilation of papers and ideas, what we wanted to do, what our purpose was, and what our past experience had been, working in my classroom, in the district. We worked really hard on it. We had a meeting with him. He is gone. The person who was going to help with the K–12 science rewrite is gone. The curriculum coordinator is gone, has changed. The only person that was consistent in that whole room, was Lou and myself, and our principal. Everybody else was gone. So how do you maintain this kind of communication? (Oberon teacher)

> There are already good people leaving that, well, I wouldn't be surprised if we are down to maybe half of our current science teachers in a couple of years. Sharon is looking elsewhere, and I know Nick has been floating his resume around. And well, Bob is going to retire in a couple of years I imagine. But who knows. Claire was completely disheartened and wasn't sure if she was going to come back next year. . . . We could be left with just a few of the current teachers in just a few years. And that is tragic. (Oberon teacher)

Not only the new site-based management but policies directly geared toward science also interfered with teachers' efforts in the collaborative and created pressures, such as a recently mandated K–12 curriculum rewrite and AAAS standards that drove state standards and hence curriculum. This is an example of district policy that competed for teachers' time and reduced participation in the design collaborative meetings. It also offered a potential resource (i.e., curriculum) that in the short term constrained teachers to rewrite but in the long term assisted them by providing a structure for teaching science for understanding. Nevertheless, teachers were not wholly enthusiastic about this policy for reasons that, once again, linked to administrative turnover.

> People are not crazy about this K–12 rewrite because it has been attempted for the last 10 years. Every couple of years they go so far with it, and then the administrator, it seems, who is working on it either leaves or just drops it for some reason or one of the other departments, something happens and they need to scurry to the front and work on theirs for a while. (Oberon teacher)

Despite the high regard teachers had for the university researchers, even design collaborative work created some tensions.

> I think there are times when that sort of conflict [arises that] I was talking about earlier, in terms of how much time do we spend on something versus how much do we get covered in the year. I think that is one of those places where there is a little bit of conflict between the two groups because the university researchers have a very strong commitment to a way of teaching. And I think especially Lou and Nick sometimes, and like I said Steve definitely, they feel some obligation. I don't know if it is to the district or to kids or where that comes from necessarily, but to just cover stuff. And so I think they get frustrated by the sort of idealistic university view on some things. (Oberon teacher)

Oberon High represents an example of long-term and apparently successful efforts to teach science for understanding. It also shows how even in situations where teachers are engaged and experienced, the policy arena in which they operate can undermine the most committed efforts. Perhaps most important, Oberon highlights the necessity of consistent leadership in sustaining these efforts.

Callisto Elementary and Middle

Historically in the urban district of Callisto, Massachusetts, the application of federally generated and state-mandated policies has taken creative or preemptive form. For example, this is one of the first school districts in the country to desegregate voluntarily. It also has been experimenting with school choice and bilingual education for some time, with two-way bilingual programs existing here for more than a decade. Additionally, science development has been aligned with the inception of the voluntary national standards. Thus, it is fair to describe Callisto as a school district on the "cutting edge."

We regard Callisto as a supportive environment for teaching for understanding because the goals of the design collaborative were in agreement with district policy. Callisto policies reflected curricular coordination at the district level that explicitly favored policies consistent with teaching for understanding in the science curriculum. Adopted 5 years ago, Callisto's science curriculum consisted of "science kits" that promote a learn-by-doing instructional approach. The curriculum largely reflected the efforts of the district's science coordinator, whose success in acquiring federal grants greatly enhanced Callisto's recent focus on science learning. This funding also supported four staff developers, each assigned to a set of schools. In a novel attempt to provide science assistance to language-minority teachers, one of the staff development positions was targeted specifically for a bilingual teacher.

For a number of reasons that are embedded in the structure of bilingual programs, teaching for understanding complemented the bilingual instruction of the teachers in Callisto's design collaborative. Language-minority teachers experienced professional and social isolation and had to negotiate often-minimal material and human resources in order to accomplish classroom goals. For example, bilingual teachers described difficulties that ranged from lack of staff development and para-professionals, to professional isolation within the school, to difficulty obtaining curricular materials. A bilingual program's size and access to material resources also influenced its goals and instruction. One teacher in the district's Spanish transitional program, a small program with few staff persons, taught four grade levels in a single science class. She characterized team teaching (and deprivatized practice) as a problem-solving device to reduce the number of science lessons. One consequence of these structural constraints was that negotiations among the bilingual teachers generated a professional community as they struggled to accommodate students and implement district policies.

Nevertheless, although district administrators endorsed and supported teaching for understanding in science, difficulties emerged in its practice, particularly for bilingual teachers. However inadvertently, the objectives of Callisto's science policy often intervened with the multiple goals embedded in its different bilingual programs. In addition to the formal goals of these bilingual programs, namely, to teach English as well as subject matter, were the informal goals dictated by student needs. These needs involved everything from learning basic skills to acculturation and the impact of these processes on identity. How does one teach science for understanding and mainstream a student within 3 years, while attending to the fact that this 10-year-old student has just arrived in the United States having never attended a school? This scenario was not uncommon, with a considerable number of Haitian immigrant children who arrived in the school district having little or no formal education despite being of school age. These goals and the dilemmas they presented to teachers are implicit in all bilingual programs.

Added to the issue of formal and informal goals, bilingual education often takes various organizational forms even within the same school district. These forms both reflect and dictate distinctive goals, and the Callisto programs differed in their structures, goals, and access to resources. For example, Callisto's transitional bilingual programs organized learning with an emphasis on mainstreaming students within a circumscribed period of time, whereas its two-way bilingual programs taught subject-matter content while encouraging the maintenance of language and culture throughout the bilingual educational experience. More important, bilingual programs, and hence bilingual teachers, did not necessarily receive the same organizational support or resources, regardless of the more broadly defined and district-endorsed goal of teaching for understanding.

The multidimensionality of the Callisto school district is manifest in teachers' access to resources. Accessing resources in Callisto required entrepreneurial skills that were rewarded by opportunities, such as workshops, that facilitated teaching for understanding. However, teachers without access to resources often found their efforts frustrated despite their interest in teaching for understanding. Teachers in the bilingual programs often had difficulty obtaining curricular materials, qualified student teachers, and paraprofessionals (see Chapter 5). The time spent translating lessons detracted from teaching time.

Lack of materials also included simple teaching tools. While few of the teachers in the design collaborative complained about the lack of curriculum materials or supplies, one language-minority elementary teacher who taught math at a "target" school found the lack of materials frustrating.

> I couldn't even get an overhead. I couldn't get calculators. So he [the principal] sent me some but that took a while. Maybe because it was my first year of teaching, but I mean this bureaucracy of going through what you have to have, you have to order at the end of the year. I didn't even get my emergency fund this year when I went into the classroom in September. So this whole year I went through without . . . unless I went out and bought them on my own or borrowed from other teachers. So those are necessary things.

Similarly, teachers were just beginning to react to the new statewide assessment and to acknowledge how it was affecting their teaching. Despite the test's reported alignment with teaching for understanding, several teachers voiced a concern regarding the lack of alignment among the science curriculum, students' prior learning, and the test. Others admitted that, while committed to teaching science for understanding, they anticipated the use of this test as part of their evaluations and allocated a portion of class time to "teach to the test." One elementary school teacher explained:

> The test takes about 18 hours of class time (just to take it) and more to prepare them for it. It is significantly above grade level even though we're testing these kids at eighth grade. . . . These are kids who come from homes where they hear words and know words, but the vocabulary in the test confounds them. Did you know that no high school student (in the district) passed the science component last year! Students must pass all three components (i.e., science, math, and reading) in order to pass the test.

Thus, while Callisto is a district that promoted teaching for understanding, bilingual teachers faced relatively more obstacles in their efforts to engage this practice. In addition, the newly implemented statewide assessment affected all teachers in Callisto.

Janus Middle

In this Tennessee urban middle school site, resources for teachers were tied to a set of assumptions about the nature of mathematics learning that are at odds with teaching for understanding. As the official district policy for Janus school reform, the City Curriculum Framework (CCF) and its associated Mathematics Scope and Sequence (MSS) resulted in the allocation of resources in very specific ways. For example, the CCF explicitly defined goals and objectives within 6-week periods for both teachers and their students, and parents received newsletters outlining these goals. Professional development time, a resource critical to teaching for understanding, was perceived quite differently by the teachers in the design collaborative and the Janus administration, with Janus principals describing professional development opportunities as plentiful in the district.

> They do technology, learning our CCF. You know, when new teachers come in, they have new teacher training. And also they do the training on the curriculum, the reading curriculum, [and] the math curriculum, so a lot is provided for the teachers. But again, the principal can suggest things, but those 5 days each person can do what he or she wants to do. (Janus administrator)

Teachers, by contrast, described professional development time as highly delimited (e.g., textbook adoption and model lessons) with little opportunity to examine or modify their teaching.

> In other words, don't set limitations and boundaries that you have to do this and you have to do that and you have to do this. Once you allow teachers to do lesson study and collaborate and begin to share with each other about excellent teaching, give them the time to do that. Trust the professionals to do it. Don't feel like you have to have big brother watching you, which I think is happening in many schools. (Janus teacher)

Nevertheless, the explicitly defined expectations for MSS aligned with teachers' traditional orientations toward teaching math as primarily the acquisition of skills along with subsequent assessments of those skills. In addition, the district's use of professional development and the additional paperwork associated with the newly adopted curriculum combined to severely limit teachers' time, redirecting their attention toward completing curricular goals as opposed to engaging the time- and labor-intensive teaching for understanding.

> CCF curriculum made a lot of us back up, regroup, rethink, adjust to more paperwork, and the hardest thing now for us, a lot of things we do is . . . after school or before school or at home. And since we're working to the clock, it's hard because we know how difficult it is for us to do our very very best and just use the hours we have at school that we're paid for. It's difficult. (Janus teacher)

School administrators also found themselves accountable to the central office, as they had to compile the CCF paperwork of individual teachers in their school. Teaching goals convey how this curriculum left little room for the innovation and flexibility required by teaching for understanding, without the support of resources from the district.

> I have a list of objectives such as my [district] requirements, things that they must be able to do, skills that I have to teach them and test them, assess them in whatever way I can to see that they are capable of completing all those [district] exit skills. Those are the main things that I want to get the kids to get. (Janus teacher)

> Well most of these students have been in the city all their lives. They have had MSS since kindergarten. And when you say MSS, they understand. My students carry blue cards, there's a blue card, it's just like mine except theirs is thin paper, it has everything that they're responsible for, and I mark it. As a matter of fact, I'm taking theirs up, I will mark, they will know exactly what they have mastered, what they still haven't. Every day, over there, there is an objective posted, right there on that sheet over there, okay. I want the objective that we're working on today written on there. I tell them, today, we're simplifying fractions. Today, we're finding the area of a polygon. So they know the objective, they know what they have to do in order to be successful. Now city sends out every 6 weeks a little newspaper. It has all the CCF in it . . . so it has everything in there for the parent to see what they're supposed to be covering that 6 weeks. (Janus teacher)

Indeed the Tennessee Comprehensive Assessment Program (TCAP), the state-mandated assessment, was cited by teachers as another constraint on excellent teaching.

> You've got TCAP. . . . So not only am I trying to do CCF, I start the day out each class period with about four problems that deal with basic skills that are usually covered with TCAP, and that's the way I start the day. . . . But again, these are, this is a test that they're going to have to take and then again they're going to take it when they get to high school. Once they pass it, of course, they don't have to see it again, but you know, it's the competency thing and yeah, they need to be able to know those things, to say that they know enough knowledge to graduate from high school. It's just that the pressure's on for both areas and just the way it has to be gone about—doing it is a lot of concern for me. It really is. (Janus teacher)

Statewide assessments were not seen as aligned with either the National Council of Teachers of Mathematics Standards (Standards) or the district's CCF. This lack of alignment in policies not only discouraged Janus teachers from engaging teaching for understanding but also limited their success with the CCF.

> I'm sorry to say that the curriculum seems at odds with the Standards to me because the Standards want you to explore and problem solve and the curriculum tests you on finding the mean. It tests you on adding rational numbers, so we haven't gotten our assessments in line, I don't think, with what we're doing for the Standards. (Janus teacher)

Not only students but also teachers were accountable to the district, which used student test scores and "work plans" to evaluate how well teachers met the CCF goals.

> We are accountable locally by, they're called work plans. Have you seen one? Our work plans . . . you choose the targeted areas that you want to improve on, identify those, and then list ways that you're going to do that. And those are checked by our administrator in the office . . . then we are held accountable by our test scores and we're rated against other teachers across the system and across the state by how our kids stack up. (Janus teacher)

The CCF curriculum and MSS were adopted under pressure from local government and business leaders in exchange for increased funding. While some teachers found them useful, the time-consuming nature of these programs as they were structured and tied to accountability, and the fact that teachers resented the lack of professional autonomy, not only directed teaching in a particular way (toward learning and practicing basic skills and away from teaching for understanding) but also generated stress.

> Probably some of our blood pressures are higher than they've been in a long time, and the doctors are going, "Why?" One thing this year, it's not that CCF is not enough to stress you out, but we have CCF and we have the board, the negotiations, which is a whole different ballgame. And they're asking us to do more and more and more and more, and then they're saying, "There's no money, or here's 1%," and you're signing for 3 years. And who knows what they're going to give me to do. They're giving me more and more and more and they're taking nothing off of me. I'm becoming more and more and more and more accountable, and more and more and more clerical, but I'm not getting any help. I'm not getting any time, and they're not wanting to pay. . . . And if they want you to be trained for something, they should give you release time from school, not after school, not on the weekends, not on your vacation during the summer, release time. And they

should provide a substitute in the building to take your classes, not teachers that are left in the building who have to cover. So that's a lot with the stress. A lot of the stress this year has to do with CCF, but a lot of it just had to do with the way that teachers see that they're being insulted, because they're not being treated as professionals. (Janus teacher)

Needless to say, the curriculum, lack of time, lack of professional development, and lack of professional autonomy combined to diminish both opportunity and incentive to teach for understanding in the Janus collaborative.

Mimas High

Mimas personifies the complexities for central-city high schools in the midst of school reform. A large school, with a predominantly poor and diverse population that traditionally has failed to achieve academically, and with a mandate from the governor to improve its student learning within 5 years, Mimas High is situated in a Wisconsin school district that engages reform in a serious way. Indeed, a multiplicity of reform efforts were being experimented with in the high school and district, with our design collaborative as only one of many programs endorsed by the administration to create change. It is possible that the lack of coherence among these projects and newly implemented policies, and the fact that they ended up competing for teachers' limited time, also played a role in participants' loss of interest in the collaborative.

For example, the various math programs/experiments such as Equity 2000, a Mathematics Urban Systemic Initiative (MUSI), and the design collaborative apparently competed not so much for funds, but for teachers' time. Whereas professional development associated with the required "banking days" and the MUSI took place intermittently and consisted mainly of large-scale workshops distributed to teachers, the Equity 2000 program met four Saturdays in semester one and four Saturdays in semester two. This program focused on the district initiative that all ninth graders would take and pass algebra. Combined with the traditional teaching orientations of so many teachers, these programs no doubt competed based on how they aligned with teachers' conceptions of pedagogy.

Simultaneous to allocating resources, the district issued mandates that acted as the stick rather than the carrot to drive reform. For example, the newly implemented proficiency exam that would soon influence students' graduation options affected teachers' performance, not only in the classroom but also in how they chose to help students to perform well on the proficiency exam. And while the new policy of student portfolios represented an alternative form of assessment, teachers acknowledged the possibility of being overwhelmed by such choices and obligations. The time-consuming nature of portfolio assessment undoubtedly would combine with existing demands on classroom instruction related to the exam to generate more stress for teachers.

I know the seriousness of it because the students, if they don't pass it, they can't graduate. And it is more work and more pressure on us if they don't pass it and then later on we have a hundred kids trying the portfolios as the alternative. So, for me, what I spend, I spend 2 weeks on proficiency and for me it was worthwhile. So that is something that they change, it changed my lessons and stuff, my time line or whatever. (Mimas teacher)

At Mimas, the newly formulated policy of interdisciplinary "families" served a dual function regarding teaching for understanding. On the one hand, families enabled relationships between students and teachers by allowing the same group of students to remain together throughout their tenure in high school, with the same group of teachers. Insofar as this policy improved social relationships in the school, it served as a resource and incentive to teach for understanding. On the other hand, this structuring of relationships between students and teachers also pulled the teachers in our design collaborative in different directions by competing for their energies. The latent effect of this resource is that subject-matter specialists (i.e., math teachers) did not have the opportunity to discuss their discipline with one another. This is tied to the fact that other "family" teachers often did not perceive that their topics intersected with math (e.g., social studies). In this way, the participants in the Mimas collaborative were isolated from one another and at odds with the objectives of the family structure.

Thus, at Mimas the piecemeal approach to "systemic reform"—experimenting with a variety of programs and policies—provided the dilemmas inherent in reform efforts, particularly in large urban systems, that affected teachers' efforts to engage teaching math for understanding.

Summary and Cross-Site Comparisons

As these case descriptions have demonstrated, educational policies are not isolated in a political vacuum. Rather, they coexist and are often incompatible, competing with one another and causing tensions for schools and teachers. More often than not, policies, as they are practiced, have results that influence other policies, and although there is a relationship among such policies, organizational resources, and teaching for understanding, it is not linear. Moreover, interactions among policies cannot be predicted by looking at a particular policy in isolation. In our study, some policies provide incentives and resources for teaching for understanding, while others detract or redirect attention away from it. We even have situations where the same state policy has a positive effect in one school district and a negative effect in another.

For example, the Wisconsin State Assessment System presents a situation where policy was seen as a positive resource in the Europa district and a constraining factor in the Mimas district. This statewide assessment (designed to meet the Wisconsin Model Academic Standards) is taken in grades 4, 8, and 10. In Europa elementary and middle schools, this test was not a concern because students performed well on it. In fact, it served to energize efforts to engage in teaching for understanding, with Europa elementary teachers using the Wisconsin standards to select their units that focused on teaching for understanding. In Mimas High, however, the state policy was a concern because students there typically had not done well on standardized assessments. Here district policy interacted with state policy, with the district threatening to take control of Mimas based on its test performance. This was also the case for Janus, where the district policy environment was similar to that at Mimas where students, teachers, and even administrators were evaluated based on test performance. These sites contain a built-in tension between accountability systems and building resources to support teaching for understanding.

However, we have evidence that, despite contradictory pressures, some of the districts attempted to create environments supportive of teaching for understanding. Callisto adopted a science curriculum that encouraged teaching for understanding, as did the Europa middle school in mathematics. And the science department at Oberon High had been engaging in this approach long before the inception of the design collaborative. Even in those districts where the efforts of the design collaboratives failed to gain momentum, we can still see how district policy makes teaching for understanding more or less feasible through its provision (or restriction) of resources and incentives and alignment among policies. We also see, however, how difficult it is for districts and schools to force teaching for understanding.

To return to a point made in the opening of this chapter, the trends reportedly occurring in the U.S. educational system (systemic change processes and the "marketizing" of school structures) appear to move in opposite directions. Systemic change centralizes change in the heart of the system, and what Apple (2001) calls the marketizing of schools spins off change in a decentralizing manner. Several of our sites were caught between these competing trends, such as Callisto, where "controlled choice" dominated a system attempting to centralize professional development and teaching for understanding; Oberon High, where site-based management was being introduced and departments were contending with one another over funds to support their teaching efforts; and Mimas High, which operated under district supervision (and possible regulation) in a "choice" environment, and where Mathematics Urban Systemic Initiative funds supported systemic change in math, while the market for math programs within the school undermined such a change.

The Mimas High school district simultaneously endorsed school choice and used MUSI funds to generate systemic change in mathematics teaching and learning. However, these efforts competed with other mathematics programs within the school, and ultimately the district (through the use of state assessment) would determine the "competitiveness" of Mimas and superimpose the district's label of "success" (or its sanction). These reforms were designed to generate wide-scale systemic reform, but they were not adopted with consideration for how each would complement other reform efforts or how they would configure into a totality of systemic change. Rather, they were put together separately, randomly, and haphazardly. Thus, the vision of an educational market coexisted with increased pressure to regulate both the content and the performance of the market (i.e., Mimas).

DILEMMAS OF TEACHING FOR UNDERSTANDING

This chapter illustrates the multiple, and sometimes incompatible or nonaligned, goals located within these structurally complex and politically charged environments that drive teachers' work. But what drives these districts and schools, if not the larger community and its demands for students and teachers? In examining the special challenges of reforms geared toward teaching for understanding, it is also important to remember the political and contextual constraints in the society at large. While our sites may not speak directly to these issues, they are nevertheless important to consider.

Social and Political Contexts

During every presidential campaign, we find education to be a top priority for the nation. However, just as in Europa's school district, with its ultimate resistance to school-expansion initiatives (a situation mirrored in many parts of the country), we consistently encounter the public's desire for educational improvements without increases in educational funds.

In addition, one of the defining features of educational policies in our country is their revolving-door character. Aside from the fact that teachers may be reticent to engage new educational practices for fear that the "new" approach will soon become yesterday's news, or that their school or district will fail to sustain their efforts by allocating resources, is the issue of the larger environment within which teachers are asked to work. Teachers are increasingly asked to engage in various reform efforts that require a great deal of time, resources, dedication, and caring, while often being regarded by their local community and portrayed by the media and politicians as the cause of children's failure in school. Similar to other reform efforts, teaching for understanding also is embedded within the larger political contexts of accountability and the professionalization of teaching.

Professionalization of Teaching and Accountability

One feature of being a *professional* is a fair degree of autonomy; however, countering this professionalization of teaching are the promulgation of nationally issued and state-controlled accountability systems and assessments, for teachers as well as for their students. For example, in the Janus school district, teachers were rated against each other and evaluated according to their students' test performance.

Part of the emphasis on accountability is due to the necessity of keeping track of systems that are partially state-funded but increasingly have become diverse in structure, and where politicians are held accountable for their performance. In his analysis of the transformation of education into a marketplace, Apple (2001) suggests that seeming inconsistencies are actually quite reasonable, as this process "signifies what initially may seem to be contradictory tendencies. At the same time as the state appears to be devolving power to individuals and autonomous institutions that are themselves increasingly competing in a market, the state remains strong in key areas" (p. 75). Apple goes on to explain just why this process is occurring:

> In essence, we are witnessing a process in which the state shifts the blame for the very evident inequalities in access and outcome it has promised to reduce, from itself onto individual schools, parents, and children. This is, of course, also part of a larger process in which dominant economic groups shift the blame for the massive and unequal effects of their own misguided decisions from themselves onto the state. The state is then faced with a very real crisis in legitimacy. Given this, we should not be at all surprised that the state will then seek to export this crisis outside itself. (p. 76)

Thus, teachers are asked to participate more fully in student learning and engage in self-regulation such as deprivatized practice, yet they increasingly must submit to competency tests, often created and imposed without their involvement in generating such assessments.

The proliferation of student assessments to determine the value of curricula and teaching provides an example of the transformation of educational policies through initiatives like voluntary national standards. These standards are supposed to provide an incentive structure for districts, and hence schools and teachers, to adopt more professional approaches to teaching and to ensure that students learn the requisite skills to perform in our society. It is worthwhile to question whether the national standards and their operationalization (i.e., state assessments) are counterproductive to teaching for understanding, since our sites demonstrate that statewide assessments generate a push toward more traditional teaching practices and *teaching to the test* rather than teaching for understanding. Such pressure, of course, should be mitigated if statewide assessments are aligned with teaching for understanding. Of our six sites, however, only in Europa and Callisto did such alignment take place, and in Callisto teachers pointed to the amount of time that the test took from class instruction (18 hours) and its degree of difficulty, which surpassed even the most capable students (e.g., one high school student passed the science component).

The teaching profession finds itself embroiled in efforts to maintain itself as a vocation in the Weberian sense of the word (with teaching for understanding personifying this effort). That is, teaching may be promoted as a profession, yet it is treated as merely a technical career or job. In his essay, "Science as a Vocation," Weber (1946) discusses the term *vocation* as it has been used historically as a "calling" in religion. Applying this concept to science, he illustrates that a vocation demands that its values, ethics, and philosophy be at the top of the hierarchy of values, guiding the beliefs, practices, and loyalty to the "calling" to the chosen profession, in all areas of life. Thus, teaching as a vocation demands a particular hierarchy of values, beliefs, and practices, and loyalty to the hierarchy in the life of the teacher. As teachers enter the profession in response to some calling, we educate them to think of themselves as professionals. However, once they are on the job, they are ignored in developing and meeting standards. Although most professions define themselves and establish criteria for success and/or failure, the critiques of teaching and the solutions suggested for educational problems come from outside the profession, offering political options rather than technical or professional solutions that were developed within the profession itself.

Adoption of the teaching for understanding framework is a process in which teachers need time not only to engage this practice through professional development, but also to engage teaching for understanding *before* the classroom becomes a contested arena in which constituencies expect rapid achievement based on standardized assessment scores. Even the best of standardized assessments fail to provide this needed time when teachers are tested, students assessed, and punitive measures (e.g., withholding diplomas for test failure and withholding salary increases to teachers) taken within a year of the adoption of the assessments. In short, long-term processes such as teaching for understanding and systemic change, which imply coherence to efforts of reform, cannot succeed with the narrow visions of our politicians or the public.

CHAPTER 9

Sustaining Teaching for Understanding in Mathematics and Science

Adam Gamoran, Charles W. Anderson, and Tona Williams

Throughout the book, we have addressed three challenges to supporting teaching for understanding: providing resources; aligning purposes, perceptions, and commitments; and sustaining change. Data from the six sites provide solid evidence pertaining to the first two, but it has been more difficult to assess how the design collaboratives met the challenge of sustainability because of the limited time frame of our observations. In this concluding chapter, we draw our analyses to a close with a focus on this third challenge.

THE POTENTIAL FOR SUSTAINABILITY

The question of sustainability is particularly important for the cases we studied, because outside experts provided a crucial stimulus to teacher change. What happens when the outsiders move on to new challenges? How can schools and districts sustain momentum on their own?

By sustainability, we mean *maintaining generative practice*. Let's unpack that phrase. First, we refer to individual teachers *maintaining the classroom practices they* have learned in their professional development experiences. Through their engagement with sustained, coherent professional development focusing on student thinking about powerful mathematical and scientific ideas, many teachers have brought new practices to their classrooms (see Chapter 1). Do these new practices persist over time?

As we have seen in the previous chapters, however, teaching for understanding changed more than teachers' classroom practices. In ongoing partnerships, the schools created or gained access to new organizational resources (Chapters 4 and 5), administrators developed new styles of leadership (Chapter 6), and teachers formed professional communities (Chapter 7). Furthermore, in all of the partnerships, teaching for understanding was an unfinished business. To sustain teaching for understanding, teachers must keep learning and growing professionally. Franke, Carpenter, Levi, and Fennema (2001) refer to this type of sustainability as *generativity*, in that the focus on teaching for understanding generates a continued growth in knowledge and understanding. Generativity means not only maintaining new practices over time, but modifying and adapting practices continually, in response to new learning and reflection that occur as a result of persistent focus on student thinking. Both maintaining practice and generativity can be observed at the level of the individual teacher, but a crucial difference between the two is that generativity occurs through collaborative inquiry rather than in isolation (Franke et al., 2001). What conditions foster self-sustaining, generative teacher change? How can districts and schools support this process?

We focus here on district and school conditions that help or hinder generative teacher change and the diffusion of change throughout the school and district. Although we studied each case for 2 or 3 years, that is still too little time to determine whether changes that occurred are self-sustaining. Consequently, we examine the *potential* for sustainability rather than evidence that sustainability occurred, and we ask whether the conditions we observed are likely to result in generative teaching for understanding.

In Chapter 2, we articulated a dynamic model in which groups, practices, and organizational resources influence one another to support multidirectional change. Throughout this book, we have argued that developing a capacity for change means providing not only material resources such as time, curriculum, supplies, and equipment, but human resources, including knowledge, skills, and commitments, and social resources, such as the interpersonal relationships that teachers draw upon to develop and sustain new norms of practice. We have claimed further that school and district leaders need to go beyond a conception of resource allocation as a means of control, to building an organization that allocates resources in response to teachers' efforts and initiatives (see Chapter 6). According to this conception, teacher professional development is a driving force for change, because it alters the nature and distribution of resources in a district and its schools. Professional development requires resources but also generates new resources, including human resources in the form of new knowledge, skills, and commitments on the part of teachers. If the professional development is ongoing, coherent, and focused on student thinking, it also may generate social resources in the form of relationships among teachers that help them develop new approaches and resolve uncertainties in their teaching (see Chapters 4 and 7).

Current writing about "professional community" and "social capital" emphasizes the need for a cohesive group of educators to engage in collaborative inquiry (e.g., Newmann & Associates, 1996). While this is important, our conception of the school and district as contexts for change suggests that a professional community cannot guarantee its own sustainability. As Gamoran, Secada, and Marrett (2000) explained, ongoing and widely diffused change is the rarest outcome of a change process in school systems; more common outcomes are conflict, accommodation without transformation, or coexistence of the innovation as an alternative structure alongside traditional arrangements. For change toward teaching for understanding to be widespread and generative, relationships and resource flows need to be strong and coherent not only among those engaged in professional development, but between the professional development community and other important actors and groups in the district.

Thus, maintaining generative practice requires a continuing flow of organizational resources to the professional community. As we have seen, professional communities can generate some human and social resources through their own practices (see Chapters 4, 5, and 7). However, it is hard to imagine a community becoming self-sustaining in the sense that it can keep going without any outside resources. At a minimum, teachers will continue to need time for professional development. Professional communities also will inevitably lose human resources over time as key members retire or accept other assignments. Thus, communities that sustain generative change must have ways of recruiting or generating new human resources—finding new members and socializing them into the norms and practices of the community.

FOUR CONDITIONS FOR SUSTAINABILITY

In his writing about social capital and economic development, Michael Woolcock (1997) developed ideas that help us examine the potential for sustainability of school reforms. His perspective focuses on relations among those involved in reform and on interdependence between that community and the larger environment. According to his account, four conditions are necessary to foster sustainable growth: integration, linkage, organizational integrity, and synergy. In our terms, these conditions are essential for teacher learning to be generative and to spread beyond a small group of initial participants.

Integration

Integration refers to trust, mutual expectations, shared values, and the potential for establishing norms within a community. This is social capital in the sense that the term is used by recent writers such as Coleman (1990) and Putnam (2000). Integration is important from Woolcock's perspective because it means that members of a community can focus collectively on common goals. In our study, when we ask about integration we inquire whether a professional community of teachers attempting to teach for understanding exists at a particular site. Integration is necessary not only because it constitutes a collective focus on common aims, but because it provides opportunities for professional collaboration, an essential aspect of fostering teaching for understanding. The importance of integration is consistent with the notion that individual action is embedded in a social context that guides it and constrains it even as the context is shaped by the action.

We found solid integration within all of the sites that showed at least some promise of sustainability (Europa elementary, Oberon, Europa Middle, and Callisto), and weak or no integration within the two unsustained cases (Mimas and Janus). In particular, the small size of the Mimas collaborative limited integration, in that a strong culture never emerged because so few teachers participated. Teacher turnover appeared to be the strongest threat to integration, and this was apparent in Europa elementary, Callisto, and Oberon, where teachers left the group and their roles had to be filled by others.

Linkage

Woolcock's insight is that if social relations are limited to a well-integrated community, that community may be cut off from its environment, preventing members from maintaining the resource flows necessary for sustained growth and diffusion. This is an apt description of what often happens in education, when a small group of teachers participates in a change process but cannot establish more than an isolated niche within a larger system (Newmann & Associates, 1996). To break out of isolation, the community needs *linkage* to the wider environment, in the form of social relations that allow members to attract material and human resources (e.g., funding, equipment, and expertise) so the community can continue to thrive. These resource flows probably depend not only on the relationships through which the linkage operates, but on the group's capacity to provide something in exchange—a product that is perceived as valuable outside the group itself.

To consider whether the design collaboratives we observed are characterized by linkage as well as integration, we ask, Does the professional community have strong social ties with key individuals and groups outside of itself? In particular, does the group have ties with those who control resources, such as district and school administrators? Is the community's "product"—teaching and learning with understanding—perceived as valuable by these and other key constituents, including parents and school board members?

Levels of linkage varied a lot across the design collaboratives and, here again, the unsustained groups differed from the others in their lack of connections at the school or district levels. Europa elementary developed the strongest linkages and showed the most promise for sustaining generative change. This finding is supported not only by interviews and observations reported earlier in the book, but also by survey data (see Table 9.1). Teachers in the Europa elementary schools reported more influence on school policy and a more supportive professional development climate than the teachers at Europa Middle, Callisto, and Oberon. Oberon, Europa Middle, and Callisto displayed some linkages but also some areas where linkage was weak. At Europa Middle, all three survey indicators of linkage are relatively high (see Table 9.1). This reflects the principal's strong commitment to integrating algebra throughout the curriculum, which became the group's central goal and major accomplishment. By contrast, Callisto teachers reported relatively small roles in influencing policies, but higher levels of administrative support for teaching and professional development. Teachers at Oberon reported slightly less influence over school policies compared with some of the other sites, and they reported much less administrative support for teaching and for professional development than the other sites surveyed. However, they maintained many connections with other science educators through participation in professional conferences

Table 9.1. Elements of Sustainability in Four Sites According to Teacher Surveys

	Europa Elementary	Europa Middle	Callisto Elementary and Middle	Oberon High	F	Scale Alpha
Linkage						
Teachers influence school policies	3.10	2.94	2.32	2.44	8.65**	.80
Administrative support for teaching	3.26	3.38	3.59	1.31	7.27**	.76
Professional development climate	1.61	1.52	1.49	1.06	3.22*	.78
Synergy						
Schoolwide vision	2.84	3.28	2.77	3.50	2.67*	.76
Support for innovation	3.34	3.28	3.16	3.00	2.85*	.60
Number of schools	4	1	4	1		
Number of respondents	75	18	45	6		

Notes. Mimas and Janus were not included in the survey because of insufficient data. No survey indicators of integration were available, because the survey focused on the school and district context, not on the professional development group. Similarly, the survey did not contain enough items relating to organizational integrity to construct a meaningful scale. See Appendix, Table A.5, for wording of survey items and construction of scales. $^*p < .05.$ $^{**}p < .01.$

and university-sponsored projects. The two high schools, Oberon and Mimas, had the weakest district linkages, and this may be due to the relatively strong internal organization of high schools.

Organizational Integrity

Even powerful linkages may have little value for sustaining growth if the context in which the community is embedded lacks the capacity to procure and distribute resources effectively. Woolcock (1997) uses the term *organizational integrity* to refer to the coherence, competence, and capacity of institutions to manage a process of change. Woolcock's conception of organization is highly compatible with ours (see Chapters 2 and 6). He begins by noting the advantages of bureaucratic organization, including efficiency and impartiality. Yet bureaucracy also can be a trap, or an "iron cage" to use Weber's (1922/1978) term, if actors adhere rigidly to rules and procedures, focusing on standard routines as ends in themselves instead of as means to an end. To avoid the iron cage, administrators need to be responsive rather than rigid. An effective organization also needs to acquire material and human resources and to have a system for deploying those resources strategically. Organizational integrity thus refers to an internal structure that provides the capacity, credibility, and flexibility to sustain meaningful change. As we think about the districts in which collaboratives were located, we ask: Is the school system well resourced and well organized, with the ability to mobilize internal advocates and external experts to support a process of change?

The degree and character of organizational integrity also varied substantially among the sites. Oberon and Europa elementary both operated within highly effective organizational environments that supported the work of the collaboratives. Europa Middle enjoyed support from the district, but its overall levels of organizational integrity were compromised by plans to split the school into two sites and divide the teachers. Callisto, although it showed promise for maintaining generativity, struggled to retain its focus within a district context that lacked coherence and consistency. The Mimas and Janus schools and districts had high organizational integrity—they articulated goals for teachers and implemented plans—but this did not help to sustain the design collaboratives because of the lack of another condition: synergy.

Synergy

A fourth condition for sustainability is the degree of *synergy* between the efforts of the community and those of the organizations in its larger environment. A focus on synergy recognizes that not only are individual actors embedded in a context, but organizations are embedded in an environment of organizations. When we search for synergy in our cases, we ask whether the efforts of professional developers and of the teacher professional community are aligned with other school and district efforts. In particular, are they consistent with formal standards set by the district and/or the state? Are they commensurate with or contradictory to decisions about resource allocation that are already occurring? Indeed, the stronger the organizational integrity of a school system—that is, the stronger its cohesiveness and capacity to procure and distribute resources—the more important synergy becomes, as a group of would-be innovators may be unable to find a niche at all unless some synergy exists. The case of Janus provides a powerful example of this. Here, a teacher describes the design collaborative's unsuccessful attempts to address both approaches at once.

> We were working on seeing if there's any way that [the city] curriculum could be worked in with this [professional development] program. And it was . . . like, "Well, okay, that's fine, but then you got to consider this, that's fine but you got to go this way, that's fine but there's this obstacle to face," . . . and [one of the researchers] was very positive, [saying,] "well, if I can do that on the computer . . . [will] that work?" "No, because you've got to do this." And it was becoming so jumbled that I was wondering at that point, is there any way? . . . I mean, it was becoming, major obstacles were being presented to try to pull both in together.

Again, the Europa elementary and Oberon collaboratives enjoyed the greatest degree of synergy with their organizational environments. In particular, Oberon teachers reported a strong school-wide (really, department-wide) vision of science teaching on the survey, and Europa elementary teachers reported a high degree of support for innovation (see Table 9.1). Overall, the data suggest that consistency with formal state and district content standards and assessments is essential over the long term. Both of these groups aligned their work with district and state standards, and the standards helped to energize the collaboratives by suggesting directions for curriculum building. The same was true of Callisto, although here the design collaborative's work was undercut by contradictions among divergent programs within the district. For instance, science kits distributed by the district science office were compatible with the inquiry-based approach undertaken in the design collaborative, but teachers utilized the materials inconsistently since they were based on several types of programs that were not explicitly coordinated. This is reflected in the relatively low level of school-wide vision that the teachers reported on the survey (see Table 9.1). Europa Middle also had positive synergy with district goals, and the work of the design collaborative was co-opted by the principal and lead teachers in their efforts to integrate algebra into the school's core mathematics curriculum. The survey indicators reflect this, as responses average between agree and strongly agree to questions about school-wide vision and support for innovation (see Table 9.1).

Interconnections Among the Conditions for Sustainability

Identifying the potential for sustainability is not simply a matter of whether a case is high or low on integration, linkage, organizational integrity, or synergy, but of the particular combination of conditions and how they may act in concert. Our sites suggest that no single element is sufficient for maintaining generative practice. Rather, each is crucial, and within a specific context some support or undercut others, creating trade-offs. Across the six sites, the variation among the four conditions brought several themes and issues into focus.

Synergy among organizational structures and group goals affects integration. In Europa Middle, for example, the impending division of the middle school diminished overall levels of organizational integrity, disrupting the group's momentum and threatening its integration and stability. In Mimas, the school's cross-disciplinary families made it difficult for the bilingual mathematics teachers to form a community. By contrast, the daily departmental meetings forged an atmosphere of collegiality among the teachers in Oberon.

We also noted that strong linkages with school administrators and highly synergistic environments encourage one another. In the Europa elementary collaborative, for instance, administrators regularly attended group meetings, participated in activities with the teachers, and shared the group's goals. The interdependence reflected in these linkages enhanced the synergy in the larger district environment. Conversely, the Janus collaborative experienced a disjuncture between its approach and the larger organizational context, and the group's participants had little opportunity to form linkages with administrators. In Oberon, difficulties in communicating with the school and district administration compromised organizational integrity through lack of official acknowledgment of the group, and this limited the degree to which a mutually supportive relationship that had synergy with other district efforts could form.

When either synergy or organizational integrity is minimal, the benefits of the other for sustainability are constrained. Although the Janus district was highly coordinated, its rigid testing schedule and top-down approach to curriculum did not synergize with the design collaborative, and this mismatch directly impeded ongoing collaboration. In Mimas, the shared desire of the school, district, and design collaborative to improve students' algebra performance created a synergy that was the group's strongest element of sustainability. Despite this promise, the collaborative's incompatibility with the organizational logic of the school—which grouped students and teachers into cross-disciplinary families— compromised the bilingual mathematics teachers' ability to collaborate with one another. The disjuncture undercut the benefits of synergy at the site. Similarly, the Callisto collaborative synergized with the district's approach to pedagogy, but the lack of coordination among multiple programs detracted from the synergy between the specific approaches of the design collaborative and those of other educators.

These assessments about the sustainability of the sites are necessarily speculative, since our data cover a relatively short time frame and we cannot directly observe the degree to which each group will maintain generative practice. However, the evidence suggests that the four elements that organized the analysis do describe the potential for design collaboratives to sustain their work. Within each organizational context, participants found that they could much more easily influence some of the elements, while they were required to adapt to others. An awareness of how these dimensions of sustainability relate to one another across divergent contexts may help other groups such as these to negotiate a course. Now that we have examined conditions that contribute to sustainability, we move to broader consideration of what these data reveal about how organizational conditions can support teaching for understanding.

DISTRICTS AND SCHOOLS CAN SUPPORT TEACHING FOR UNDERSTANDING

We know that individual teachers are able to teach students for understanding (see Chapter 1). The question motivating our study is whether and how districts and schools can support such teacher development. When teachers focus on student understanding, must they invariably do so *despite* the circumstances of the organizational contexts in which they work? Or is it possible to reorganize resources, roles, and relationships to *enhance* the prospects for teaching for understanding?

Our study shows that districts and schools *can* foster an environment conducive to teaching for understanding. The Wisconsin suburban and Massachusetts urban cases make this most clear, and they also show that there are at least two routes to establishing a supportive context. One strategy is to nurture teacher autonomy, while the other involves promoting programs that are compatible with teaching for understanding.

In all three Wisconsin suburban sites high levels of teacher autonomy, coupled with material resources such as time for teachers to meet and district funding of teacher administrative roles, created contexts in which teacher-driven change could emerge and flourish. The change processes unfolded differently in each case (Europa elementary, Europa Middle, and Oberon High), but high levels of support and strong prospects for generative change were common to all three. These patterns contrasted with Mimas, the Wisconsin urban high school, where a lack of resources and a fragmented school structure made it difficult for the change process to take root, despite teachers' classroom autonomy.

Callisto school district in Massachusetts also provided a context in which teaching for understanding took hold. Here, the key ingredient did not appear to be teacher autonomy, but rather that district science programs did not contradict the efforts of teachers and researchers in the design collaborative. Callisto teachers had autonomy in their classrooms, but much less influence over school policies compared with the suburban teachers. This meant that there was enough synergy between the design collaborative and other district initiatives to provide a hospitable niche for the reforms, even though individual teachers varied in their levels of participation. This pattern contrasted with the Janus middle school initiative in Tennessee, where district mandates that were incompatible with the researchers' and teachers' vision of teaching for understanding made it impossible for potential changes to commence. The finding of a supportive context in Callisto is especially important because it shows that even in a complex, challenging urban environment, district and school leaders can work with teachers and researchers to move toward teaching for understanding.

What lessons can we draw from these cases? Establishing that schools and districts *can* support teaching for understanding is a useful first step, but its value is limited unless we can show *how* this support was exercised.

WHAT DOES IT TAKE TO SUPPORT TEACHING FOR UNDERSTANDING?

Our research suggests three steps to help ensure a supportive context for teacher development toward teaching for understanding: commitment from the teaching profession, responsiveness from school systems, and improving the research base. Each of these steps includes all the actors we have discussed in this book: teachers, administrators, researchers, and professional groups. It would be a mistake to assume, for example, that school system responsiveness involves only administrators, or that developing a research base is a responsibility of researchers alone. Enhancing the capacity for change requires a response that crosses the boundaries of organizations and occupational roles.

Commitment from the Teaching Profession

One of the most encouraging features of our study was the willingness of many teachers from a wide range of backgrounds to commit themselves to ongoing study and collaboration toward teaching for understanding. By focusing together on students' thinking about powerful mathematical and scientific ideas, these teachers improved their own knowledge and skills (human resources) and enhanced their professional relationships with other teachers (social resources). Yet these individuals and groups worked in larger environments in which teaching generally is regarded as a task for an individual teacher, whose responsibility begins and ends with the particular group of students to which she or he is assigned. Many of the teachers we observed developed strong social relationships within their professional development communities, but the communities were not always well connected to their larger contexts. This lack of linkage contributed to the demise of the professional development group in Mimas and constituted a major challenge for Oberon. To create a more supportive context for teaching for understanding, we need a more radical rethinking within our teaching profession of the key elements of the teacher's role. These elements would include a commitment, among most teachers, to coherent, collaborative, sustained inquiry into student thinking, so that this professional development would be *part of the teacher's regular job* instead of something only unusual teachers do. Our findings suggest that a *culture of generative change* among teachers would help establish a supportive environment for teaching for understanding. By this, we mean a culture in which ongoing investigation about student thinking is a professional responsibility for any teacher—a norm whose salience is exhibited in everyday practice.

Research on teachers in Japan sheds light on what might characterize such professional commitment. According to Stigler and Hiebert (1999), Japanese teachers have time built into each school day to work together to plan teaching activities. In these meetings, they commonly discuss their instructional intentions and obtain feedback from colleagues. This sort of activity occurred in the design collaboratives we studied, but it was unusual, not characteristic of most teachers and not seen as part of their regular jobs. Beyond daily planning, Japanese teachers engage periodically in "lesson study," in which they observe and critique a colleague's practice. They also have access to lesson books that recount the variety of responses from students that teachers are likely to encounter in response to their teaching. The lore of specialized knowledge is a valuable resource for Japanese teachers, and it is a hallmark of professionalism that is largely missing from the teaching profession in the United States. Commitment to the development and dissemination of such knowledge among American teachers would help foster a more supportive environment for teaching for understanding in this country.

Our study shows that supporting such teacher development in districts with diverse student populations poses special difficulties. In our urban sites, we saw how competing policies and scarce resources make it hard for teachers of diverse students to collaborate, especially when bilingual and language-minority teachers seem isolated from others in their schools. For the same reasons, however, support for teacher development is especially valued in these settings when it does occur, as in the case of Callisto. A commitment to ongoing inquiry among teachers—the culture of generative change—would help break the isolation and reduce the fragmentation that we observed in urban sites, and thus improve the prospects for an environment that supported teaching for understanding.

Our study was not designed to show how to create commitment to change among teachers where none exists, because the cases we studied all began with groups of teachers who wanted to pursue teaching for understanding in science and/or mathematics. Moreover, all the cases we studied except Janus, the short-lived group in Tennessee, involved preexisting professional ties, either among researchers and one or more teachers (Europa elementary, Callisto, and Mimas), among teachers (Europa Middle), or both (Oberon). Thus, some level of social as well as material and human resources facilitated collaboration in each of these sites from the outset. Future research will have to address the difficult question of how to create professional bonds where none exist, to lay the foundation for a culture of generative change. A school in which teachers both are professionally isolated from one another and lack other professional ties, would seem to lack the social resources even to begin the process we observed.

Responsiveness from School Systems

A central thesis of our work has been that to understand how schools can increase their capacity for change, we need to think more broadly about what we mean by resources and about how resources are acquired and allocated. For this reason we considered human and social as well as material resources, and we explored how resources could be generated and distributed from within teacher groups outward as well as from the school system to teachers. Our findings provide consistent support for both of these ideas, and they point directly toward steps that school systems can take to support teachers who are committed to teach for understanding. These steps suggest how districts and schools can remove barriers and enhance the prospects for teaching for understanding.

Our analyses indicate that, as we anticipated in our dynamic model of organizational change (see Chapter 2), schools support teaching for understanding primarily by *responding to* teacher activity. Two aspects of school system responsiveness seem particularly important. First, schools can allocate resources in response to teachers' efforts to learn and collaborate with their colleagues. Thus, for example, the Europa school district provided $15,000 annually to support the design collaboratives. This may seem simple, but it is not the usual way schools operate. Typically, staff development is prearranged at the school and district levels, and teachers commonly lack input into its design, let alone plan the whole process independently. In our study, schools and districts that allocated resources such as time for meetings, materials and supplies, and the flexibility for teachers to pursue their own professional development, helped teachers develop their capacities for change. These resources, moreover, paid off more than one might expect, because instead of being used up, they generated new social and human resources that helped create the potential for generative change. Resources that support coherent, sustained, collaborative professional development do not depreciate over time like material objects, but are transformed into other, long-lasting resources and have the potential to contribute to their own regeneration.

Sustainability is not ensured even when resources are allocated in response to teacher development. Teacher turnover can undermine the new human and social resources stimulated by professional development; this was a major concern at Oberon and Europa, the sites with the highest potential for sustainability because of their material resources and home-grown leadership. Also, structural conditions can pose barriers to creating and sustaining social ties; witness the departmental fragmentation induced by the family system at Mimas, and the impending division of teachers into two schools at Europa Middle. Furthermore, districts that lack synergy between teachers' efforts and other system commitments, as at Janus, cannot provide hospitable ground for the growth of human and social resources that support teaching for understanding. Thus, allocating resources in response to teacher needs is likely to generate new resources when teachers have the flexibility and stability to learn and act collectively, and the district is not undermining their efforts through competing initiatives.

A second way school systems can respond to teacher development is by extending leadership opportunities beyond persons in positions of formal authority. In our study, cases in which teacher-leaders played a major role in directing the change process (Callisto, Europa, and Oberon) showed signs of increasing capacity to support teaching for understanding. Distributed leadership is enhanced by administrators who redefine their roles as facilitators, creating room for teachers to take charge of their own learning. From the teachers' perspective, it often appeared that administrative support consisted of not interfering with teacher initiatives, but our research indicated that supportive principals and district officials took more active roles, including allocating resources in response to needs, creating connections with experts who could offer new knowledge about teaching for understanding, and bringing together teachers with common interests to form productive relationships.

By providing resources in response to teachers' needs and providing space for distributed leadership, school districts can nurture professional communities among their educators. In our study, the viable professional communities we observed created many of the resources they needed to ensure their own sustainability, including new leaders, new professional knowledge, and social norms and relationships that supported new practices. However, they also relied on an ongoing flow of material resources to continue their growth and development.

All participants in the process of supporting teaching for understanding—administrators, teachers, and researchers—can enhance the prospects for sustaining new practices by becoming articulate spokespersons for the value of teaching for understanding. By demonstrating to the public that they have created a product of value, participants can help form the linkages necessary for maintaining long-term support for teacher change.

Improving the Research Base: Creating New Knowledge About Student Thinking

The researchers in these professional development groups were engaged in extraordinary activity. Instead of studying teacher behavior and reporting on it as outside observers, they worked with teachers to try new approaches to teaching and reported on teachers' changing knowledge and perceptions and on the learning of their students. The point of these "design experiments" was not to test hypotheses, but to document how teachers and students respond to new instructional approaches that emphasize student thinking, center on powerful ideas in mathematics and science, and occur in equitable classroom communities. This evidence is contributing to a new body of knowledge about teaching for understanding that is sorely needed in American schools.

Consider the contrast between Japanese and American teachers provided by Stigler, Fernandez, and Yoshida (1996). Both were teaching fifth-grade students how to figure out the area of a triangle. For the American teachers, the lesson plan consisted of the various steps the teachers would take: review of recent work, demonstration of the new concept, and assigning exercises. Most of the Japanese teachers' lesson plan, however, consisted of thoughts about how the students would respond to instruction. It is precisely this information—how students think about math and science problems—that is missing from the resources of American teachers and can be developed only through systematic research.

Calling for more research, though, is not to place the burden solely on researchers. On the contrary, teachers and administrators have important roles to play. First, they can make their practices visible and their classrooms open so that researchers can help them document student thinking. In our study, this was a key requirement for establishing the design collaboratives, and where this was limited through low rates of teacher participation (Mimas) or discouraged because of competing demands on teachers (Janus), the groups atrophied. Second, and perhaps more important, teachers can become researchers themselves. "Action research" by teachers is becoming widely practiced (e.g., Mills, 1999), and it is hard to imagine a more appropriate role for action research than documenting student thinking in the context of particular curricular content and activities. In this way, administrators, teachers, and researchers can become partners in moving toward the vision of teaching for understanding as the standard practice in American schools. In our study, the cases where teachers were most involved in the research process through authoring papers and presenting at conferences (Europa elementary and Oberon) also demonstrated the greatest capacity for maintaining generative practice. This focus stimulated the development of new classroom projects and provided these teachers with ongoing opportunities to interact with colleagues outside the design collaboratives.

Here, too, the comparison with Japanese teachers is instructive. Japanese teachers accept the task of systematically studying their students' learning and sharing their findings with other educators as part of their job duties. As Stigler and Hiebert (1999) report:

> Japan has succeeded in developing a system that not only develops teachers but also develops the knowledge about teaching that is relevant to classrooms and sharable among members of the teaching profession. . . . The process of designing and critiquing lessons is an integral part of the larger professional activity of both teachers and researchers. (p. 126)

The authors quote a teacher as saying, "If we didn't do research lessons, we wouldn't be teachers" (p. 127). Like their Japanese peers, American teachers are uniquely situated to produce knowledge about how particular lessons work in the classroom, and how students think about powerful mathematical and scientific ideas in the classroom context. Recording and sharing what they have learned would be a new and valuable contribution for most American teachers.

What vision of teaching mathematics and science will prevail in American schools? The rise of standards-based reforms has placed teachers under pressure to demonstrate that their teaching practices are effective and their students are learning. By some accounts, teachers are responding to this pressure by narrowing their teaching to focus on little more than the test items that are used to assess their students' achievements (e.g., McNeil, 2000). If this response becomes general, American schools will fall far short of the vision embraced by professional organizations such as the National Council of Teachers of Mathematics (2000) and the American Association for the Advancement of Science (1993). Members of these groups imagine mathematics and science teaching and learning that is richer and deeper than mere mastery of routine test items. To reach this vision, teachers will need better access to professional knowledge and practices than current systems allow.

By increasing the commitment to ongoing collaborative inquiry, securing more responsiveness from schools and districts, and building a better research base, schools can begin to address the challenges of supporting teaching for understanding: providing resources for classroom teaching; aligning purposes, perceptions, and commitments; and sustaining change. In doing so, we can move toward a vision of teaching that embraces new professional responsibilities and focuses on student understanding. These steps will not be easy, and they are context-bound; they are sure to play out a little differently in each district in which they are tried. Nonetheless, if teaching for understanding is the goal, there is much that schools and districts can do to improve the prospects for advancing this agenda.

Methodology

Our data collection followed a multisite case study approach. We combined qualitative and quantitative longitudinal data from five school districts and 13 schools
to examine whether and how the districts and schools posed barriers and supports
to the teacher–researcher partnerships. The sites selected were those initiated and
underway at the National Center for Improving Student Learning and Achievement in Mathematics and Science. As explained in Chapter 3, this constraint on
our selection of sites invoked both benefits and costs for our study. Partnerships
that were already under way (Callisto, Europa elementary) we studied for 3 years;
partnerships that began later we studied for 2 or 3 years, as time allowed.

DATA SOURCES

We collected data from four sources: observations of meetings, interviews with
teachers, interviews with school and district administrators, and a survey of teachers. Table A.1 summarizes our observational and interview data collection. All
district, school, and personal names are pseudonyms.

Observations

As Table A.1 indicates, during 4½ years of data collection we observed 106 meetings across the five sites that had active design collaboratives. We were not able to
observe any meetings in Janus, because the design collaborative did not become
fully established. The observational data consisted primarily of field notes that
members of our research team produced after attending meetings of the design
collaboratives. In a typical meeting that we observed, a member of our team would
participate minimally in the group's activities while taking notes and sometimes
tape recording. We occasionally supplemented our observations with notes produced by other members of the design collaboratives, and in a few cases, we attended
other meetings in the school or district that enabled us to gather more information about a site. Most of the design collaborative meetings that occurred during
the school year were approximately 2 hours long. Longer meetings were held dur-

Table A.1. Sources of Observational and Interview Data

	Callisto Elementary and Middle	Europa Elementary	Europa Middle	Janus Middle	Mimas High	Oberon High	Total
Observations							
Time frame	11/97–7/98	6/96–5/99	1/98–1/00	—	12/97–3/99	7/98–12/99	6/96–1/00
Design collaborative meetings observed	6	26	19	0	18	33	102
Other meetings observed	0	1	3	0	0	0	4
Teacher interviews							
Time frame	8/97–8/99	4/97–8/99	6/99–7/00	10/98–11/00	2/98–6/99	3/99–7/00	4/97–11/00
Number of interviews	25	72	17	7	20	14	155
Number of individuals	15	34	11	4	4	8	76
Administrator interviews							
Time frame	12/97–7/99	9/96–5/99	1/98–4/00	2/00	2/98–6/99	3/99–8/00	9/96–8/00
Number of interviews	17	14	3	3	2	3	42
Number of individuals	15	8	2	3	1	2	31

Note. The administrator interviewed at Mimas was a department chair who was also a participating teacher, as was one of the administrators interviewed at Oberon.

190

ing the summer, on weekends, or during school release days, and these lasted approximately 4 to 6 hours. While the majority of the field notes summarized and paraphrased the activities and conversations that took place, some also included entire or partial transcriptions of the cassette tapes.

Interviews

Teacher Interviews. We conducted 155 interviews of 76 teachers across the six sites over multiple years (see Table A.1). All of these teachers were design collaborative members. We interviewed some teachers only once, and others two or even three times. Since participation was voluntary, we were not able to interview every teacher in each collaborative every year. Interviews took from 1 to 2 hours to complete, and most were cassette tape recorded and fully transcribed. Table A.2 lists the core questions that we asked in each interview. Although we maintained a high degree of consistency to facilitate comparisons across sites, we adapted the wording and particular questions for each site so that they resonated with the local context. All the interviews were concerned with teachers' perspectives on the design collaboratives, professional communities, group leadership, collaborative efforts, learning from colleagues, professional development, relationships with the administration, resources, and influences of the design collaboratives on teaching practice.

Administrator Interviews. To gain perspective on the school and district contexts of the sites, we conducted 42 interviews of 31 administrators who worked in the schools and districts that housed the design collaboratives (see Table A.1). These interviews lasted approximately 1 hour, and were cassette tape recorded and fully transcribed. Initially, we planned to interview only the principals of the elementary and middle schools, and department chairs in the high schools. As the data collection progressed, however, it became apparent that it would be useful to speak with the high school principals and district-level administrators. Although we refined our interview schedule to reflect this decision at most of the sites, we were not able to interview any administrators except for the department chair at Mimas. Unfortunately, this is a data limitation of that site. As with the teacher interviews, we based the administrator interviews on a set of core questions, while the details were tailored to fit each setting. Table A.3 lists these core questions, which cover the areas of leadership, teaching innovations, professional development, standards, and important issues in math or science teaching.

Surveys

Survey Respondents. While the interviews gathered detailed information from design collaborative participants and key administrators, our surveys provided a broader data source that incorporated the perspectives of teachers who were

Table A.2. Core Teacher Interview Questions

OVERALL PERSPECTIVE

1. If another teacher were to ask you what the professional development project is all about, what would you say?

DEFINING THE MEMBERSHIP, SHAPE, AND BOUNDARIES OF THE PROFESSIONAL COMMUNITY

2. People talk about teachers' forming communities when they share common values and beliefs about the nature and purposes of teaching. Would you say that you and your colleagues form a cohesive group or community in this way? (a) Who, specifically, are your colleagues in the group? (b) Do you think that, within this group, you share common values and beliefs about teaching [math/science]? (c) How would you describe those common values and beliefs? (d) What kinds of things help develop these common values and beliefs? What kinds of things get in the way? (e) Please describe a recent event or discussion that focused on these common values and beliefs.

LEADERSHIP WITHIN THE GROUP

3. Are there any leaders in your group's efforts to improve how they teach [math/science]? (a) Who are they? (b) Why do you think of them as the leaders?

COLLECTIVE EFFORT

4. Has professional collaboration been different for you in recent years? Explain.
5. What benefit has collaboration been to you as a teacher?
6. Are there any drawbacks to collaboration?

COLLABORATIVE LEARNING

7. If you were to have any questions, ideas, or concerns about teaching [math/science], who would you go to, to discuss those ideas?
8. Think back to an event when you discussed something with one of the people whose names you just mentioned. Could you recount the incident—what was the issue? (a) How did the discussion go? (b) Did you go into each other's classrooms to observe? (c) How were things eventually resolved?
9. How do you make sure that the [math/science] program flows from year to year? This includes things that you, yourself, do on an individual level and things that you do as a group of teachers in your [school/department].

PROFESSIONAL DEVELOPMENT

10. What are the main kinds of professional development experiences related to [math/science] teaching that you have participated in during the past year?
11. Has your [school/department] supported your professional development? Has it gotten in the way? How?
12. Have other teachers supported your professional development? Have they gotten in the way? How?

(continued)

Table A.2. (*cont.*)

RELATIONSHIP WITH ADMINISTRATION

13. How well do the school administration and the district office support your efforts to teach [math/science]? (a) What kinds of support or concerns have they expressed? (b) What additional resources do they provide? (c) What opportunities for ongoing professional development have they provided? (d) Have they expressed any other expectations of the [math/science] program, of your group's efforts to improve the [math/science] program, or of your own personal involvement in these efforts?

RESOURCES AND OTHER CONSTRAINTS

14. What resources have been helpful or important to you this year for supporting your [math/science] instruction?
15. What resources do you think are necessary for you and your colleagues to maintain your efforts to improve your program and teaching? How does the group plan to get those resources?
16. Do you, personally, have adequate resources to teach [math/science] in the ways you think are best?

THE PROFESSIONAL DEVELOPMENT COLLABORATIVE AND TEACHING PRACTICES

17. Have you learned anything over the past year that made you less certain about your teaching practices?
18. When you tried out ideas from the professional development collaborative in your classroom, did you encounter any problems or did you have any questions? What were they?
19. Has your participation in the program led to changes in the way you respond to equity or diversity issues? These might involve things like student achievement and race, language background, gender, culture, or other issues of inclusion.
20. Based on your experience as a [math/science] teacher undergoing change, what advice would you give to another teacher who wanted to make similar changes? What questions, obstacles, or surprises might that teacher encounter and how could the teacher address these concerns?

not part of the professional development groups as well as those who were. In the Europa elementary and Callisto sites, we surveyed everyone classified as a regular classroom teacher who taught mathematics and/or science. This encompassed four schools at each of these two sites. In Europa Middle and Oberon, we surveyed all of the teachers in the math and science departments, respectively. The particular contexts of Janus and Mimas made it impossible to collect usable sets of surveys from either of those sites. Table A.4 summarizes the data collection across the four sites that we utilized for Chapter 6, "Leadership for Change," and Chapter 9, "Sustaining Teaching for Understanding in Mathematics and Science." The response rates across the sites ranged from 66% to 86%. Because response rates varied by

Table A.3. Core Administrator Interview Questions

LEADERSHIP

1. How do you know when teachers in your school are having success with their students?
2. How do you communicate that vision of success among your staff? Is it widely shared?
3. What do you do to support that success?
4. How much control do you (or your staff) have over hiring and retaining new staff?
5. Has anyone ever left the school because they were dissatisfied with the direction the school [or their department] was going? Were there particular concerns for [math/science]?

TEACHING INNOVATIONS

6. How much innovation in teaching occurs among the teachers in your school? How about in [math/science]?
7. To the extent that teaching involves innovations, what role do you as principal play? How about curriculum coordinators? What is the role of parents or other community members?
8. When teachers are working out innovations in their practice, does that tend to pull them together, or push them apart?
9. What, if anything, has impeded the efforts of teachers to improve their teaching in [math/science]?

PROFESSIONAL DEVELOPMENT

10. How would you characterize the level of district support for professional development?
11. Do you have a model of professional development in mind for teachers in your school?
12. Are teachers in your school similar in the amounts and types of professional development they obtain, or is there a lot of variation?
13. If professional development plays a prominent role in teaching innovations, how does that affect the role of administrators?

STANDARDS

14. How do formal content standards affect [math/science] teaching at your school?

OTHER IMPORTANT ISSUES

15. What is the most controversial issue in [math/science] teaching in your school right now? Choose one to talk about. (a) What are the conflicting sides? (b) Who is involved? (c) Who will have the main power to influence the conclusion? (d) How do you think the issue will be resolved? How are you likely to feel about it?
16. What do you see as the most important or pressing "next steps" for [math/science] in your school?

Table A.4. Sites and Years Included in the Survey Analyses

Site	Year	Number of Schools	Number of Respondents	Response Rate (%)
Europa Elementary	1997/1998	4	75	83
Europa Middle	1998/1999	1	18	86
Europa Elementary and Middle Combined	1997/1998	5	91	83
Callisto Elementary and Middle	1997/1998	4	45	66
Oberon High	1998/1999 1999/2000	1	6	75

Note. We collected about 500 surveys in total between 1996 and 2000, but used in our analyses only the ones listed here.

year and we surveyed each site across multiple years, we were able to focus our analyses on the years that provided the most robust data. Because Chapter 6 combines the elementary and middle school data for the Europa district and Chapter 9 does not, we report the details of the Europa elementary and Europa Middle surveys both separately and together.

Survey Items. To facilitate direct comparisons, our survey items had a high degree of consistency across sites and years. The primary distinctions were between the high school instruments and the combined elementary and middle school instruments, since the high school surveys included items that referred specifically to departments. Table A.5 lists the items used in Chapters 6 and 9. There is some overlap in the questions utilized in each chapter, although Chapter 6 compares them individually while Chapter 9 combines them into scales. The items range across the seven categories of classroom autonomy, influence, school-wide vision, support for innovation, administrative support for teaching, principal's leadership, and professional development climate.

Schools and Staffing Survey Comparisons. The Schools and Staffing Survey is a national study of students, teachers, administrators, and school districts conducted by the National Center for Education Statistics. In Chapter 6, we used the SASS teacher surveys in order to compare our survey results with a national sample. We restricted the SASS sample to elementary and middle school teachers in public schools who were classified as regular classroom teachers and taught math or science at least part of the time. We utilized data from two cross-sectional waves of the survey: 1987–88 and 1993–94. The 1987–88 data included 14,011 respon-

Table A.5. Survey Items Used in the Analyses

CLASSROOM AUTONOMY

Scale from 0 = no influence to 5 = great deal of influence

How much control do you feel you have in your classroom over each of the following areas of your planning and teaching?

Selecting textbooks and other instructional materials. (used in Chapter 6)

Selecting content, topics, and skills taught. (Chapter 6)

Selecting teaching techniques. (Chapter 6)

INFLUENCE

Scale from 0 = no influence to 5 = great deal of influence

At this school how much actual influence do you think teachers have over school policy in each of the following areas?

Setting discipline policy. (Chapter 9)

Determining the content of inservice programs. (Chapters 6 and 9)

Hiring new full-time teachers. (Chapters 6 and 9)

Deciding how the school budget will be spent. (used in Chapters 6 and 9)

Evaluating teachers. (Chapter 9)

Establishing curriculum. (Chapters 6 and 9)

SCHOOL-WIDE VISION

Scale from 1 = strongly disagree to 4 = strongly agree

Teachers in this school exhibit a focused commitment to student learning in mathematics and science. (Chapter 9)

A vision for student learning in mathematics and science is shared by most staff in this school. (Chapter 9)

SUPPORT FOR INNOVATION

Scale from 1 = strongly disagree to 4 = strongly agree

In this school I am encouraged to experiment with my teaching. (Chapter 9)

Teachers in this school are continually learning and seeking new ideas. (Chapter 9)

ADMINISTRATIVE SUPPORT FOR TEACHING

Scale from 1 = no help to 6 = extremely helpful

To what extent has each of the following people helped you improve your teaching or solve an instructional or class management problem?

Principal or head of this school. (Chapters 6 and 9)

School curriculum specialist. (Chapters 6 and 9)

District curriculum specialist. (Chapters 6 and 9)

Other teachers at this school. (Chapter 6)

Other teachers in this district. (Chapter 6)

(continued)

Table A.5. (*cont.*)

PRINCIPAL'S LEADERSHIP

Scale from 1 = strongly disagree to 4 = strongly agree

Please indicate how strongly you agree or disagree with each of the following statements about your school.

  The principal lets staff members know what is expected of them. (Chapter 6)

  The principal does a poor job of getting resources for this school (reverse-coded). (Chapter 6)

  The principal knows what kind of school he/she wants and has communicated it to the staff. (Chapter 6)

PROFESSIONAL DEVELOPMENT CLIMATE

Scale from 0 = rarely or never occurs to 3 = always occurs

  When my school initiates a change (e.g., decision making, curriculum), it supports the change with professional development opportunities. (Chapter 9)

  Teachers are left completely on their own to seek out professional development opportunities (reverse-coded). (Chapter 9)

  Teachers here help one another put new ideas from professional development to use. (Chapter 9)

  Most professional development in this school enables us to build on our teaching experiences. (Chapter 9)

  This school draws upon teachers' knowledge and practical experience as resources for professional development. (Chapter 9)

  The school principal encourages teachers to participate in professional development. (Chapter 9)

dents, and had an 86% response rate. The 1993–94 data included 12,676 respondents, and had an 88% response rate. The administrative support items in Chapter 6 were taken from the 1987–88 survey, and the classroom autonomy, influence on school policy, and principal's leadership items came from 1993–94.

CODING AND ANALYSIS OF QUALITATIVE DATA

We used the QSR NUD*IST software to organize the interviews, observations, and open-ended responses to the surveys. Members of the research team used a combination of prespecified codes and open-ended coding to apply over 60 conceptual categories to the data. This procedure allowed us to incorporate our ongoing insights into the coding strategy even after the process was underway. We held several coding sessions in which we established comparability of coding decisions across the research team. As we became more familiar with the data, we refined our theoretical framework and added more nuances to the coding schema. Although the group as a whole developed the focus of the book, the authors of each chapter conducted separate searches within the database for each individual chapter analysis. This required a tremendous amount of time and some duplication of effort, but it also encouraged a broad and intuitive familiarity with the data.

References

American Association for the Advancement of Science. (1989). *Science for all Americans.* Washington, DC: Author.

American Association for the Advancement of Science. (1993). *Benchmarks for science literacy.* New York: Oxford University Press.

Apple, M. W. (2001). *Educating the "right" way: Markets, standards, God, and inequality.* New York: Routledge Falmer.

Ball, D., & Rundquist, S. (1993). Collaboration as a context for joining teacher learning with learning about teaching. In D. K. Cohen, M. W. McLaughlin, & J. E. Talbert (Eds.), *Teaching for understanding: Challenges for policy and practice* (pp. 13–42). San Francisco: Jossey-Bass.

Barr, R., & Dreeben, R. (1983). *How schools work.* Chicago: University of Chicago Press.

Beaton, A. E., Mullis, I. V. S., Martin, M. O., Gonzalez, E. J., Smith, T. A., & Kelly, D. L. (1996). *Science achievement in the middle school years: IEA's third international mathematics and science study.* Chestnut Hill, MA: Boston College, TIMSS International Study Center.

Berman, P., & Giles, N. (2000, April). *Teacher collaboration: An essential link between organizational resources and professional development.* Paper presented at the annual meeting of the American Educational Research Association, New Orleans.

Boser, U. (2000, June 7). Teaching to the test? *Education Week,* pp. 1, 10.

Bryk, A. S., Lee, V. E., & Holland, P. B. (1993). *Catholic schools and the common good.* Cambridge, MA: Harvard University Press.

Carpenter, T. P., & Lehrer, R. (1999). Teaching and learning mathematics with understanding. In E. Fennema & T. A. Romberg (Eds.), *Mathematics classrooms that promote understanding* (pp. 19–32). Mahwah, NJ: Erlbaum.

Cobb, P. (2001). Supporting the improvement of learning and teaching in social and institutional context. In S. Carver & D. Klahr (Eds.), *Cognition and instruction: 25 years of progress* (pp. 455–478). Mahwah, NJ: Erlbaum.

Cobb, P., & Bauersfeld, H. (1995). *The emergence of mathematical meaning: Interaction in classroom cultures.* Hillsdale, NJ: Erlbaum.

Cohen, D. (1988). Teaching practice: Plus ça change . . . . In P. Jackson (Ed.), *Contributing to educational change: Perspectives on research and policy.* Berkeley: McCutchan.

Cohen, D. K., McLaughlin, M. W., & Talbert, J. E. (Eds.). (1993). *Teaching for understanding: Challenges for policy and practice.* San Francisco: Jossey-Bass.

Coleman, J. S. (1990). *Foundations of social theory.* Cambridge, MA: Harvard University Press.

Coleman, J. S., Campbell, E., Hobson, C., McPartland, J., Mood, A., Weinfield, F., & York, R. (1966). *Equality of educational opportunity.* Washington, DC: U.S. Government Printing Office.

Doyle, W. (1983). Academic work. *Review of Educational Research, 53*(2), 159–200.

Doyle, W. (1986). Classroom organization and management. In M. C. Wittrock (Ed.), *Handbook of research on teaching* (3rd ed., pp. 392–431). New York: Macmillan.

Elmore, R. F. (1997). *Education policy and practice in the aftermath of TIMMS.* Cambridge, MA: Harvard University and Consortium for Policy Research in Education.

Erlwanger, S. H. (1973). Benny's conception of rules and answers in IPI Mathematics. *Journal of Children's Mathematical Behavior, 1*(2), 7–26.

Fennema, E., & Romberg, T. A. (Eds.). (1999). *Mathematics classrooms that promote understanding.* Mahwah, NJ: Erlbaum.

Franke, M. L., Carpenter, T. P., Levi, L., & Fennema, E. (2001). Capturing teachers' generative change: A follow-up study of professional development in mathematics. *American Educational Research Journal, 38*, 653–689.

Fullan, M. G. (2001). *The new meaning of educational change* (3rd ed.). New York: Teachers College Press.

Gamoran, A. (1987). The stratification of high school learning opportunities. *Sociology of Education, 60*, 135–155.

Gamoran, A. (1996a). Goals 2000 in organizational perspective: Will it make a difference for states, districts, and schools? In K. Borman, P. Cookson, A. Sadovnik, & J. Z. Spade (Eds.), *Implementing federal legislation: Sociological perspectives on policy* (pp. 429–443). Norwood, NJ: Ablex.

Gamoran, A. (1996b). Student achievement in public magnet, public comprehensive, and private city high schools. *Educational Evaluation and Policy Analysis, 18*, 1–18.

Gamoran, A., & Dreeben, R. (1986). Coupling and control in educational organizations. *Administrative Science Quarterly, 31*, 612–632.

Gamoran, A., Secada, W. G., & Marrett, C. B. (2000). The organizational context of teaching and learning: Changing theoretical perspectives. In M. T. Hallinan (Ed.), *Handbook of research in the sociology of education* (pp. 37–63). New York: Kluwer Academic/Plenum.

Gee, J. P. (1991). What is literacy? In C. Mitchell & K. Weiler (Eds.), *Rewriting literacy: Culture and the discourse of the other* (pp. 3–12). New York: Bergin & Garvey.

Giroux, H. A. (1992). *Border crossings: Cultural workers and the politics of education.* New York: Routledge.

Goldring, E. B., & Rallis, S. (1993). *Principals of dynamic schools: Taking charge of change.* Newbury Park, CA: Corwin.

Greenwald, R., Hedges, L., & Laine, R. D. (1996). The effects of school resources on student achievement. *Review of Educational Research, 66*, 361–396.

Grodsky, E., & Gamoran, A. (in press). The association between professional development and professional community in American high schools. *School Effectiveness and School Improvement.*

Hallinan, M. T. (2001). Sociological perspectives on black–white differences in schooling. *Sociology of Education* [Extra issue], pp. 50–70.

Hanushek, E. (1994). *Making schools work: Improving performance and controlling costs.* Washington, DC: Brookings.

Heath, S. B. (1983). *Ways with words: Language, life, and work in communities and classrooms.* New York: Cambridge University Press.

Herman, R. (1999). *Approaches to schoolwide reform: Taking a critical look.* Washington, DC: American Institutes for Research.

Hiebert, J., Carpenter, T. P., Fennema, E., Fuson, K., Human, P., Murray, H., Olivier, A., & Wearne, D. (1997). *Making sense: Teaching and learning mathematics with understanding.* Portsmouth, NH: Heinemann.

Jackson, P. W. (1968). *Life in classrooms.* New York: Holt, Rinehart, and Winston.

Kennedy, M. M. (Ed.). (1991). *Teaching academic subjects to diverse learners.* New York: Teachers College Press.

Labaree, D. F. (1997). Public goods, private goods: The American struggle over educational goals. *American Educational Research Journal, 34*(1), 39–81.

Lampert, M. (1986). Knowing, doing, and teaching multiplication. *Cognition and Instruction, 3,* 305–342.

Lampert, M. (1990). When the problem is not the question and the solution is not the answer: Mathematical knowing and teaching. *American Educational Research Journal, 27*(1), 29–64.

Latour, B. (1990). Drawing things together. In M. Lynch & S. Woolgan (Eds.), *Representation in scientific practice* (pp. 19–49). Cambridge, MA: MIT Press.

Lee, V. E., & Smith, J. B. (1997). How high school organization influences the equitable distribution of learning in mathematics and science. *Sociology of Education, 70,* 128–150.

Lehrer, R., Carpenter, S., Schauble, L., & Putz, A. (2000). Designing classrooms that support inquiry. In J. Minstrell & E. H. Van Zee, *Inquiring into inquiry learning and teaching in science* (pp. 80–99). Washington, DC: American Association for the Advancement of Science.

Lehrer, R., Schauble, L., Carpenter, S., & Penner, D. (2000). The inter-related development of inscriptions and conceptual understanding. In P. Cobb, E. Yackel, & K. McClain (Eds.), *Symbolizing and communicating in mathematics classrooms: Perspectives on discourse, tools, and instructional design* (pp. 325–360). Hillsdale, NJ: Erlbaum.

McClain, K. (2000, April). *An analysis of the teacher's learning: A case from statistics.* Paper presented at the annual meeting of the American Educational Research Association, New Orleans.

McLaren, P. (1994). Multiculturalism and the postmodern critique: Toward a pedagogy of resistance and transformation. In H. A. Giroux & P. McLaren (Eds.), *Between borders: Pedagogy and the politics of cultural studies.* New York: Routledge.

McNeil, L. (2000). *Contradictions of school reform: Educational costs of standardized testing.* New York: Routledge.

Meyer, J. W., & Rowan, B. (1977). Institutionalized organizations: Formal structure as myth and ceremony. *American Journal of Sociology, 83,* 340–363.

Meyer, J. W., & Rowan, B. (1978). The structure of educational organizations. In M. Meyer & Associates (Eds.), *Environments and organizations* (pp. 78–109). San Francisco: Jossey-Bass.

Mills, G. E. (1999). *Action research: A guide for the teacher-researcher.* New York: Prentice Hall.

National Center for Education Statistics. (1999). *The condition of education, 1999.* Washington, DC: US Department of Education.

National Council of Teachers of Mathematics. (1989). *Curriculum and evaluation standards for school mathematics.* Reston, VA: Author.

National Council of Teachers of Mathematics. (1991). *Professional standards for teaching mathematics.* Reston, VA: Author.

National Council of Teachers of Mathematics. (2000). *Principles and standards for school mathematics.* Reston, VA: Author.

National Research Council. (1996). *National science education standards.* Washington, DC: National Academy Press.

Newmann, F. M., & Associates. (1996). *Authentic achievement: Restructuring schools for intellectual quality.* San Francisco: Jossey-Bass.

Olneck, M. R. (1993). Terms of inclusion: Has multiculturalism redefined equality in American education? *American Journal of Education, 101,* 234–260.

Olson, D. R. (1986). Intelligence and literacy: The relationships between intelligence and technologies of representations and communications. In R. J. Sternberg & R. K. Wagner (Eds.), *Practical intelligence: Nature and origins of competence in the everyday world* (pp. 338–360). Cambridge: Cambridge University Press.

Perrone, V. (1998). Why do we need a pedagogy of understanding? In M. S. Wiske (Ed.), *Teaching for understanding: Linking research with practice* (pp. 13–38). San Francisco: Jossey-Bass.

Peterson, P. L., McCarthey, S. J., & Elmore, R. F. (1996). Learning from school restructuring. *American Educational Research Journal, 33,* 119–153.

Putnam, R. D. (2000). *Bowling alone: The collapse and revival of American community.* New York: Simon & Schuster.

Rosebery, A. S., & Puttick, G. M. (1998). Teacher professional development as situated sense-making: A case study in science education. *Science Education, 82,* 649–677.

Rosebery, A. S., Warren, B., Conant, F. R., & Hudicourt-Barnes, J. (1992). Cheche Konnen: Scientific sense-making in bilingual education. *Hands On! 15*(1), 16–19.

Rowan, B. (1990). Commitment and control: Alternative strategies for the organizational design of schools. In C. Cazden (Ed.), *Review of research in education* (Vol. 16, pp. 353–389). Washington, DC: American Educational Research Association.

Smylie, M., & Hart, A. (1999). School leadership for teacher learning and change: A human and social capital perspective. In J. Murphy & K. S. Louis (Eds.), *Handbook of educational administration* (pp. 421–441). New York: Longman.

Spillane, J. P., Diamond, J. B., Walker, L., Halverson, R., & Jita, L. (2001). Urban school leadership for elementary science instruction: Identifying and activating resources in an undervalued subject. *Journal of Research in Science Teaching, 38*(8), 918–940.

Spillane, J. P., Halverson, R., & Diamond, J. B. (2001). Investigating school leadership practice: A distributed perspective. *Educational Researcher, 30*(3), 23–28.

Steele, C. M. (1992, April). Race and the schooling of black Americans. *The Atlantic Monthly, 269*(4), 67–78.

Steele, C. M. (1999, August). Thin ice: "Stereotype threat" and black college students. *The Atlantic Monthly, 284*(2), 44–54.

Stigler, J., Fernandez, C., & Yoshida, M. (1996). Traditions of school mathematics in Japanese and American elementary schools. In L. P. Steffe, P. Nesher, P. Cobb, G. Goldin, & B. Greer (Eds.), *Theories of mathematical learning* (pp. 149–175). Mahwah, NJ: Erlbaum.

Stigler, J. W., & Hiebert, J. (1999). *The teaching gap.* New York: Free Press.

Swales, J. M. (1990). The concept of discourse community. In Swales, *Genre analysis:*

English in academic and research settings (pp. 21–33). Cambridge, England: Cambridge University Press.

Tyack, D., & Cuban, L. (1995). *Tinkering toward utopia: A century of public school reform.* Cambridge, MA: Harvard University Press.

Vygotsky, L. S. (1978). *Mind in society.* Cambridge, MA: Harvard University Press.

Walsh, C. E. (1996). Introduction. In C. E. Walsh (Ed.), *Education reform and social change: Multicultural voices, struggles and visions* (pp. i–xvii). Mahwah, NJ: Erlbaum.

Warren, B., Ballenger, C., Ogonowski, M., Rosebery, A. S., & Hudicourt-Barnes, J. (2001). Rethinking diversity in learning science: The logic of everyday sense-making. *Journal of Research in Science Teaching, 38*(5), 529–552.

Weber, M. (1946). Science as a vocation. In H. H. Gerth & C. W. Mills (Eds.), *From Max Weber: Essays in sociology* (pp. 129–156). New York: Oxford University Press.

Weber, M. (1978). *Economy and society* (G. Roth & C. Wittich, Eds.). Berkeley: University of California Press. (Original work published 1922)

Weick, K. E. (1976). Educational organizations as loosely coupled systems. *Administrative Science Quarterly, 21,* 1–19.

Weick, K. E. (1982). Administering education in loosely coupled systems. *Phi Delta Kappan, 63,* 673–675.

Wertsch, J. V. (1991). *Voices of the mind: A sociocultural approach to mediated action.* Cambridge, MA: Harvard University Press.

Whitty, G. (2000). Sociology of education and urban education policy. In K. A. McClafferty, C. A. Torres, & T. R. Mitchell (Eds.), *Challenges of urban education: Sociological perspectives for the next century* (pp. 79–96). Albany: State University of New York Press.

Wiske, M. S. (Ed.). (1998). *Teaching for understanding: Linking practice with research.* San Francisco: Jossey-Bass.

Woolcock, M. (1997). Social capital and economic development: Toward a theoretical synthesis and policy framework. *Theory and Society, 27,* 151–208.

About the Authors

Adam Gamoran is Professor of Sociology and Educational Policy Studies at the University of Wisconsin at Madison, where he has taught and conducted research since 1984. Gamoran's studies have focused on inequality in education and the organizational context of teaching and learning, and he has published widely on these topics. From 1996 to 2001, Gamoran served as the chair of the Organizational Support Study Group and a member of the Management Team at the National Center for Improving Student Learning and Achievement in Mathematics and Science (NCISLA/MS). He is also a principal investigator at the Center on English Learning and Achievement and the Institute for Research on Poverty. In 1992–93, Gamoran was a Fulbright Scholar at the University of Edinburgh, Scotland, and in 1998 he was a visiting professor at Tel Aviv University. A member of the National Academy of Education, Gamoran serves on several national panels, including the Board on International Comparative Studies in Education, a committee of the National Research Council.

Charles W. Anderson is a Professor in the Department of Teacher Education, Michigan State University, where he has held a position since 1979. Before coming to Michigan State, Anderson was a Peace Corps volunteer in Korea and a middle school science teacher; he received his Ph.D. in science education from the University of Texas at Austin. Anderson's primary research interest is in using conceptual change and sociocultural research on student learning to improve classroom science teaching. He has published numerous articles and book chapters on research on student learning. Anderson was the lead consultant to the State of Michigan for the development of the Michigan state science objectives, published in 1991. He is serving in 2003–04 as president of the National Association for Research in Science Teaching. He was formerly co-editor of the *Journal of Research in Science Teaching* and is currently associate editor of *Cognition and Instruction.*

Pamela Anne Quiroz is Associate Professor of Education at the University of Illinois at Chicago. She received her Ph.D. in sociology from the University of Chicago and has taught sociology at the University of Massachusetts at Amherst. Her research focuses on the manifestation and reproduction of socioeconomic, racial, and ethnic inequality in educational institutions. She has published both qualitative and quantitative studies, addressing topics such as teachers' working conditions and school organization, educational successes of Latino students, and differential participation in extracurricular activities. She was a Summer Fellow of the Center for Advanced Studies in the Behavioral Sciences and is involved in a long-term study of the educational careers of disadvantaged urban high school students, focusing on the development of ties among students and between teachers and students, and the relation between these ties and student success.

Walter G. Secada is Professor of Curriculum and Instruction in the School of Education at the University of Wisconsin at Madison, where he directs an NSF Center on Learning and Teaching: Diversity in Mathematics Education. He directed the Hispanic Dropout Project on behalf of the Office of the Under Secretary of Education and was senior author of its final report, *No More Excuses* (1998). He has been director, associate director, and principal investigator on numerous projects involving mathematics education reform, school restructuring, bilingual education, and professional development for teachers. He edited the AERA *Review of Research in Education*, NCTM's 6-volume *Changing the Faces of Mathematics*, and other books and journal special issues. Current research involves the nature of student engagement in school, the quality of education provided in Peru's altiplano to indigenous populations, the role of high-stakes assessment in preservice teacher education programs, and the mathematics achievement of diverse learning populations.

Tona Williams is a doctoral candidate in sociology at the University of Wisconsin at Madison and project manager for the Organizational Support Study Group at NCISLA/MS. Recent projects have focused on curriculum change and the cultures of school subject areas, the organizational context of educational reform, and parent involvement in education. She also has provided technical assistance to the Urban Institute for the Urban Systemic Initiative Effective Schools Study. Her other research and teaching interests include the sociology of culture, social movements, combining qualitative and quantitative data, and developing visual and web-based methods of data collection and presentation.

Scott Ashmann is Assistant Professor of Science Education at the Illinois Institute of Technology in Chicago. He earned his Ph.D. in curriculum, teaching, and educational policy with an emphasis in science education from Michigan State University in 2002. His research interests focus on the professional development of science teachers. He currently is involved in a research study that is examining the development of leadership in mathematics and science education in the United States. Previously, he taught chemistry, physics, earth science, and ecology at the high school level. From 1992 to 1996, he directed the Regional Center for Math and Science at the University of Wisconsin at Green Bay.

Index